FACIAL
EXPRESSIONS
FOR ARTISTS

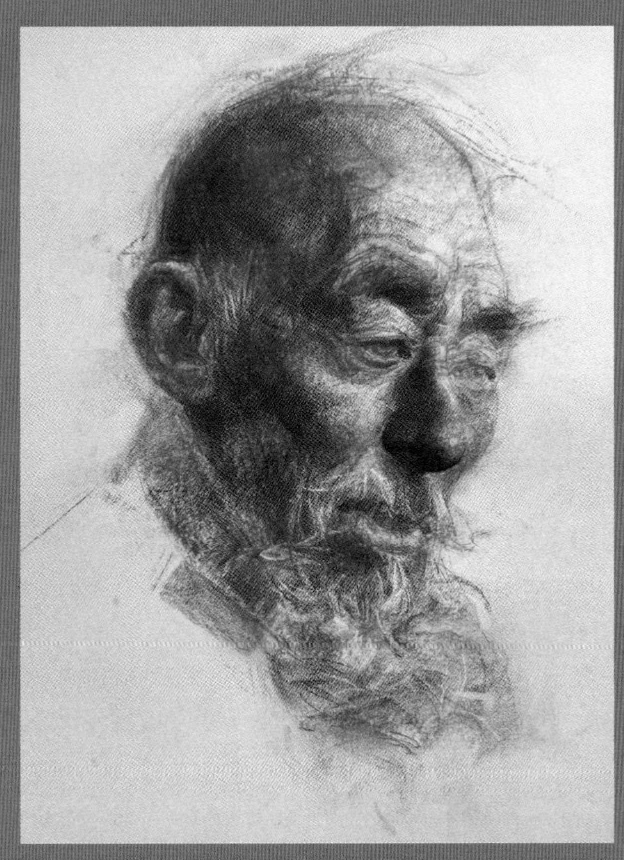

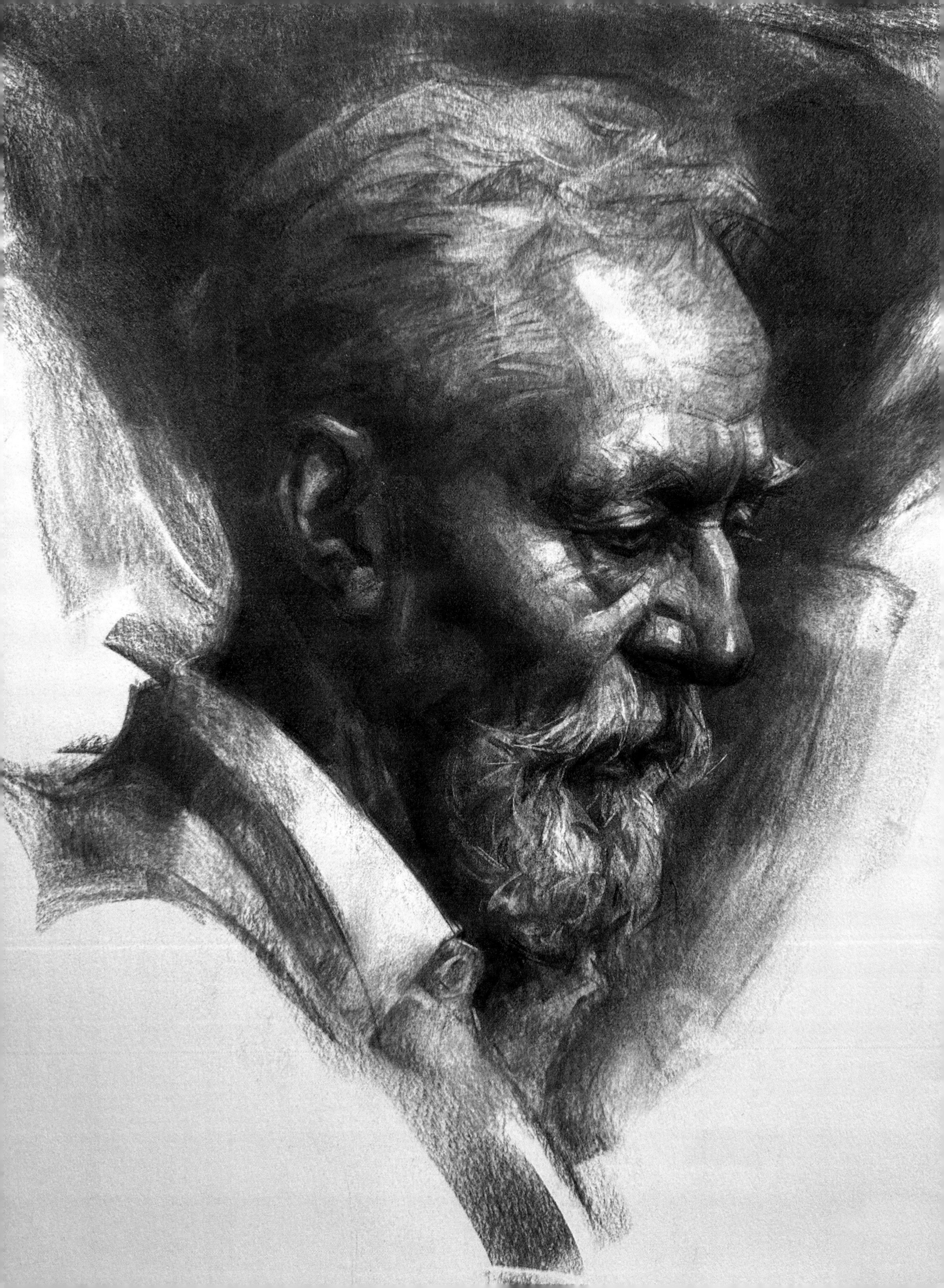

FACIAL
EXPRESSIONS
FOR ARTISTS

Techniques for Capturing
Emotion and Mood in Portrait
and Character Drawings

OLIVER SIN

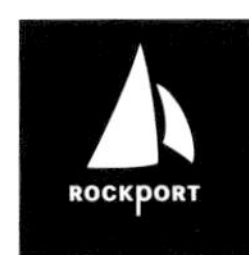

Quarto.com

© 2025 Quarto Publishing Group USA Inc.

Text and illustrations © 2025 Oliver Sin

First published in 2025 by Rockport Publishers, an imprint of The Quarto Group,
100 Cummings Center, Suite 265-D, Beverly, MA 01915, USA.
T (978) 282-9590 F (978) 283-2742

EEA Representation, WTS Tax d.o.o.,
Žanova ulica 3, 4000 Kranj, Slovenia.
www.wts-tax.si

Rockport Publishers titles are also available at discount for retail, wholesale, promotional, and bulk purchase. For details, contact the Special Sales Manager by email at specialsales@quarto.com or by mail at The Quarto Group, Attn: Special Sales Manager, 100 Cummings Center, Suite 265-D, Beverly, MA 01915, USA.

10 9 8 7 6 5 4 3 2

ISBN: 978-0-7603-8240-0
Digital edition published in 2025
eISBN: 978-0-7603-8241-7

Library of Congress Cataloging-in-Publication Data Available

Design: Megan Jones Design
Cover Image: Oliver Sin
Page Layout: Ashley Prine, Tandem Books

Printed in Huizhou City, Guangdong, China TT032026

This book is dedicated to my many students whom I have
had the privilege of teaching.

You have given me fresh perspectives and unwavering
support, which has been a fountain of strength to me.
As an artist, you might need to create ten thousand bad
drawings before making one that looks good.

Consider this book a testament to our shared journey
of learning and fun. Let's keep drawing!

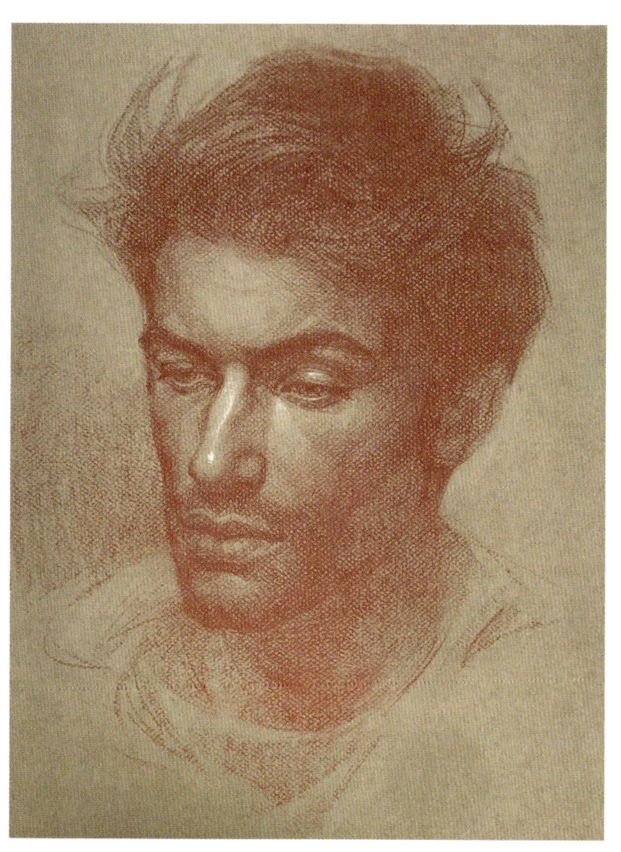
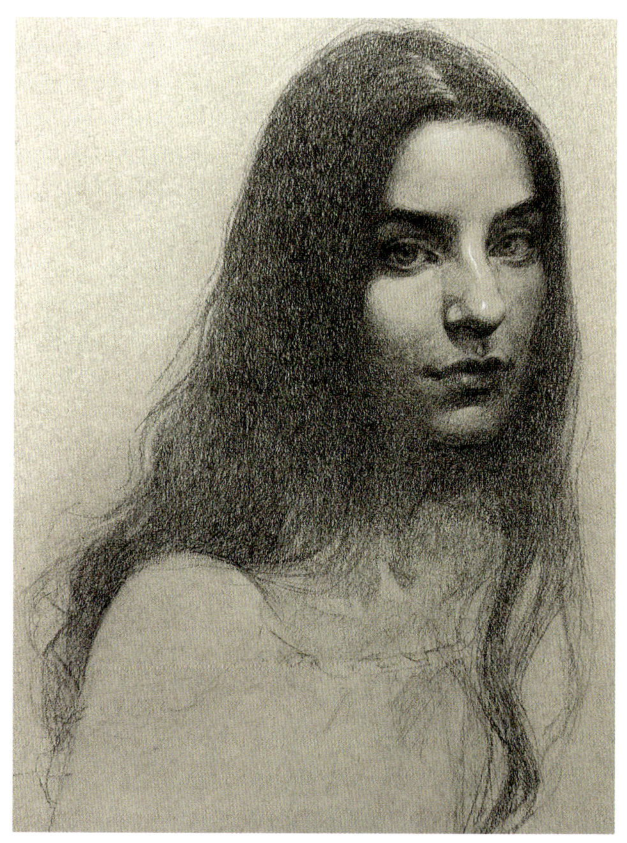
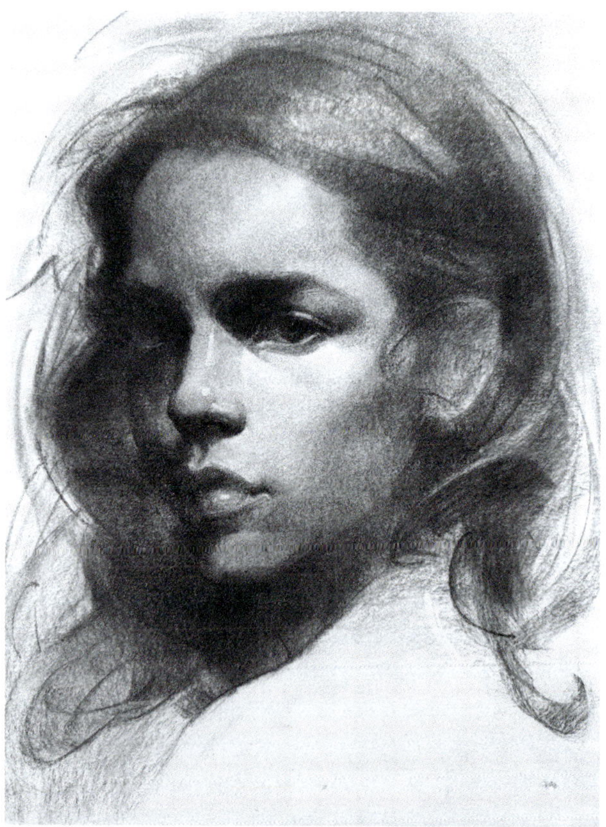
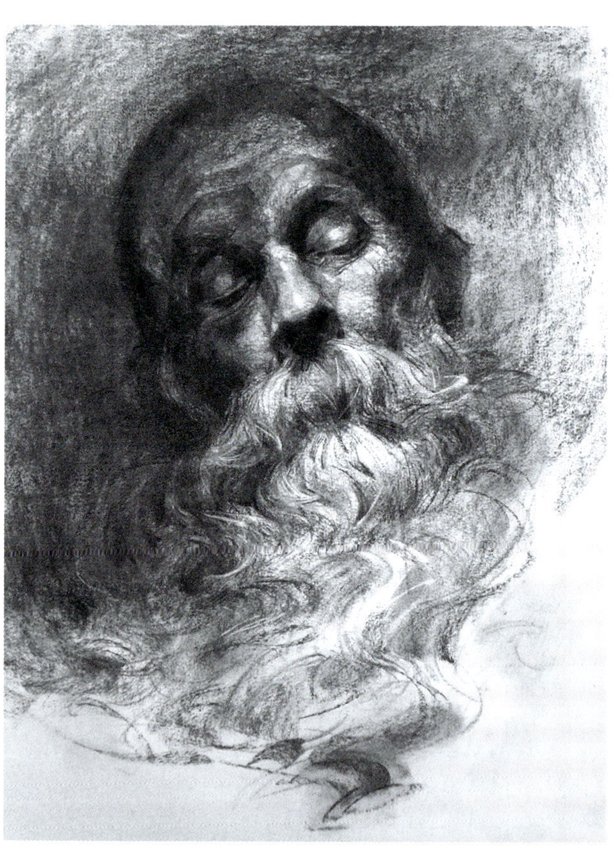

CONTENTS

Preface 8

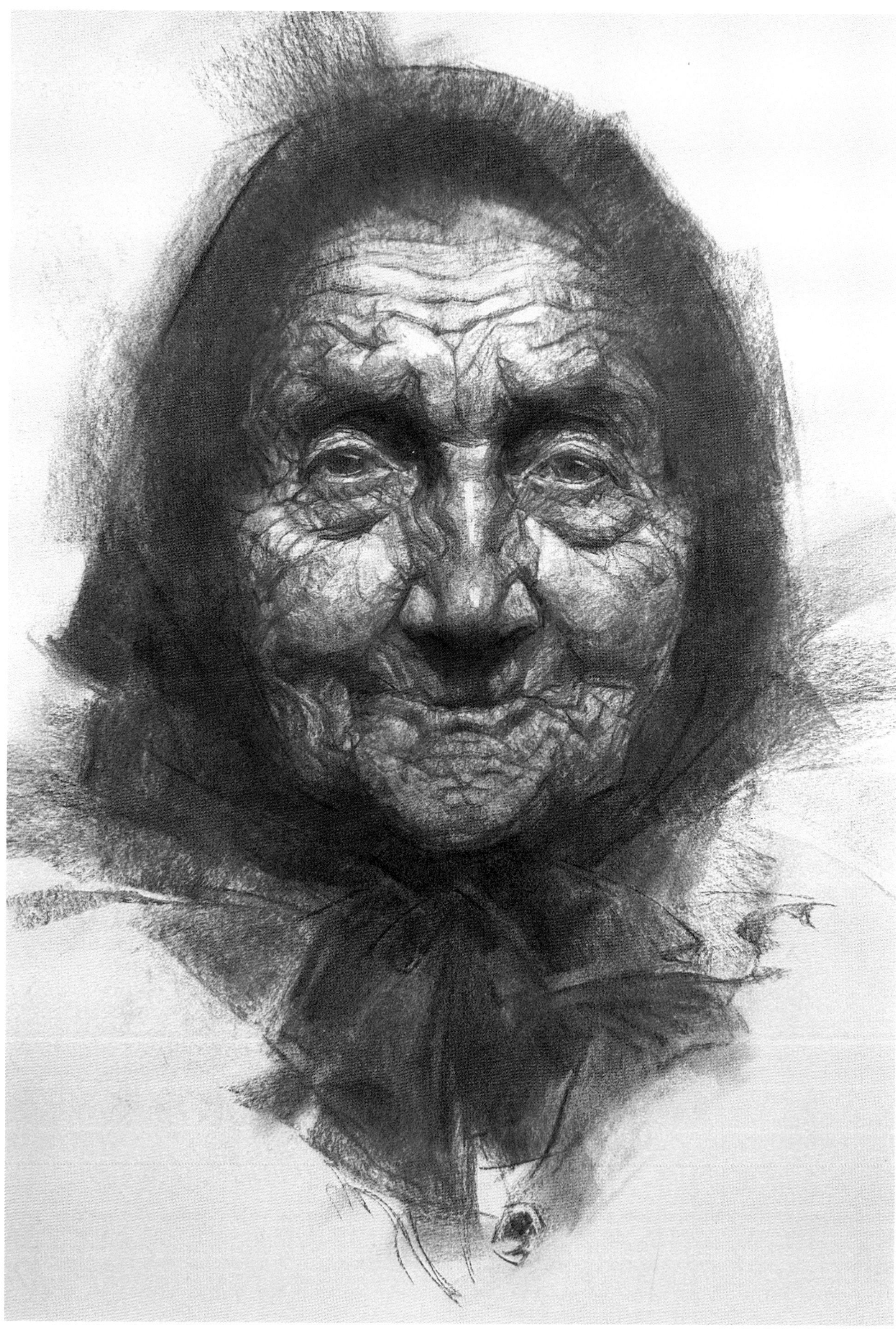

PREFACE

THE IMPORTANCE OF ANATOMY FOR ARTISTS

The study of anatomy is hugely important for all artists, whether you're a beginner or a professional. Every artist, past, present, and into the future, has and will benefit from anatomical knowledge.

When you understand the anatomy of the head, how the head moves and functions, you're able to draw it without reference, and the head that you draw will feel natural and alive. With knowledge of anatomy, you can sketch and try out different head designs and play with different compositions. Not only will that knowledge help you learn to draw the face better, you'll also certainly be reminded of how wondrous our faces are. The face is, after all, our humanity.

To me, people are the most fascinating subjects to study and to draw. There are millions of different faces in this world, and not one of them is boring. Even the same person can take on many looks through different expressions, lighting, and clothing. All heads look different, and yet they all have two eyes, two ears, a nose, and a mouth.

STUDYING ANATOMY

As an artist, you don't need to study anatomy in as much depth as a doctor would, since you only need to be concerned with its visible details. However, it's also not enough to just study the front, side, and back of the head. You need to really understand the function of the muscles so that you'll be able to draw the head in any kind of motion and expression you can imagine. Thus, you need a three-dimensional understanding of the anatomy of the head.

Learning surface anatomy is essential for artists. It helps in understanding the form and structure, leading to more accurate and expressive drawings. Whether it's human figures, animals, trees, plant life, or even inanimate objects like machinery, having a strong grasp of their underlying structure allows artists to capture the essence and details more effectively. We can not draw what we do not know.

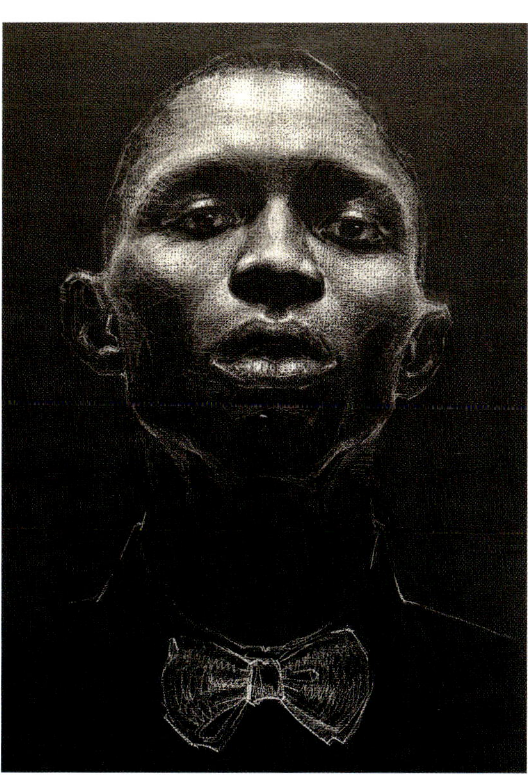

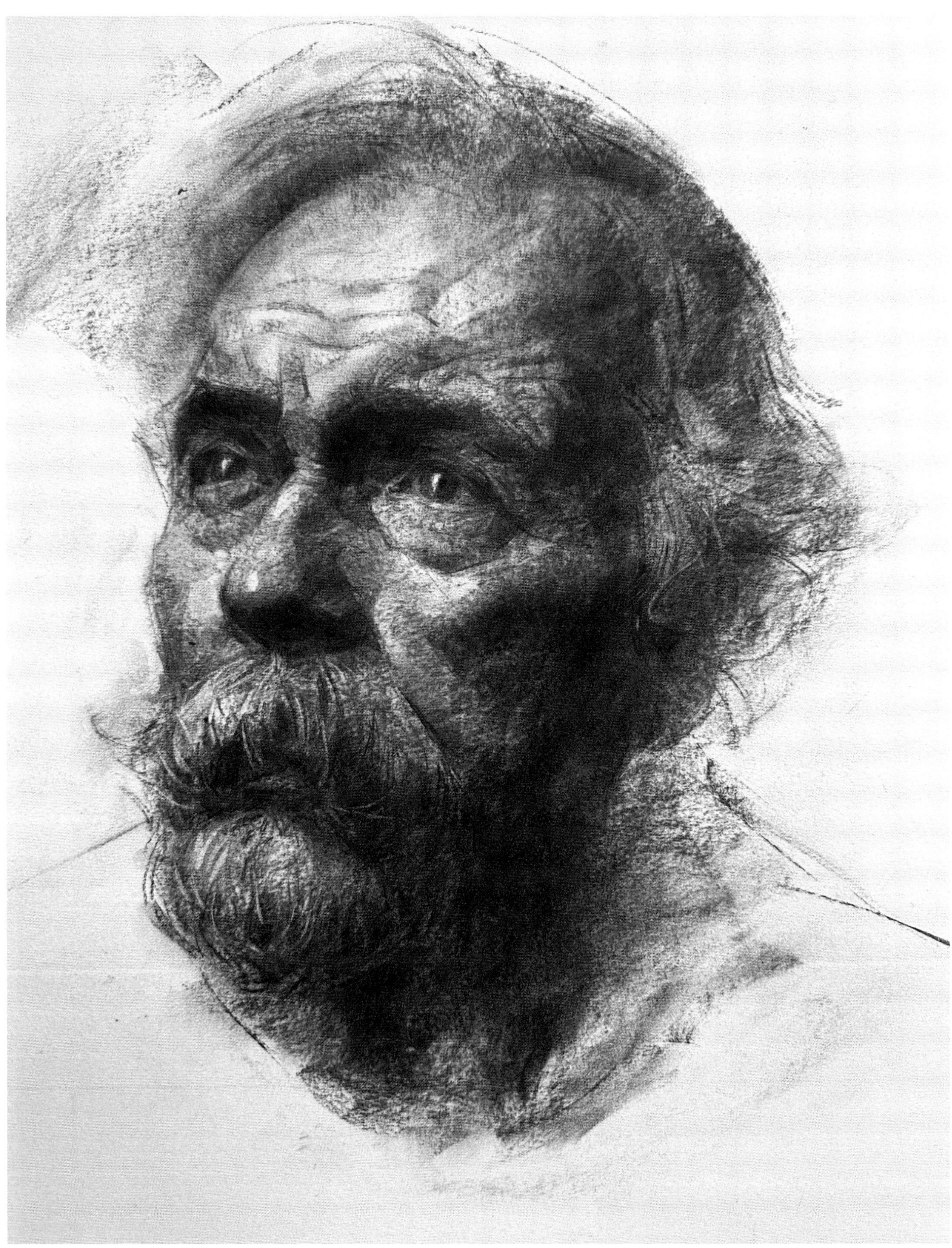

1

THE SKULL AND THE ESSENTIAL MUSCLES OF THE HEAD

THE SKULL: THE UNDERLYING FRAMEWORK

I do believe you should know the basic anatomy of the head, including the names of all the muscles and bones, as well as where they are, where they attach and connect, and what they do.

The skull and how its proportions relate to an individual forms the basis to reconstructing our facial appearance. From watching those popular forensic investigation shows, we've learned that based on the bone mass of a skull, we can re-create a decedent's face by adding facial muscles with convincing accuracy.

THE STRUCTURE OF THE SKULL

The structure of the skull can be roughly divided into two main parts: the facial skeleton, or facial bone (viscerocranium), and the braincase (neurocranium).

Of the twenty-two bones in the head, eight bones make up the braincase, and fourteen bones make up the face.

The **skull**, which is our facial skeleton, consists of the following fourteen individual bones. They provide the basic structure where all our facial soft tissues attach: one vomer, two inferior nasal conchae, two nasal bones, two maxillae, one mandible, two palatine bones, two zygomatic bones, and two lacrimal bones.

The **braincase** forms the cranial cavity, a complex structure that encloses and protects the brain and brainstem. This protective casing is composed of several bones that interlock to create a robust barrier against physical impacts and other external threats, ensuring the safety of the brain's delicate tissues.

The braincase consists of eight bones: the occipital bone, two temporal bones, two parietal bones, the sphenoid bone, the ethmoid bone, and the frontal bone. These bones are joined together with cranial sutures, forming a protective vault around the brain.

PARTS OF THE SKULL

To draw the head intelligently, you should know at least the elementary facts about the skull and the facial muscles.

Here are the names of the different parts of the skeleton of the head, the skull:

1. **Frontal bone:** This is the forehead, or front part of the skull.
2. **Nasal cavity:** The nasal structure consists of two oblong halves that meet to form the bridge of the nose.
3. **Zygomatic bone:** The zygomatic bone, generally known as the cheek bone, includes the lower eye socket.
4. **Maxilla:** The maxilla is a bone that contributes to the structure of the skull. Located in the midface, it forms the upper jaw and helps separate the nasal cavities. The maxilla plays a crucial role in the anatomy of the face by supporting the upper teeth and forming part of the orbit of the eye.
5. **Mandible:** The mandible, the largest bone in the human skull, forms the lower jawline. It's the only mobile bone of the skull. It's shaped like a horseshoe, with the ends anchoring into the temporal portion of the ear. It operates like a hinge, mainly moving up and down as the mouth opens or closes, with limited sideways and forward movement.

6. **Sphenoid bone:** The sphenoid (wasp
   bone) is part of the base of a skull and
   is located behind the eye and below the
   front part of the brain.

7. **Temporal bone:** The temporal region
   refers to the side parts of the skull.

8. **Parietal bone:** The parietal bones are a pair
   of irregular, quadrilateral skull bones that
   form the sides and roof of the cranium,
   making up the top part of the skull.

9. **Occipital bone:** This is the lower part and
   base of the skull.

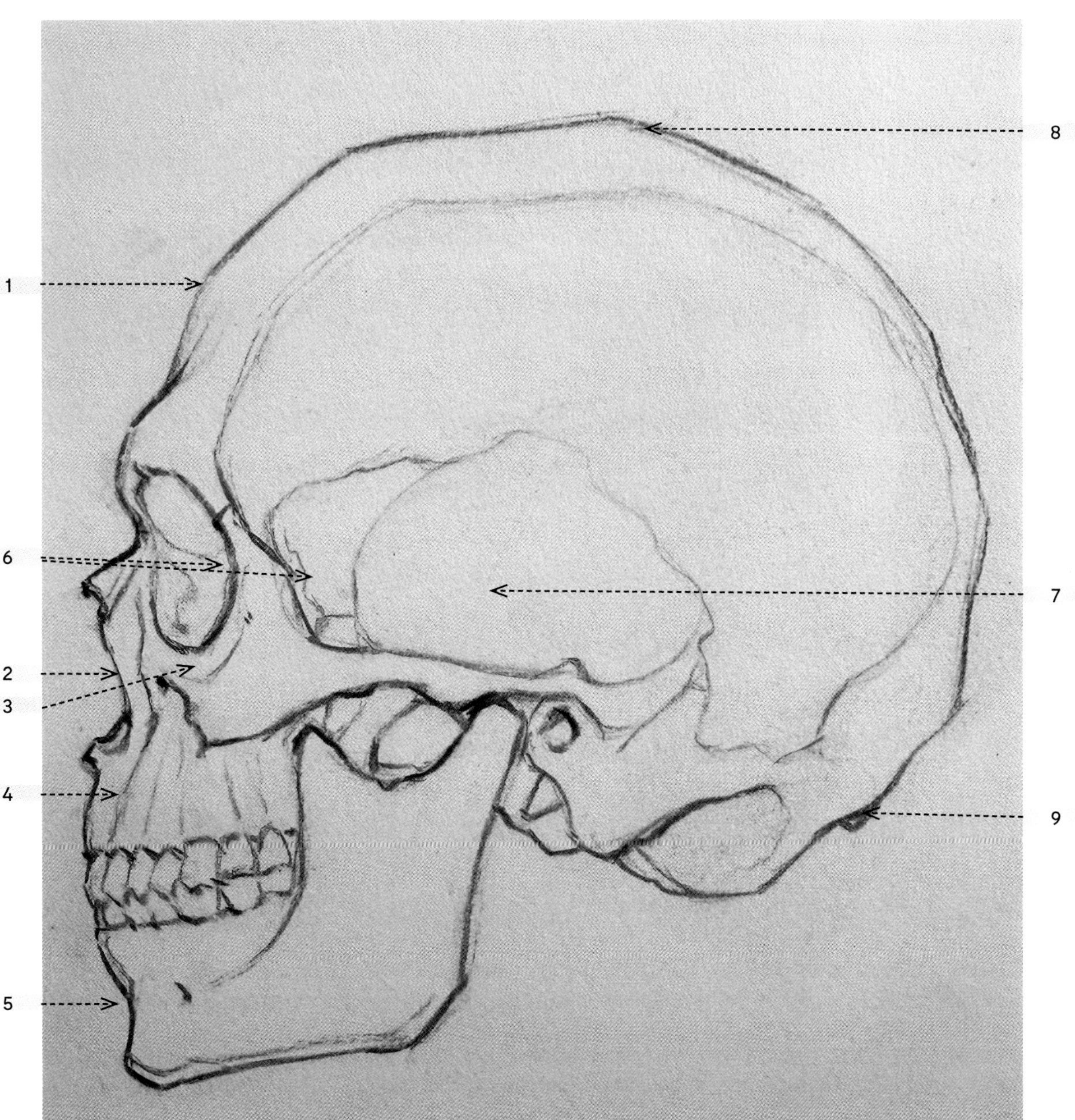

1. FRONTAL BONE
2. NASAL CAVITY
3. ZYGOMATIC BONE
4. MAXILLA
5. MANDIBLE
6. SPHENOID BONE
7. TEMPORAL BONE
8. PARIETAL BONE
9. OCCIPITAL BONE

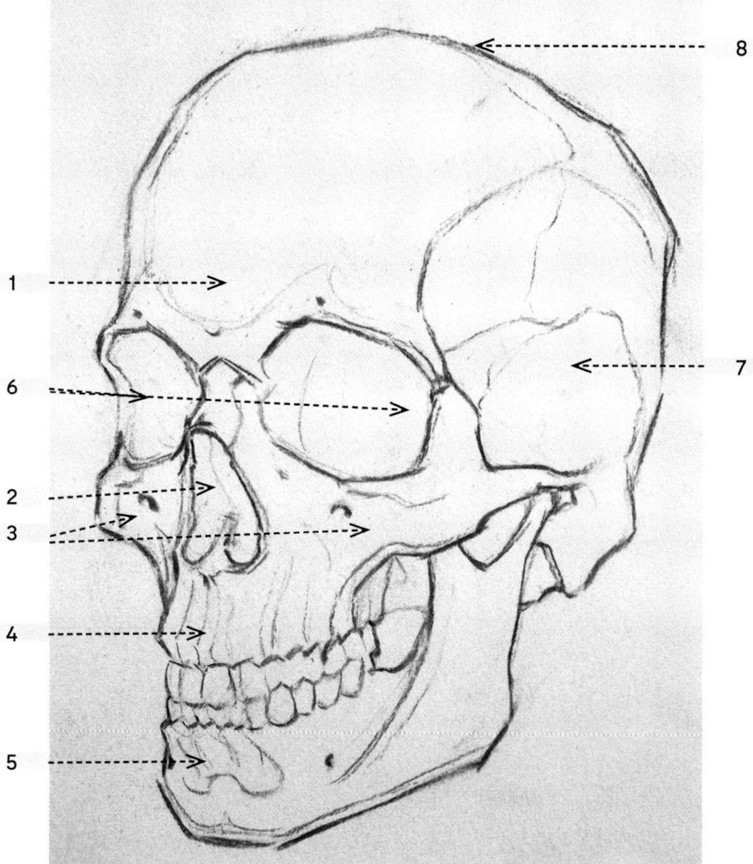

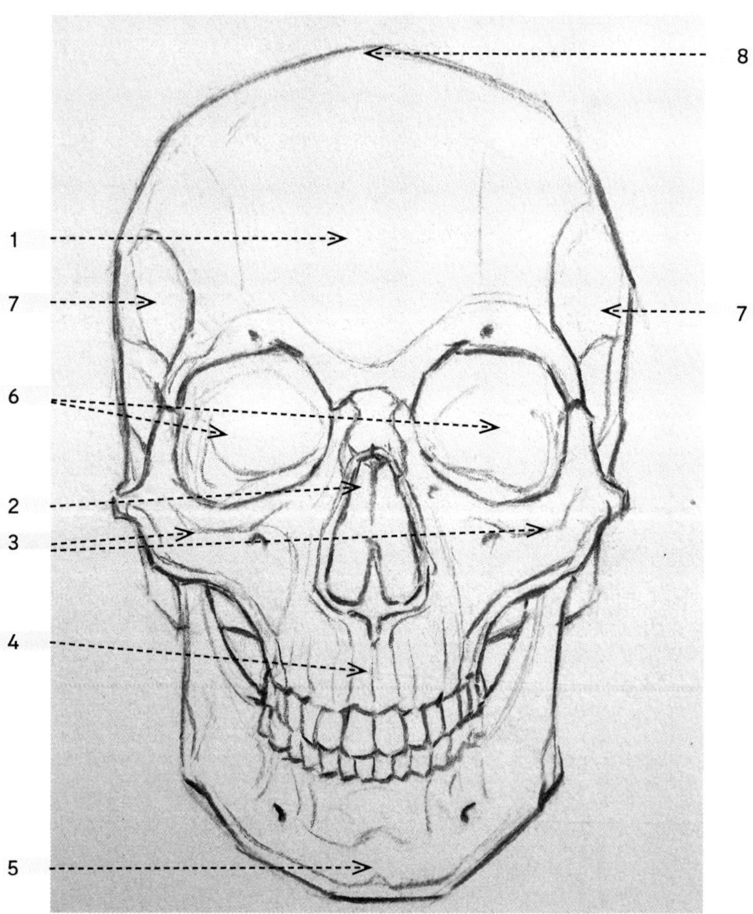

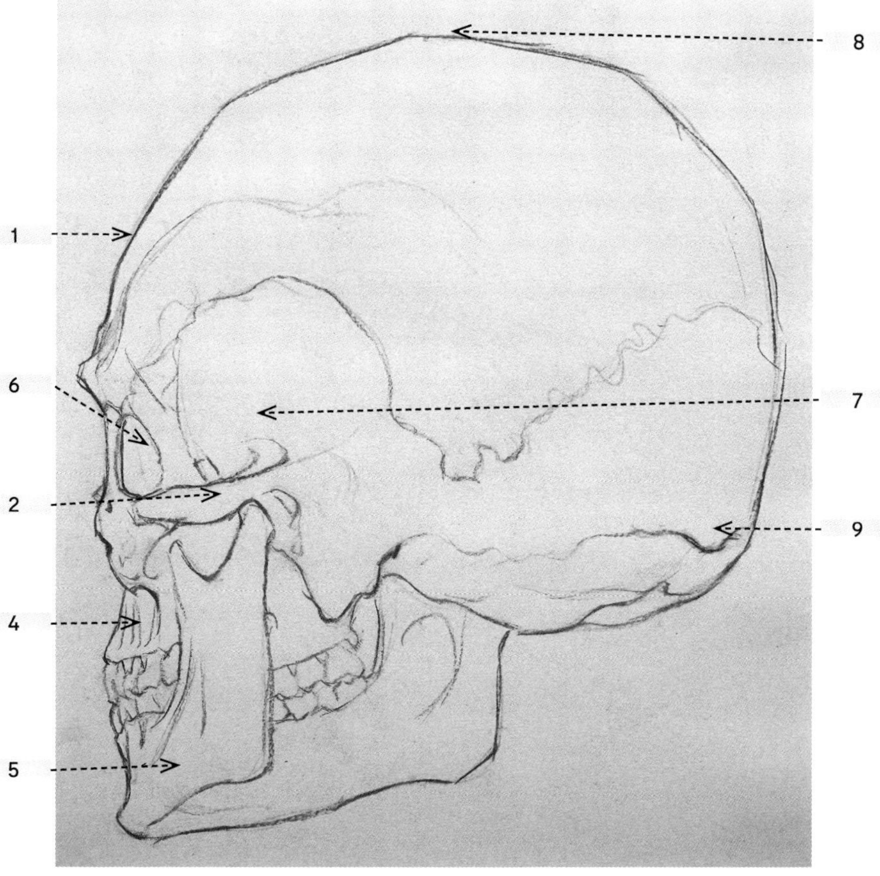

ROUND AND SQUARE FORMS OF THE HEAD

The skull is rounded on both sides of the head directly above the ears, creating a globular shape. The nose lies at the center of this formation. Just imagine how a square line naturally outlines a square form, while a round line outlines a round form. The classic beauty of all drawing is based on the harmonious combination or contrast of these forms. Conversely, partially rounded square forms or partially square rounded forms lack power or style.

HEAD WIDTH VERSUS FACE WIDTH

The **head width** is measured at the points where the two parietal eminences are located. Each parietal bone has a prominent bulge, called the *parietal eminence*, located slightly above and behind the ears.

The **face width** is broadest part of the face located between the two zygomatic arches. Anatomically, the zygomatic arch is a structure formed by the union of the zygomatic process of the temporal bone and the temporal process of the zygomatic bone. These arches are located on either side of the face and contribute significantly to the facial width and overall structure.

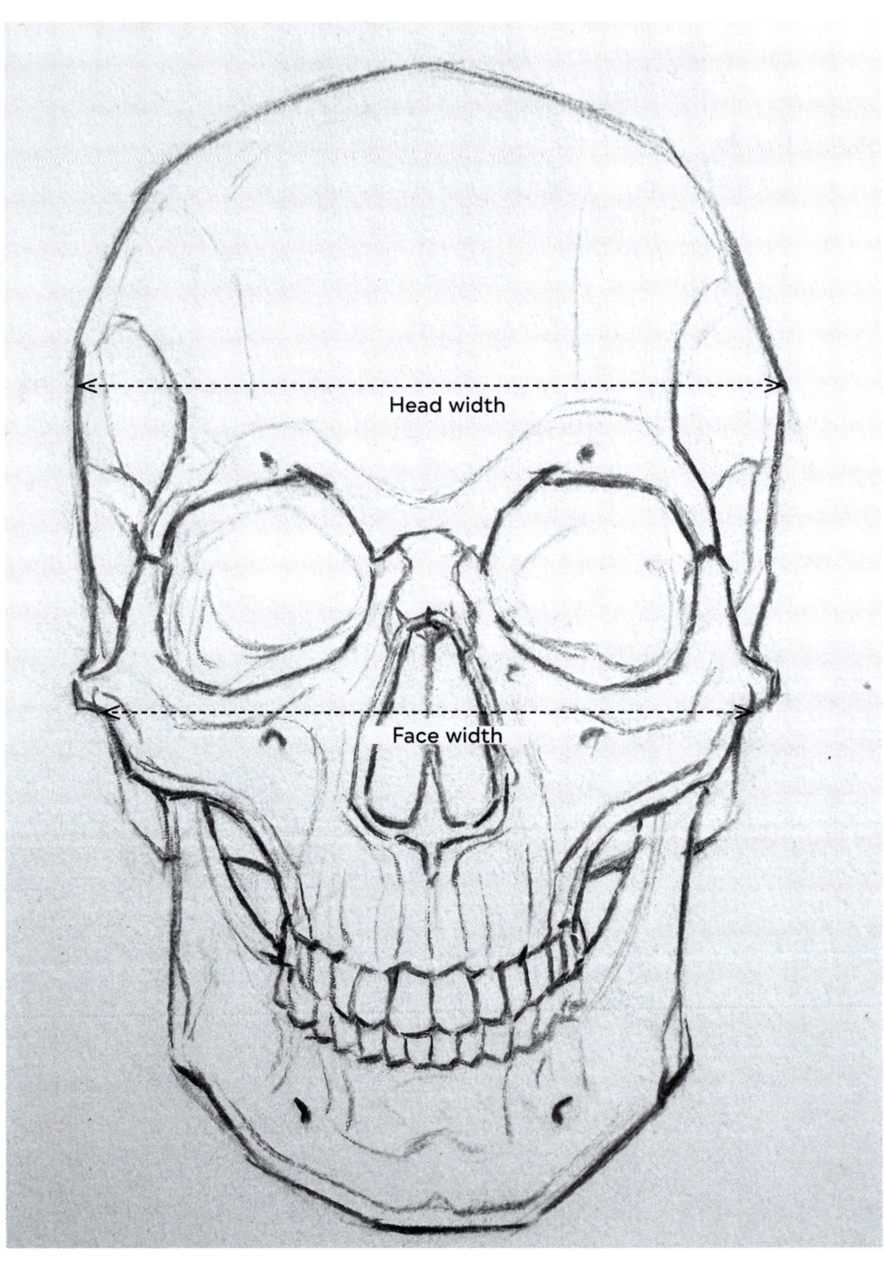

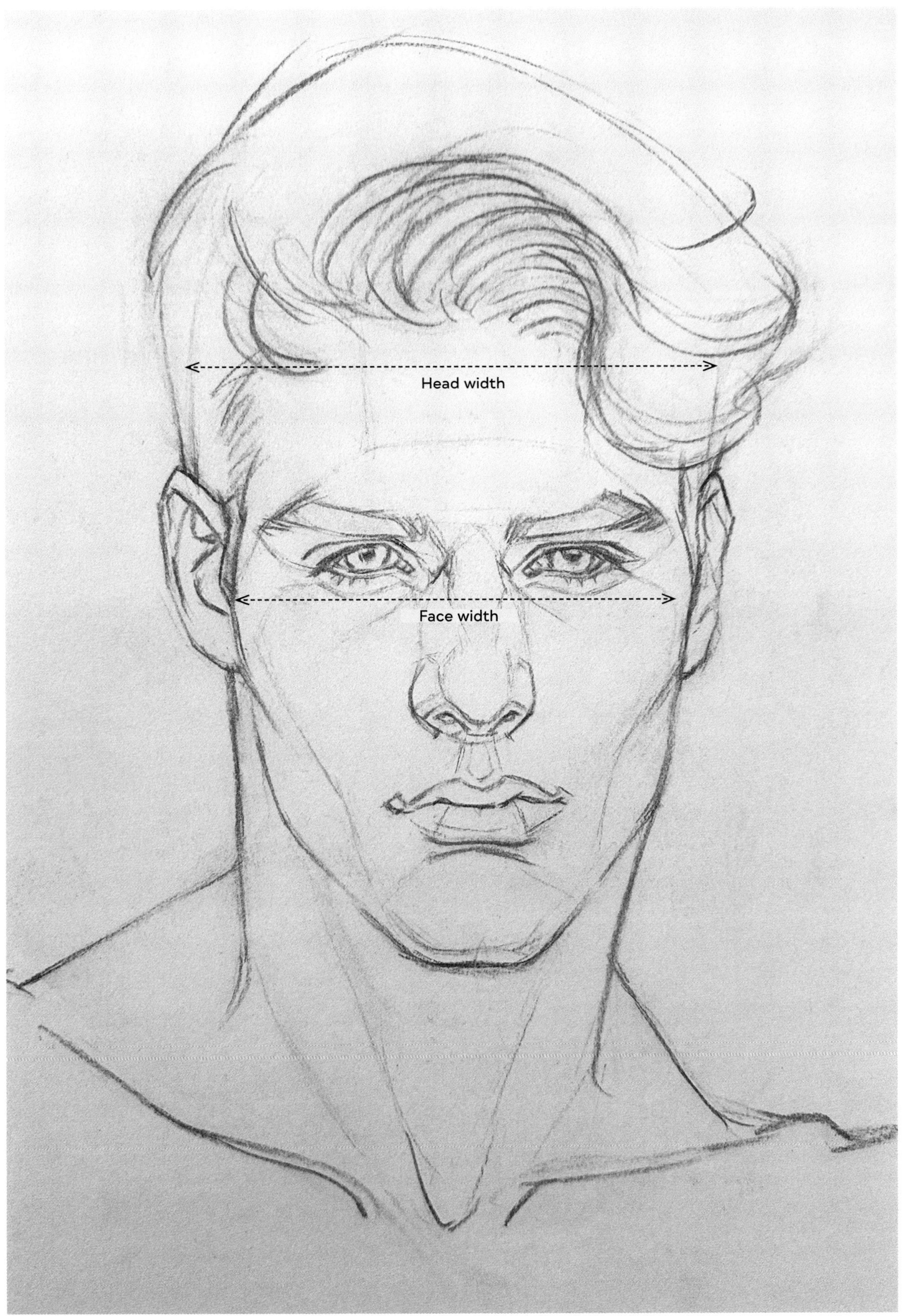

Head width
Face width

BASIC HEAD SHAPES: EGG VERSUS HELMET

The skull is the skeleton of the head. It comprises the bones of the cranium, the face, and the mandible (lower jaw). The skull is composed of twenty-two bones that are joined together by immovable joints called cranial sutures. The one exception to this rule is the mandible, the only mobile portion of the skull. The primary functions of the skull are to protect the brain from harm and to support the structure of the face. The skull acts as a hard, protective shell around the brain, safeguarding it from external impacts and injuries. It forms a solid barrier that

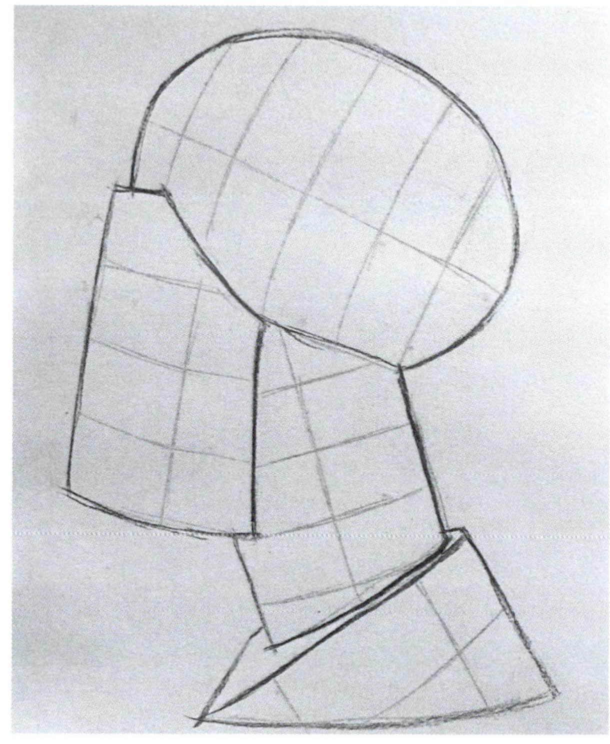

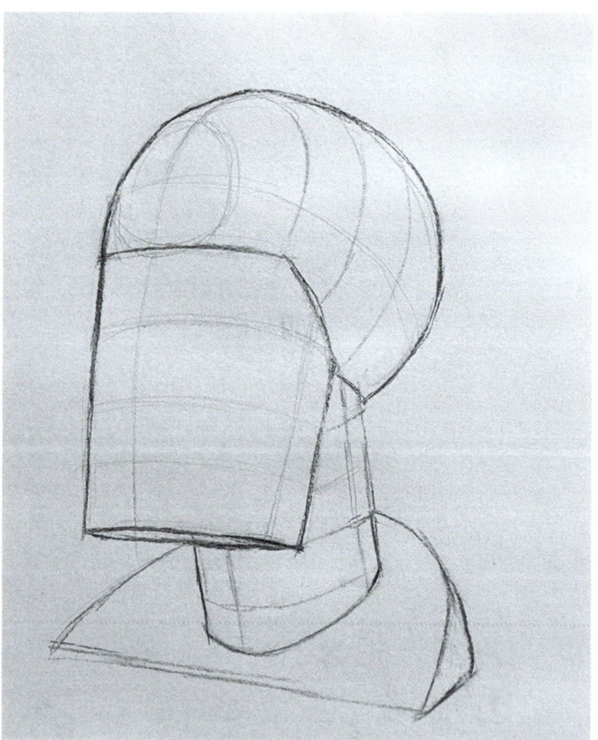

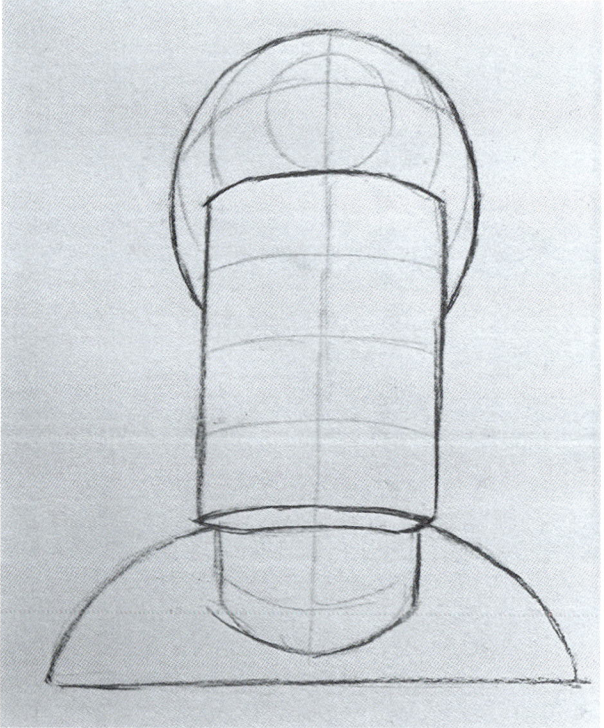

The egghead is constructed from two cylinders and a twisted egg.

reduces the risk of damage to the delicate brain tissue from external mechanical forces. The skull provides the framework for the face, supporting the facial bones and maintaining the overall shape and structure of the face. This structural support is essential for functions such as chewing, speaking, and facial expressions. The skull holds the eyes and ears in place, giving the brain sensory information, and shapes the head.

The head's shape can be simplified as an oval or egg shape, often referred to as either an **egghead** or **helmet head**.

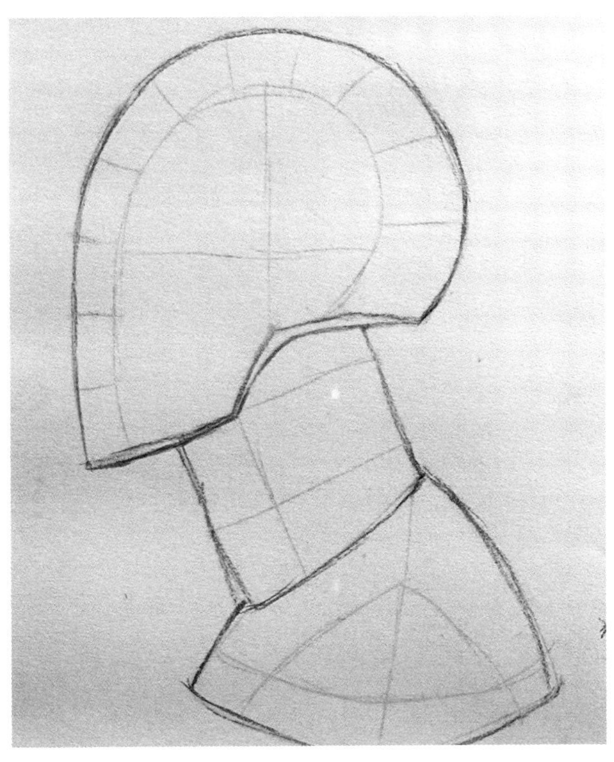

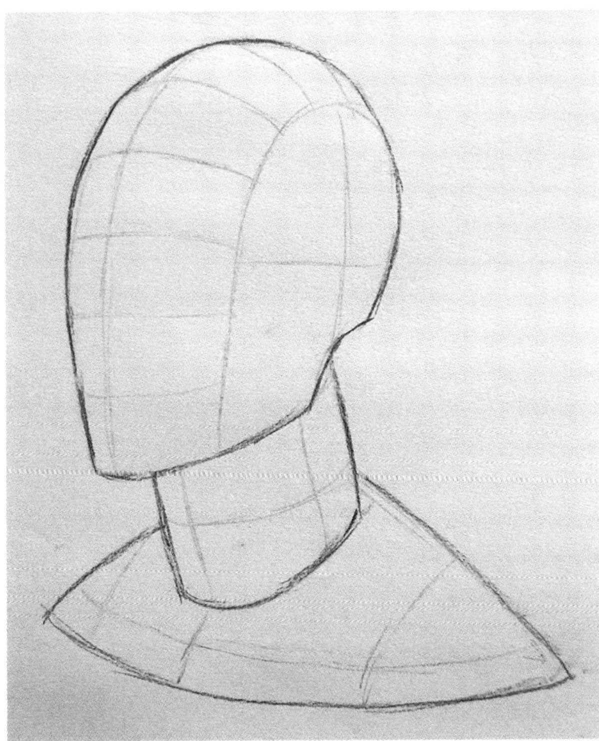

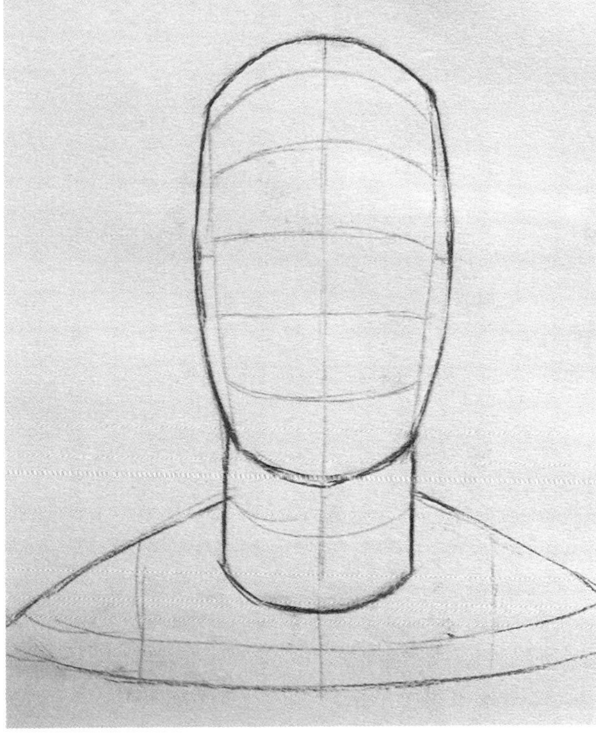

The helmet head is basically a smoothed-out head and neck with no details, resembling a motorcycle helmet.

After drawing the helmet head, the next step is to block out the main features of the face and neck. This is called the *planes change head*, where the basic shapes, such as the forehead, cheeks, and chin, become noticeable before adding realistic details. A plane is a flat surface. When the direction changes, a new plane is created. For example, a cube has six planes (top, base, two sides, and front and back) that define its form. The planes of the head are the surfaces formed by the bones and the muscles that overlay them.

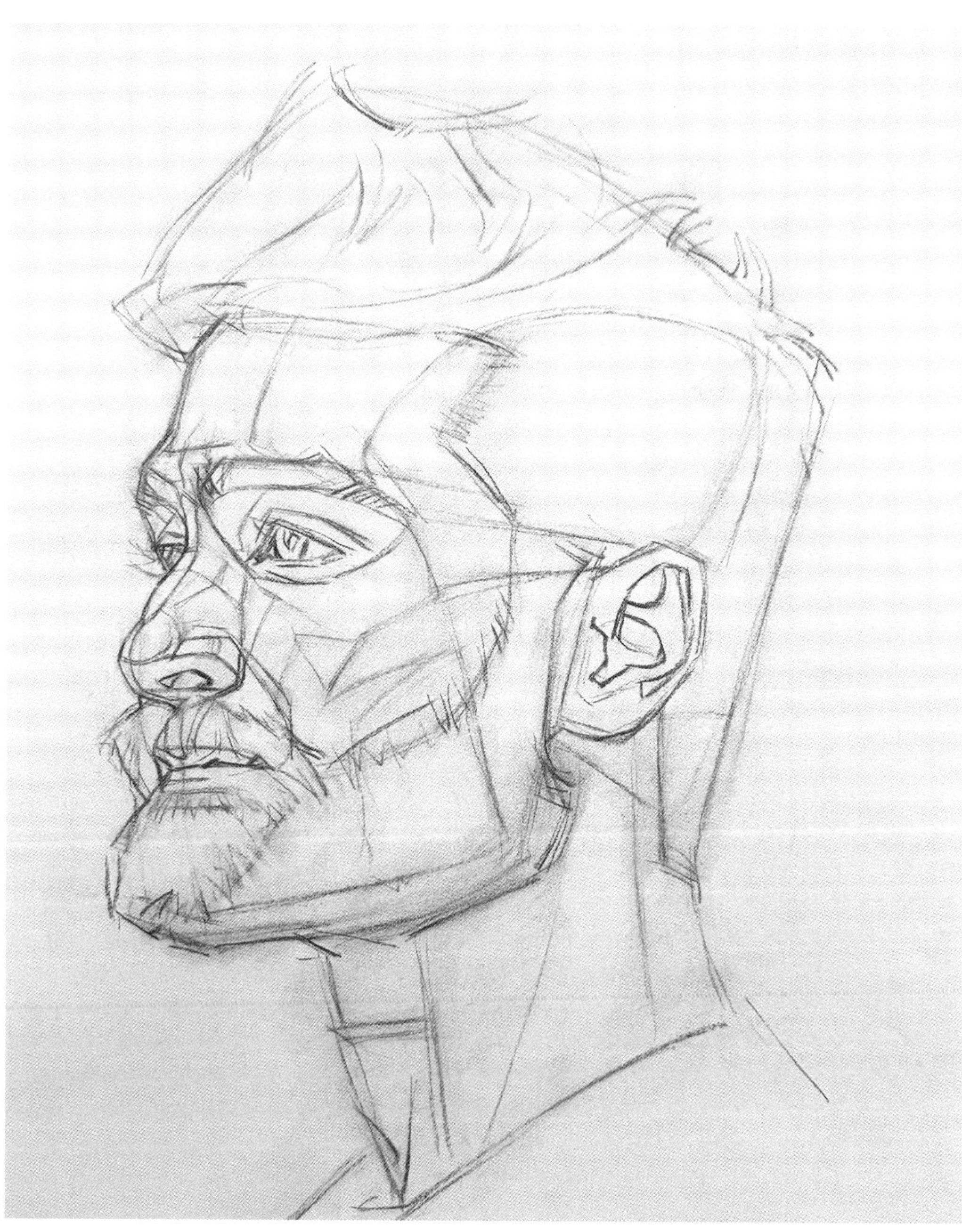

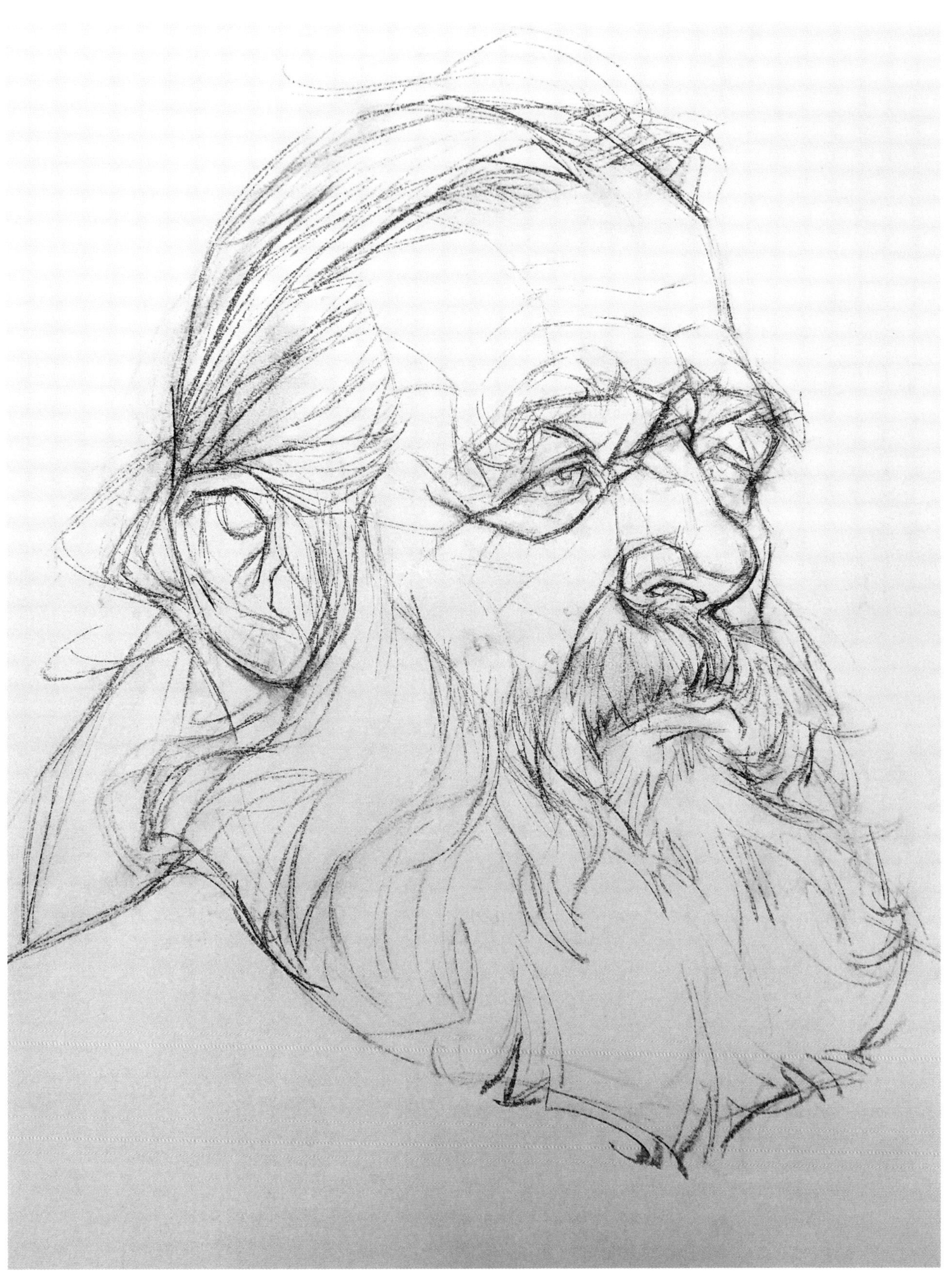

PROPORTIONAL VARIATIONS OF THE SKULL

Facial skeleton and braincase proportion change during early development and during the aging process. In adulthood, the facial skeleton is the largest size. In old age, its size generally decreases, primarily due to the reduction of the mass of the mandible. This reduction in mandibular mass leads to noticeable changes in the facial structure and overall appearance.

GENDER DIFFERENCES

The female skull is more gracile and relatively smaller and smoother than the male skull. In contrast, the male skull is larger and more rugged, reflecting the differences in overall skeletal robustness between the sexes. These variations include differences in the brow ridges, mastoid processes, and overall bone density and structure.

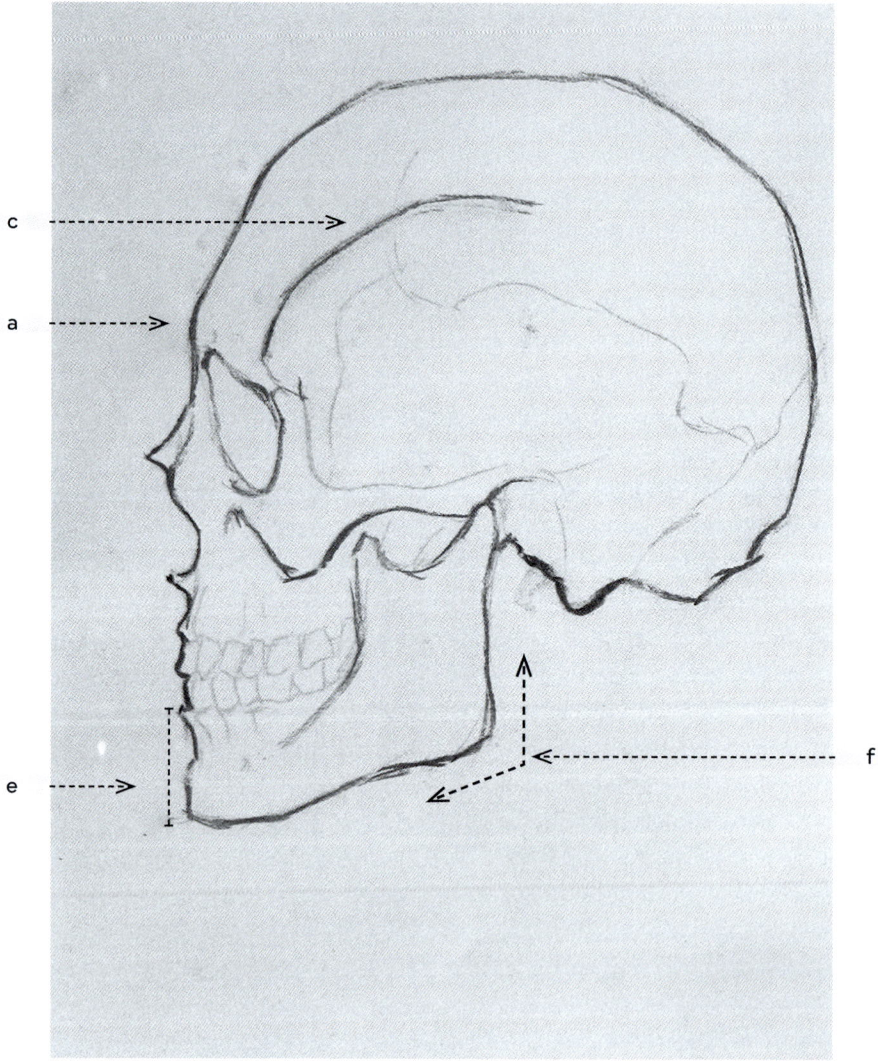

Male

Forehead: Male skulls have a more prominent glabella and brow ridge (see a, on the previous page), making the forehead look flat and oblique. In contrast, the female forehead is higher, more vertical, and rounded due to the larger frontal eminences (see b, below). These differences contribute to the distinct overall appearances of male and female skulls.

Temporal line: Male skulls have more prominent and well-demarcated temporal lines (c) compared to female skulls where it's relatively poorly defined.

Eye orbits: Female skulls have rounder, higher eye orbits with sharper supraorbital margins (d), and male skulls have squared, lower, blunt margins.

Jaws: The male chin is broad and more square-shaped, featuring a wider mandible (e) and a steeper angle (f). In contrast, the female chin is typically narrower and more pointed, with a mandible that has a less pronounced angle. In males, the angle of the jaw could be 90 degrees, but it's usually 100 to 120 degrees, more of a vertical angle as opposed to a right angle. In contrast, the angle of the female jaw is wider (g) and it can measure 120 to 140 degrees.

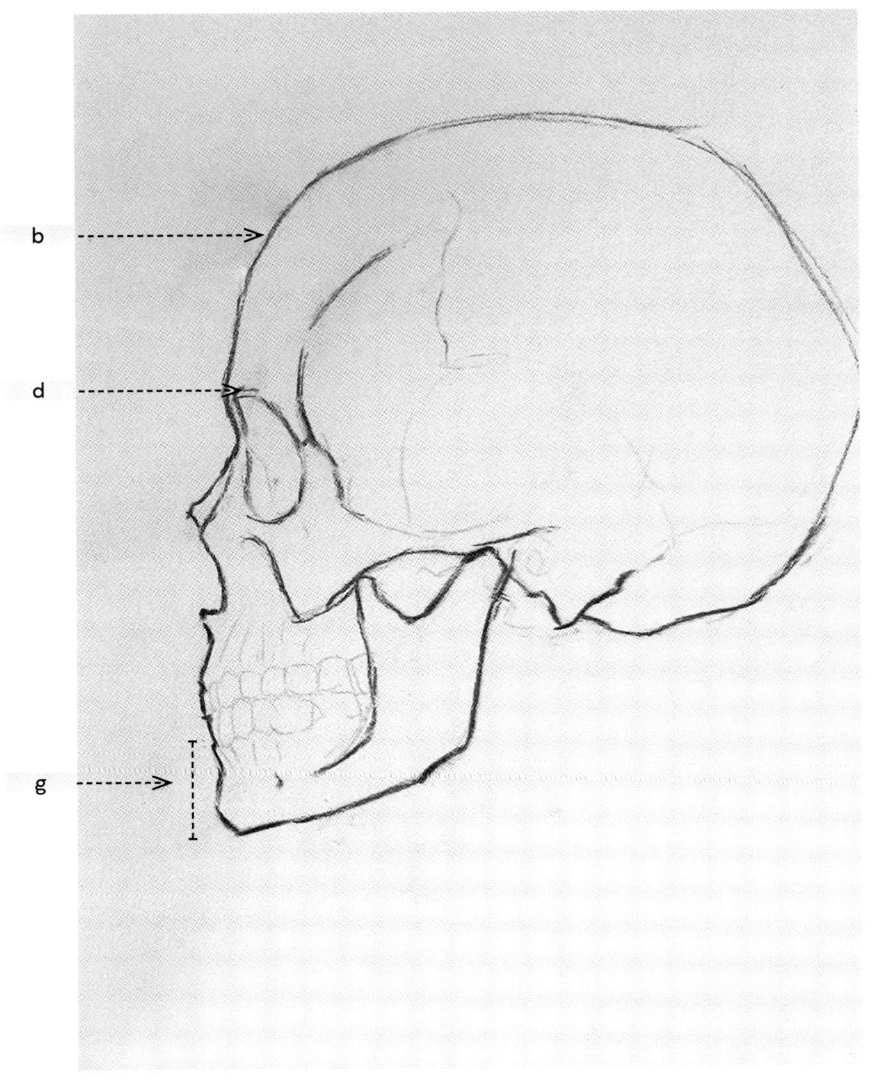

Female

FACIAL MUSCLES

When studying facial muscles, stand in front of a mirror and observe your own mannerisms. This practice will help you understand how expressions are formed and the role that the facial muscles play.

Here are the names of the facial muscles and their basic functions:

1. **Frontalis:** The forehead muscle that elevates the eyebrows, wrinkles the forehead, and plays a crucial role in facial expressions.

2. **Temporalis:** A fan-shaped muscle on each side of the head that's responsible for the retraction and elevation of the mandible. Along with the masseter, it's one of the two pairs of major chewing muscles with significant volume.

3. **Orbicularis oculi:** The muscles in the eyelids that encircle the eye socket, close the eyelids, and stretch the skin of forehead.

4. **Levator labii superioris alaeque nasi:** This muscle lifts the upper lip upward and outward.

5. **Zygomaticus major:** This muscle raises the upper lip and pulls it upward, such as when we laugh.

6. **Masseter:** This thick, rectangular-shaped muscle is one of the strongest facial muscles. It elevates the jaw bone and brings thc teeth together with great force to facilitate chewing.

7. **Buccinator:** This muscle keeps the cheek tight against the teeth while chewing to prevent you from biting your cheek. It's also responsible for controlling airflow passing in and out through the mouth.

8. **Orbicularis oris:** This muscle encircles the mouth and allows you to close and to pucker your lips, which is why it's also known as the *kissing muscle*.

9. **Depressor labii inferioris:** This muscle draws the lower lip down and to the side. It's also referred to as the *sneering muscle*.

10. **Levator labii inferioris:** This muscle depresses the lower lip and protrudes it forward. It also wrinkles the chin.

11. **Nasalis:** This muscle located within the nose compresses the bridge of the nose, depresses the tip of nose, and elevates the corners of nostrils, flaring the nostrils.

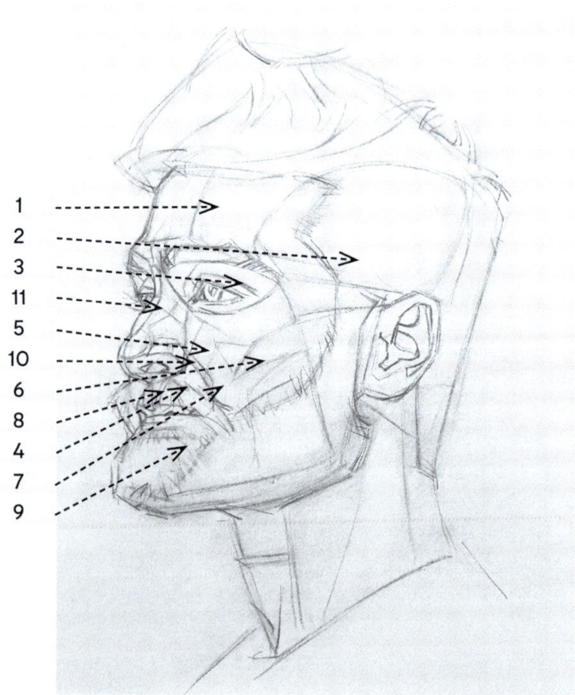

BONY LANDMARKS OF THE HEAD

As we get more in depth, painstakingly learning the relationship between the skull and the facial soft tissues, even tissue thickness, it will gradually define the anatomical accuracy of the face. Study anatomical landmarks and the key points of the head's anatomy carefully. They provide important criteria for evaluating consistency. These landmarks are important for ensuring your drawings are precise and coherent, keeping them from looking flat and shapeless.

1. **Temporal line:** This curved ridge runs along the external surface of the parietal bone.
2. **Superciliary arch (brow ridge):** This is the prominence of the frontal bone, also called the brow ridge.
3. **Nasal bones:** These two small bones form the bridge of the nose.
4. **Zygomatic arch:** This bridge of bone extends from the side of the head at the temporal bone to around the maxilla and includes the zygomatic bones. This is the area we refer to as a person's cheeks.
5. **Orbital margin:** This is the side of the orbital cavity that opens toward the front of the face.
6. **External occipital protuberance:** This is the slight bump located at the back of your skull just above your neck.
7. **Superior nuchal line:** This is the bony ridge that's located on the occipital bone at the back of the skull.
8. **Zygomatic bone:** This is the cheekbone.
9. **Mental protuberance:** This is the area we refer to as the chin.
10. **Jawline (base of the mandible):** This is the outline of the mandible.

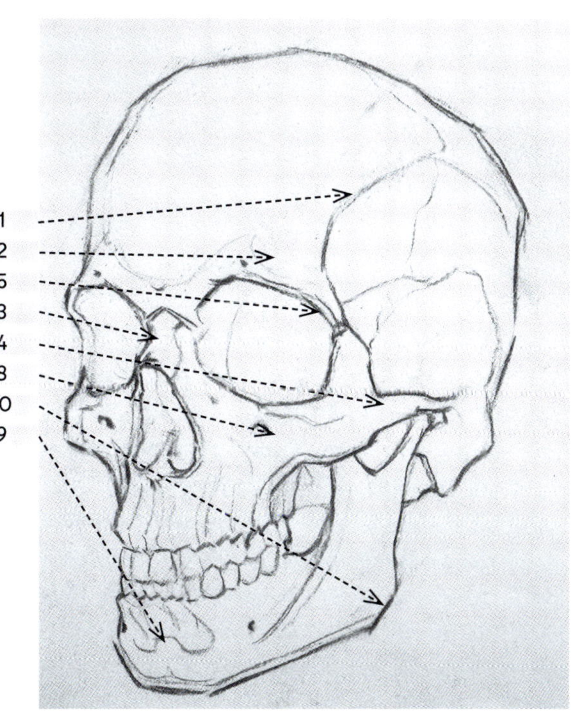

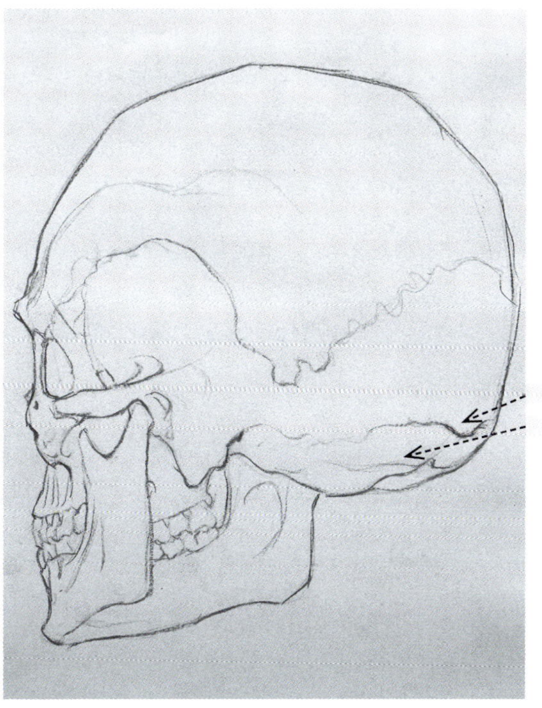

GENERAL MORPHOLOGY OF THE NECK

The neck connects to the front-top side of the trunk, not just at the top. To set the neck properly, imagine drawing a necklace around it. This line shows where the neck and trunk meet.

ANATOMY OF THE NECK

Consider the neck as the pedestal upon which the head rests. It's highly flexible and allows the head to turn and move in all directions. It forms the bridge between the head and the torso.

The **sternocleidomastoid muscle** consists of two diagonal muscles that turn the head. These muscles are attached to the skull just behind the ears at the top and to the sternum, or breastbone, between the two clavicles, or collarbones, at the bottom. The sternocleidomastoid muscle attaches to the back of the head, underneath the skull, helping to hold the head up or tip it backward. It passes obliquely across the neck, from the sternum of the breastbone and clavicle below to the mastoid process and superior nuchal line above. The pair of muscles come together to form the classic *V* shape that frames the throat. The muscle's bottom portion splits in two and divides the neck into two large triangles.

This muscle spirals like a thick rope, inserting into the mastoid process of the skull. Its primary function controls the rotation of the head, during which the medial tendon becomes prominently defined. This *V* shape, known as the *suprasternal notch*, or the pit of the neck, is an important landmark for measuring. The triangular space in front of the sternocleidomastoid muscle is the anterior triangle of the neck. The area behind it, laterally, is the lateral triangle of the neck.

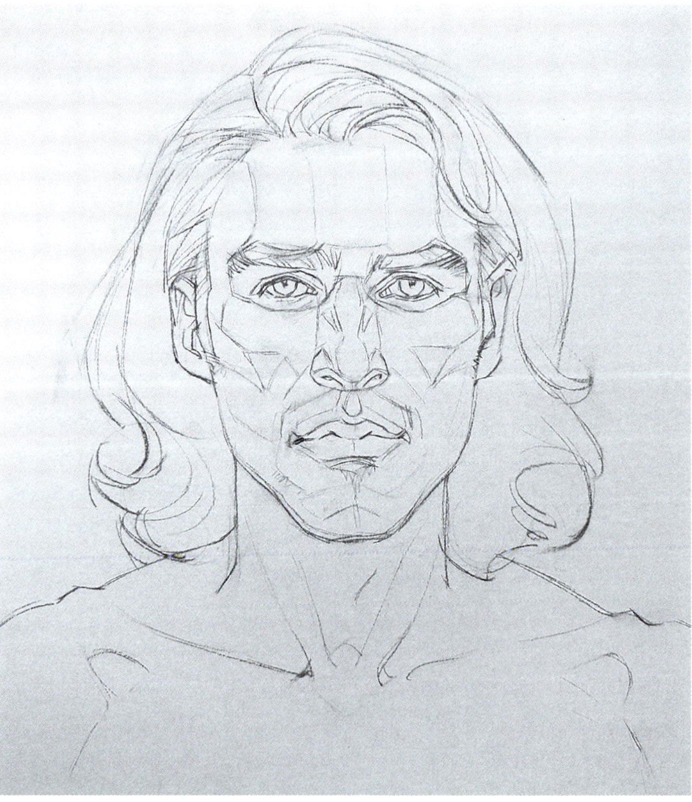

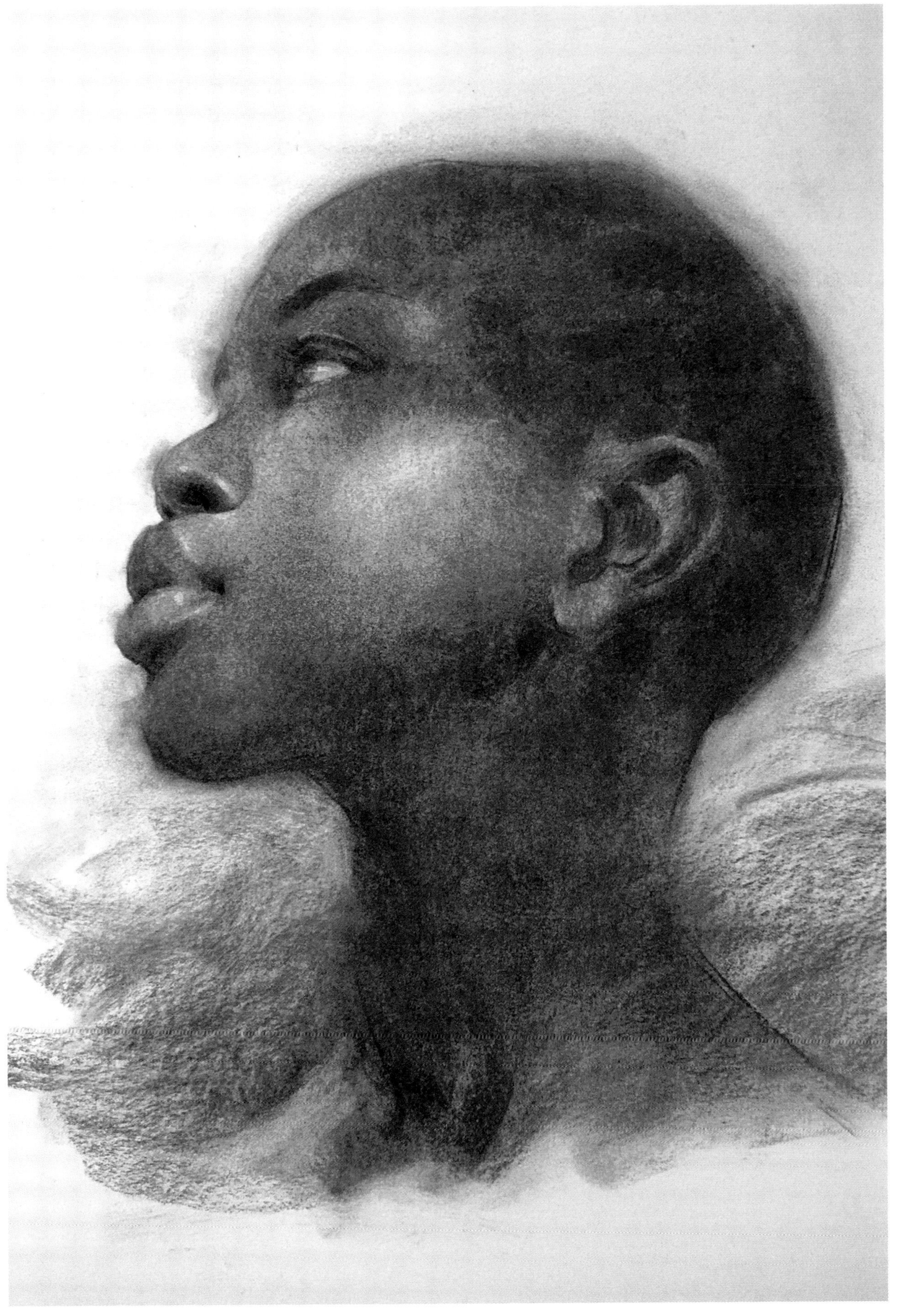

From the front, observe the *V* shape of the pit of the neck. As the model rotates their head, alternately, the opposite side pops out as it functions. On the male model, it's where the Adam's apple is, which distinctly changes the contour of the throat. Whereas on a female model, it is much more subtle. From the three-quarters view, see how the neck tilts forward, allowing the head to lead the way. From the rear, when the face rotates backward, the neck develops distinct crease lines due to the bunching up of the skin.

The neck connects to the head mostly at the superior nuchal line. This line provides an origin for the neck muscles, such as the trapezius muscle. The superior nuchal line extends from the midline to the occipitomastoid sutures. At its midline is a prominence called the *external occipital protuberance*.

The most important muscle on the back of the neck is the trapezius. Named for its trapezoidal shape, the trapezius is one of the largest flat muscles in the body. Due to its size and multiple segments, it can perform many different functions, including muscle movements such as shrugging your shoulders or turning your neck.

I often visualize the neck as a simple cylinder, like a coffee can. When we try to build up the neck, these muscles wrap around in a spherical manner. Keep this tubular form in mind when we observe the neck, no matter from which angle. This cylinder doesn't just sit on top of the shoulder, but is embedded into the shoulder girdle, with the muscles built up around it, particularly in the back. Furthermore, it's inclined toward the front and forms a tilt, which is crucial for achieving the proper posture and balance of the figure.

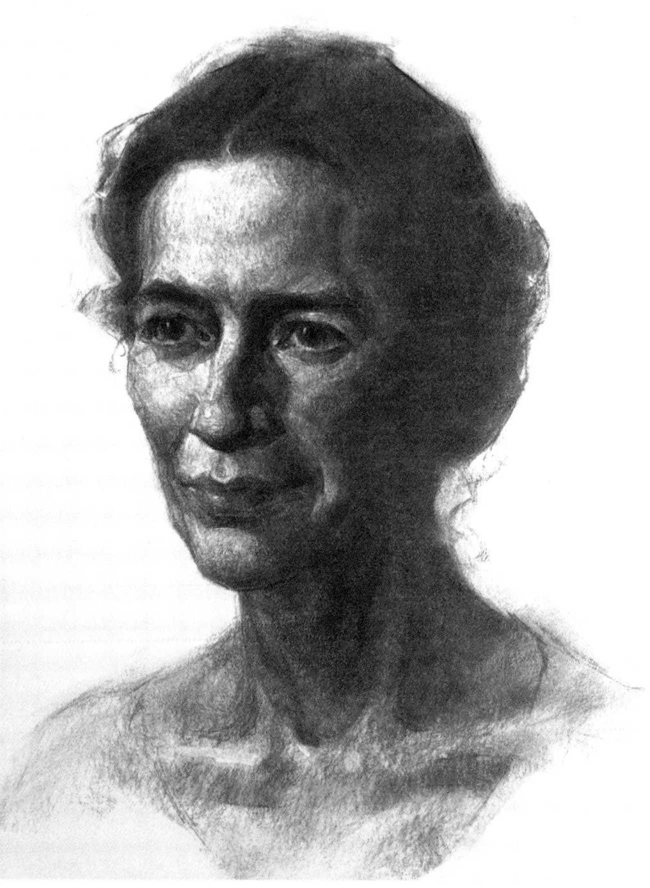

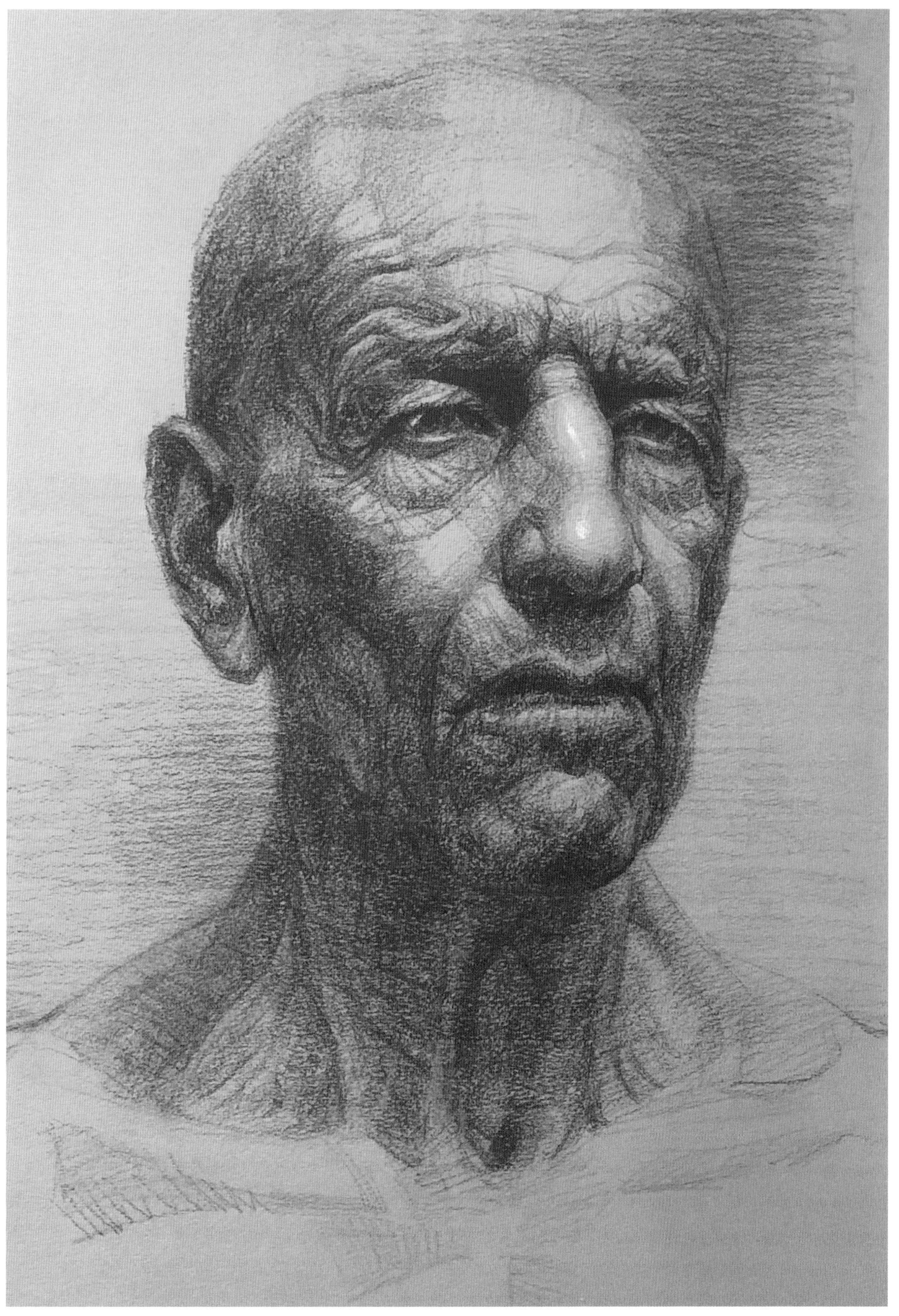

EVERY HEAD IS ITS OWN ARTISTIC CHALLENGE

Drawing the human face takes practice, but it isn't work. Try not to see it as drudgery. There's never a shortcut in mastering art. To me, people are the most fascinating subjects to study and draw. Every head is a unique assemblage of shapes, lines, and spaces. Every person has a unique face. Even the same person, with different expressions, lighting, and clothing, provides an endless array of portraits to capture. There is never a boring face to draw, only a lack of skills to appreciate the fun and challenges of drawing a portrait.

Because of the diversity of skulls and features, together with variations of spacing, millions of combinations occur. Accent the individual forms wherever you can and try to draw unique characters. The personality in a head is shaped by the distinctive bones and muscles, as revealed through careful construction and spacing of the facial features.

SMILING HEAD

Smiles that radiate happiness are much easier to render in an outline drawing than a tonal rendered drawing. I highly recommend that you draw a smiling head from picture references, as models can rarely maintain a genuine smile for an extended period. Pay particular attention to the forms around the corners of the mouth and the shapes of the cheeks.

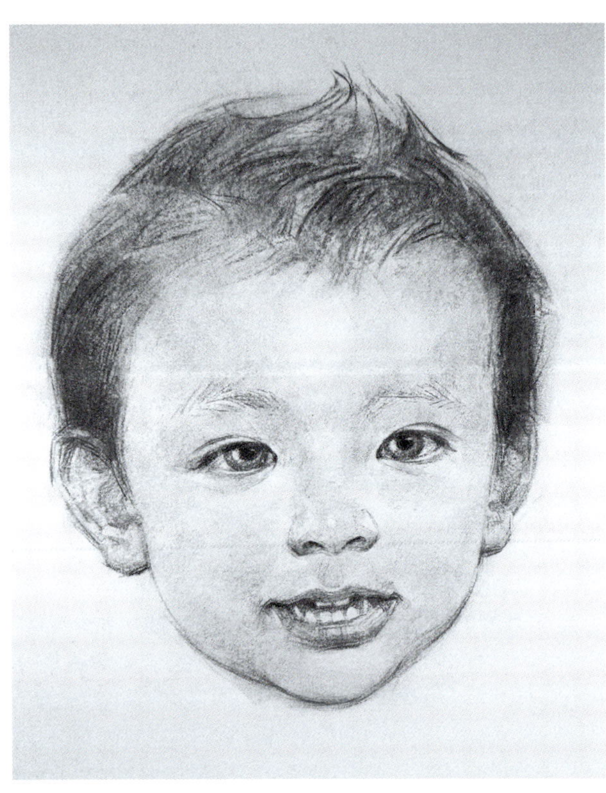

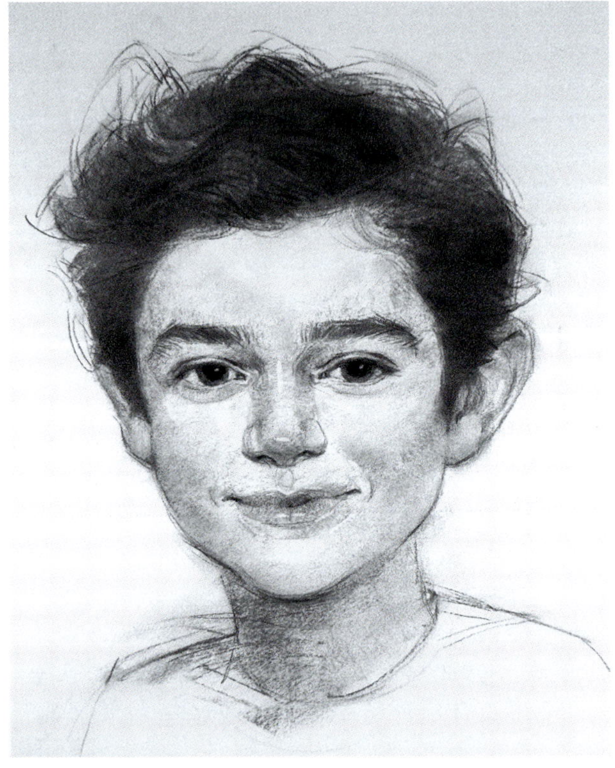

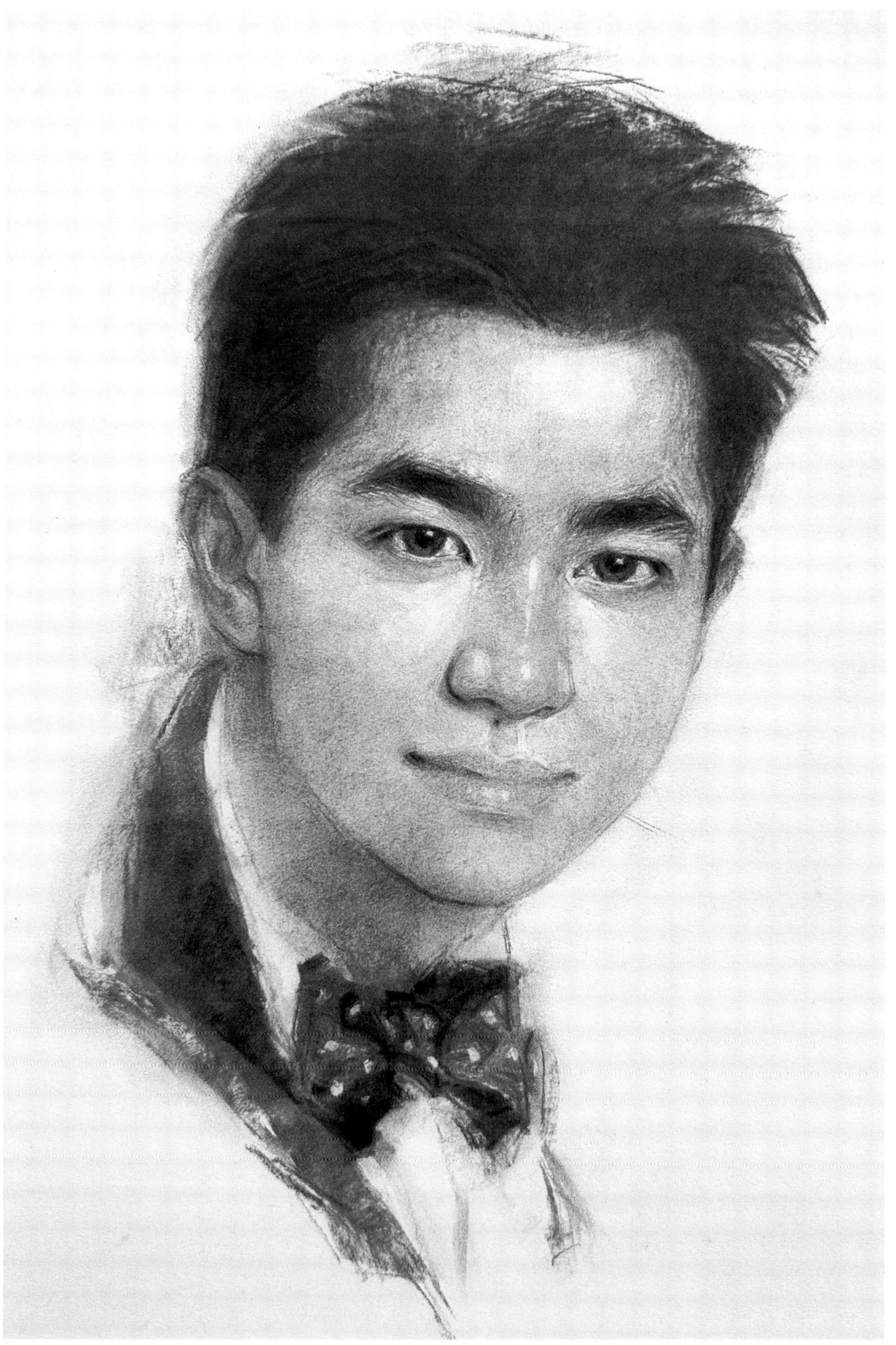

OLDER HEAD

The faces of older models give the artist more to "get hold of" in the way of form and lines. The impression of age is primarily influenced by the intricate network of surface wrinkles and fine lines on the face. These visible signs of aging are the result of the cumulative effects of environmental factors, genetic predispositions, and the natural loss of skin elasticity and collagen over time.

For additional details, see chapter 4, "Expressions and the Aging Face," pages 70–99.

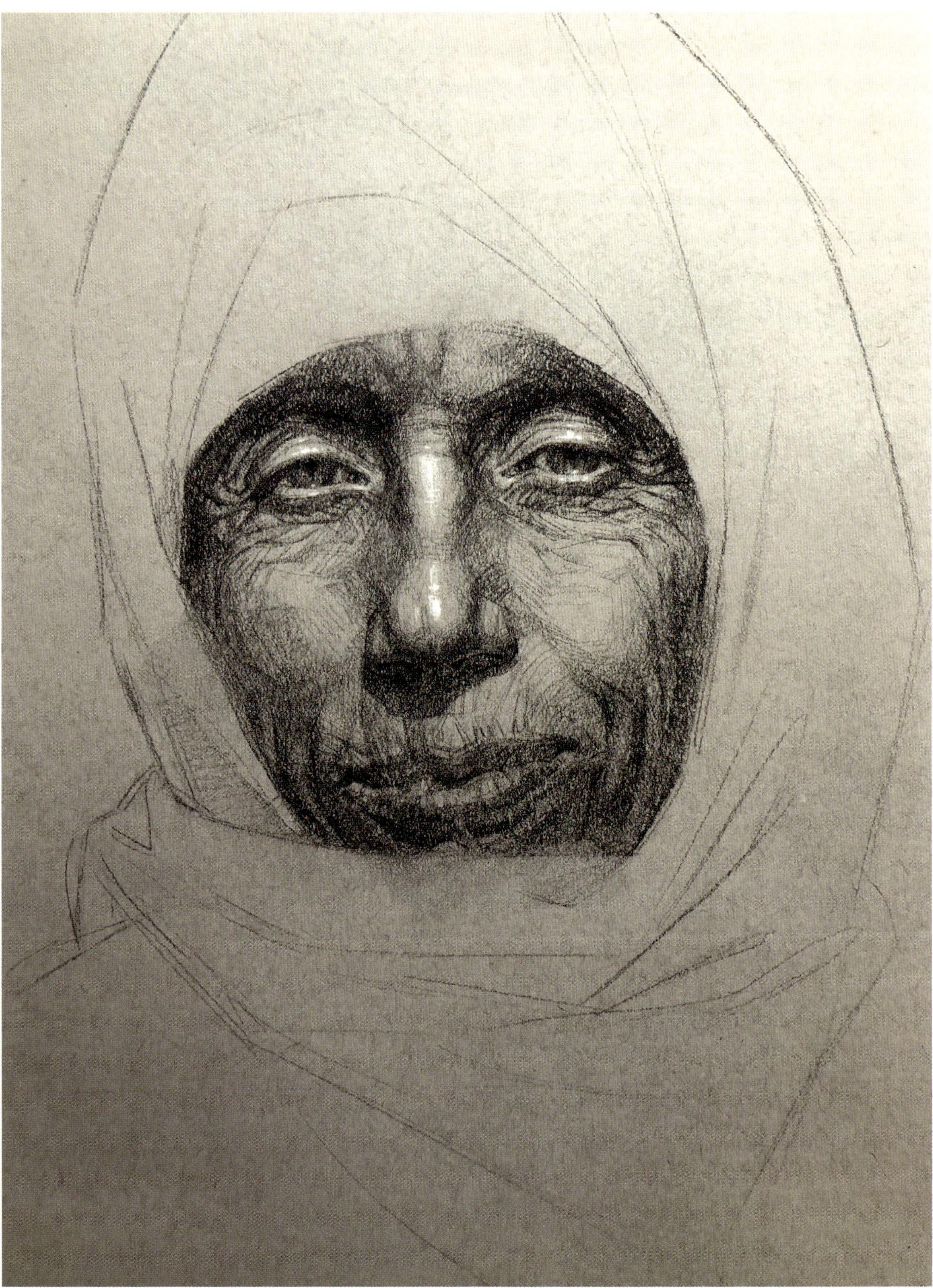

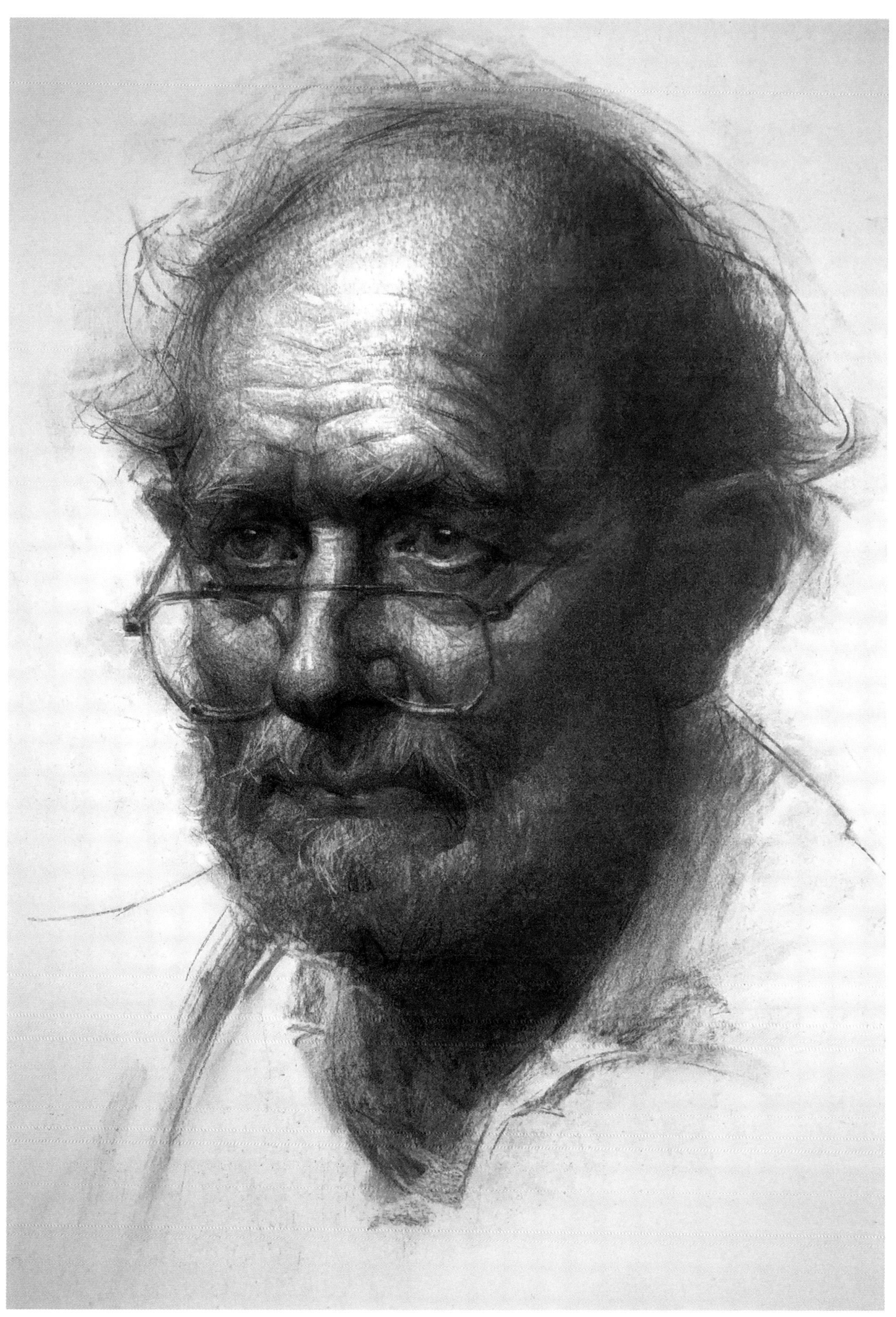

CHARACTERIZATION HEAD

This is characterization, the way a face looks at a given moment with the construction, lighting, and expression combined. Expression is essentially a distortion of the face's relaxed forms. This distortion is caused by movement of the muscles beneath the surface, leading to consequent changes on the skin's surface. Therefore, it's crucial to understand how facial muscles move and interact. By studying the underlying muscle structure and how these muscles contract and relax, one can accurately depict a wide range of expressions, capturing the nuances and subtleties of human emotion.

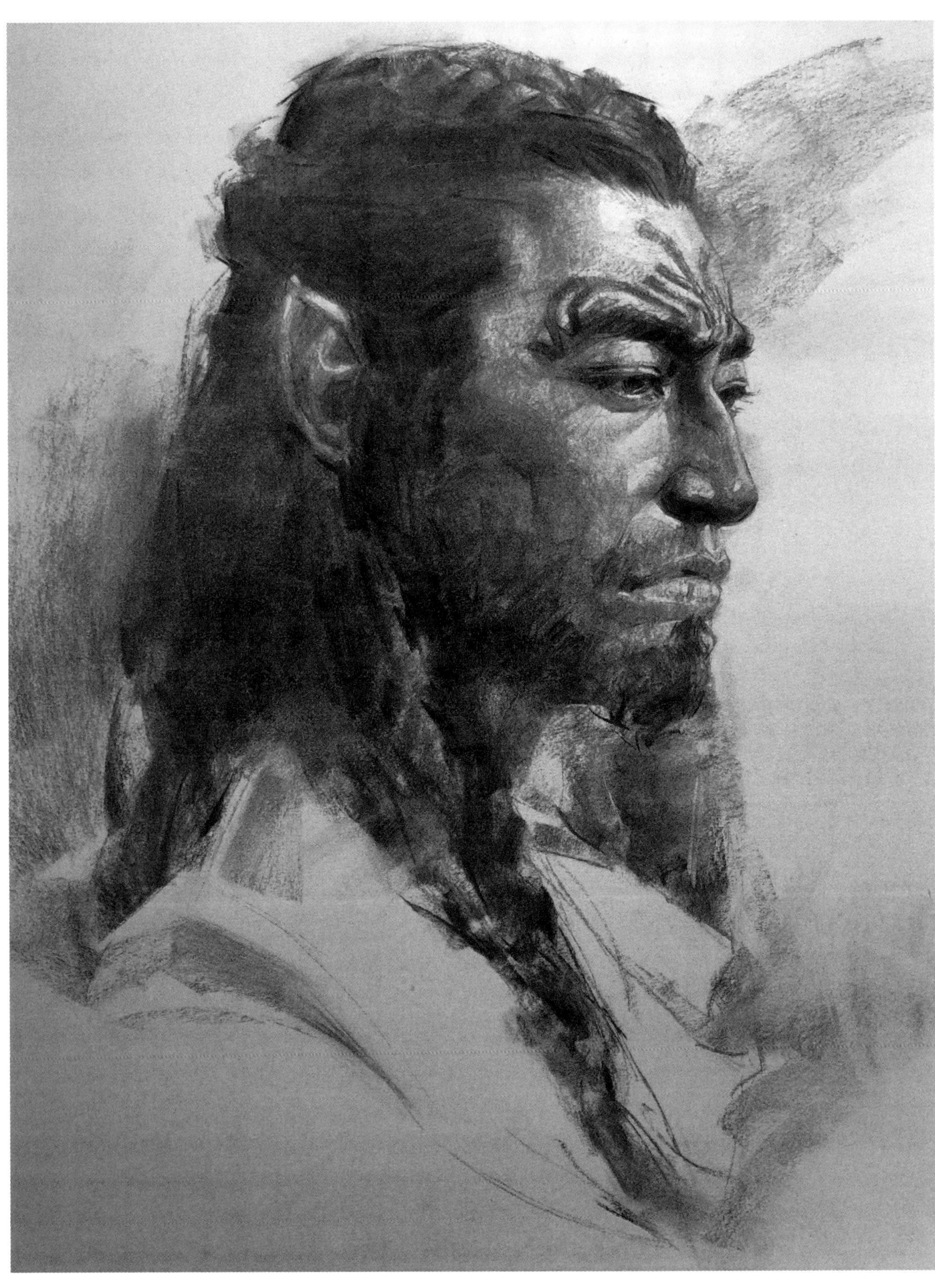

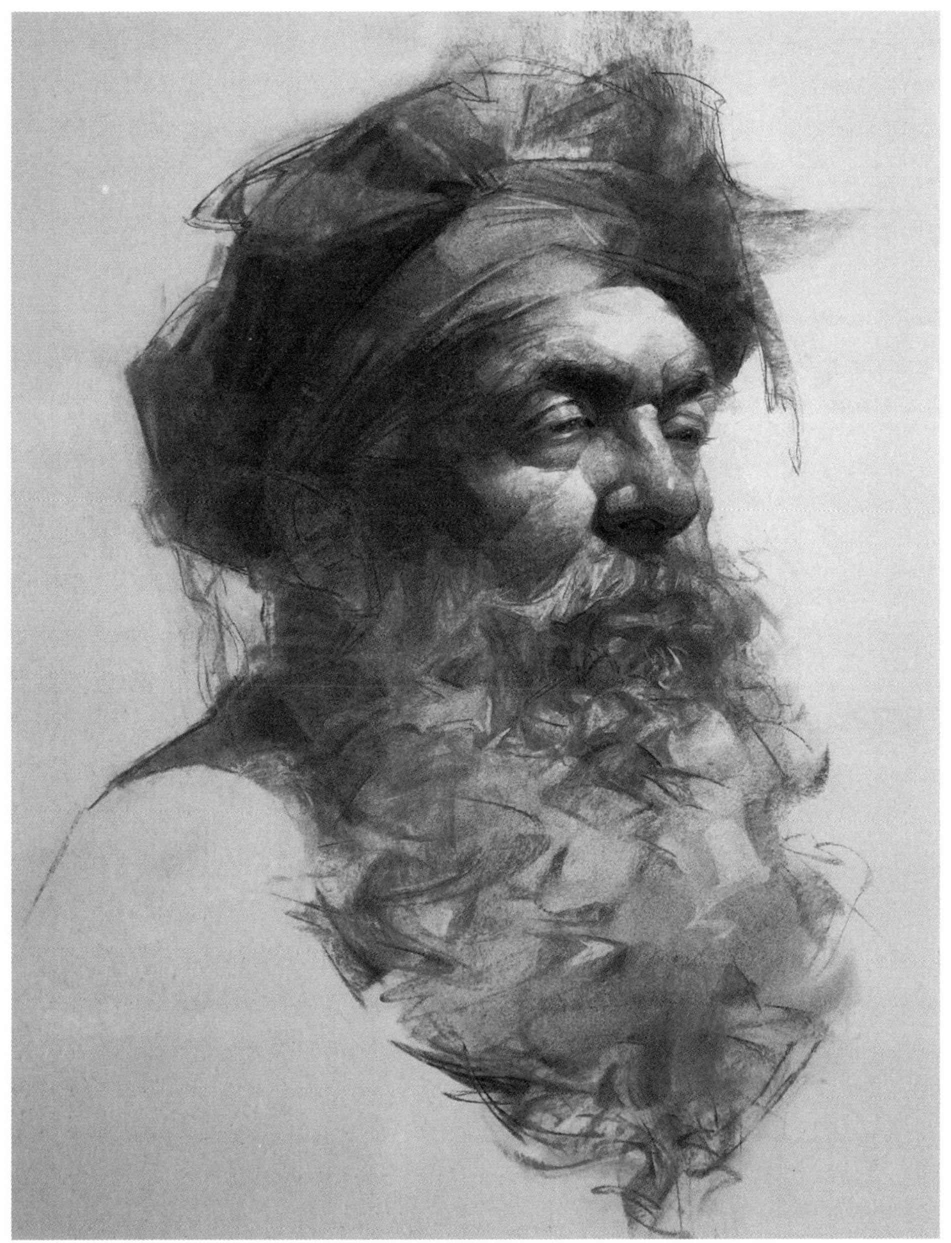

THE SUBTLETY OF FACIAL EXPRESSION

Human facial expressions are continuously changing, like a kaleidoscope, shifting swiftly with the slightest movements. Each expression is a combined result of the contraction of certain muscles, in relation to the relaxation of their opposing muscles.

Both the eyes and mouth are surrounded by circular muscles. The main function of these muscles is the action of closing either the eye or the mouth. They are operated by two distinct classes: those that control and those that oppose. When the mouth is stretched laterally and the muscles of the cheek are raised to the lower eyelid, a smile is produced. Whereas during a frown, the mouth curves downward, revealing the teeth. These facial muscles facilitate different expressions of despair, fear, anger, rage, and other emotions. While the lips can move in many ways, the mouth is usually the focal point of most expressions.

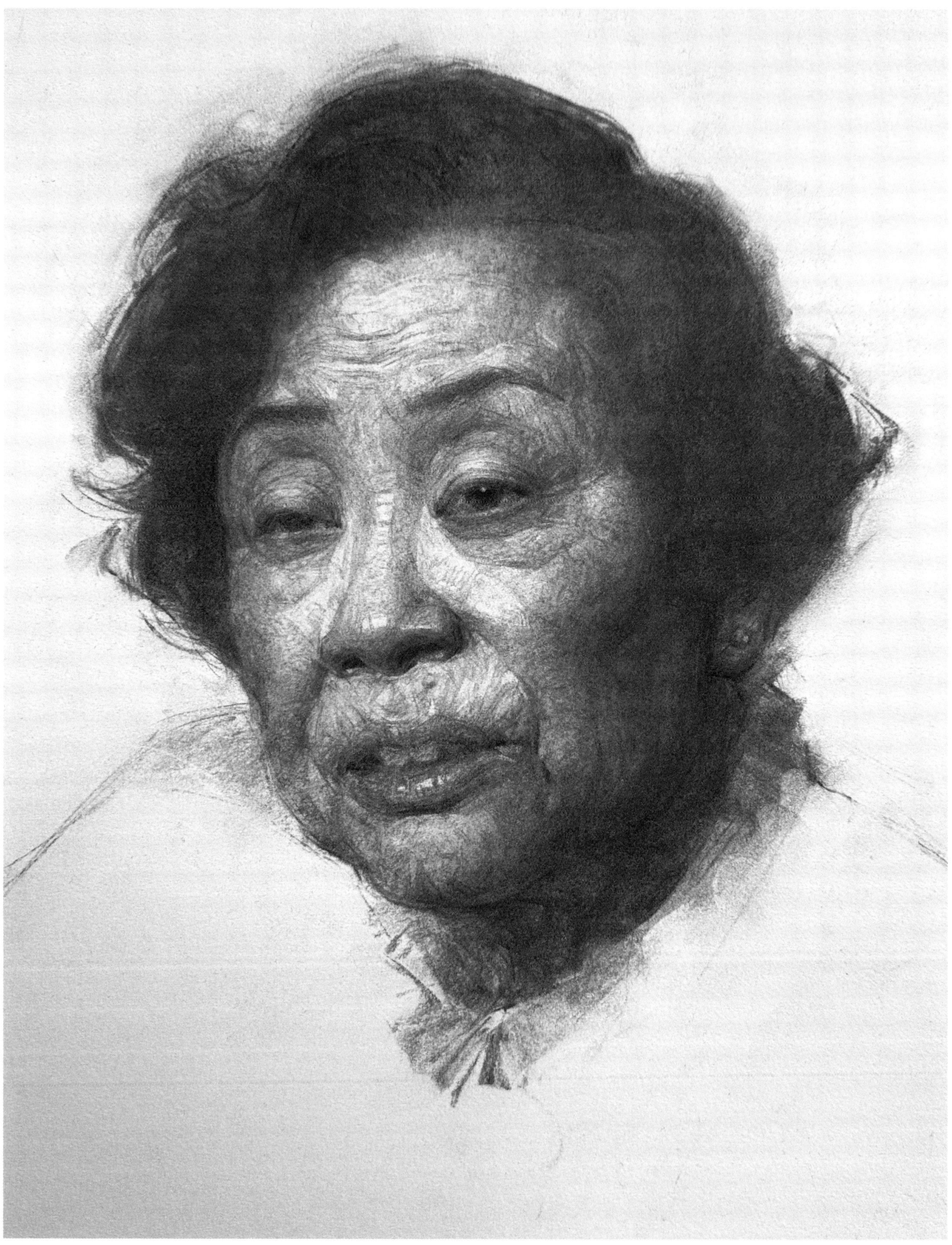

2

—

ANATOMY OF THE EYE

The eyes have often been referred to as the "windows to the soul" because they convey a vast range of emotions and personality traits. This makes them the most crucial element of a good portrait. When drawing a portrait, the eyes play a key role in capturing a person's spirit, expression, likeness, characteristics, personality, and mood. They add emotion and depth to the artwork, making the portrait more engaging and impactful.

The most expressive and memorable portraits often emphasize the emotions conveyed through the eyes, drawing the viewer's attention and creating a connection. The expression in the eyes can tell a story and set the overall mood of the portrait. Therefore, it's essential to capture the unique eyes of the subject accurately, rather than relying on generic or imagined eyes, to truly reflect their individuality and essence.

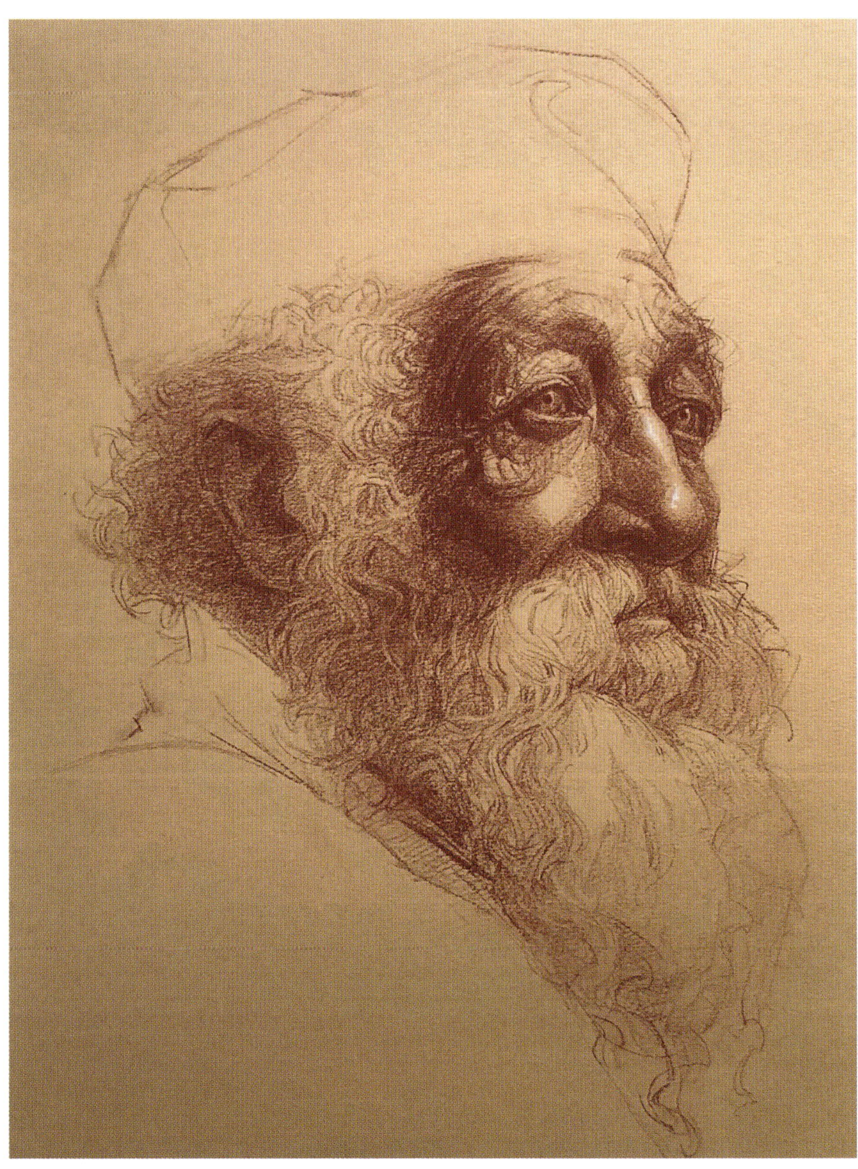

EYE ANATOMY

PARTS OF THE EYE

1. **Iris:** This is the colored part of the eye. It's a flat disc that contracts and expands to accommodate light.
2. **Pupil:** This is the circular-shaped diaphragm with a black hole in the iris with a lens covering it.
3. **Cornea:** The cornea protects the iris and pupil. It's covered by a dome-shaped transparent "bubble." The cornea usually reflects some bright light—which makes the eyes appear brilliant and at times even glassy—and is always wet in appearance.

FORMS SURROUNDING THE EYE

- **Eyelids**: The eyelids are made up of soft tissue and are divided into the **upper eyelid** and **lower eyelid**, which meet at the corners of the eye, or the canthi. The eyelids cover the surface of the eyeball and provide protection and maintain lubrication. The upper eyelid is like an awning, creating a shadow across the eyeball and is responsible for most of the movement. The lower eyelid catches the light.

- **Brow area:** The eyebrows are areas of short hairs that are located at the junction of the upper eyelid and the forehead.
  - Zygomatic process of frontal bone: This is the part of the frontal bone that extends to the cheekbone.
  - Brow bone: This is the bony ridge above the eyes, forming the arch of the eyebrows.
  - Hood: This is skin that may overhang the upper eyelid.
  - Eye cover fold: This is the fold of skin covering the upper eyelid.

- **Tear duct:** The tear ducts are located in the inside corners of your eyes and are part of the tear drainage system.

- **Tear trough:** The area called the *tear trough* is the area between the lower eyelid and the upper cheekbone.

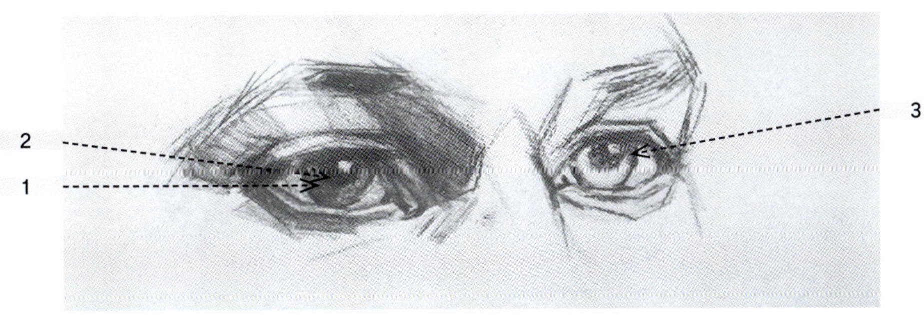

TIPS FOR DRAWING THE EYE AREA

In general, you won't see the entire eyeball when looking at someone's eyes. Typically, only about a quarter of it is visible between the eyelids. The eyeballs are spherical. The curved shape of the eyeball is apparent from one corner of the eyelids to the other.

To visualize this, imagine the eyes as two balls connected by a stick. As you slightly rotate the stick, both eyes move simultaneously. When the iris of one eye is positioned at the inner corner, the iris of the other eye will be at the outer corner. This synchronized movement ensures that both eyes are always aligned, reflecting the natural coordination of eye movement.

Here are some other guidelines to consider:

- The eyeball is exactly what it says: eye + ball. So, think a ROUND, not a FLAT, plane.
- Note the thickness of eyelids and how they wrap around.
- Eyelashes emanate from the outer edges of the eyelids. The upper lashes sweep down and out, and the lower lashes grow out and down.
- The upper lid overlaps the lower lid at the outside corner.
- From a frontal view, the space between the eyes is equal to one eye width.
- Note the hair pattern of the left and right eyebrow.

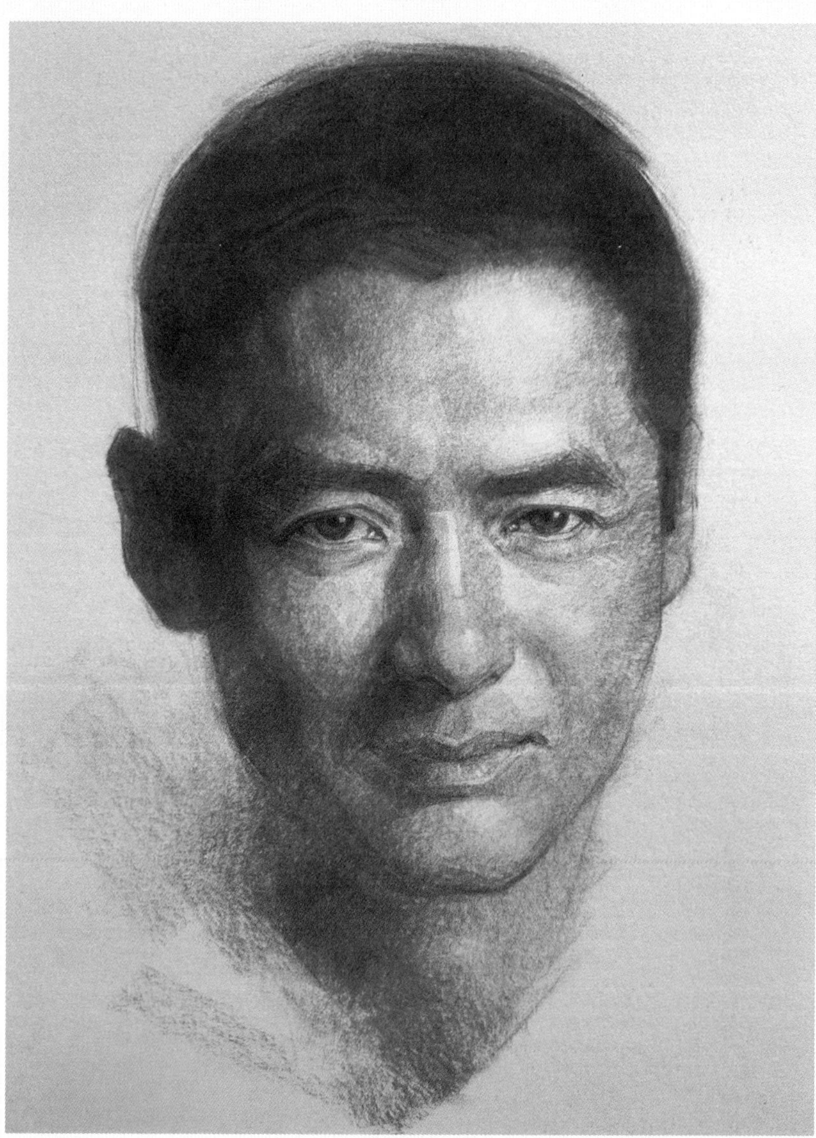

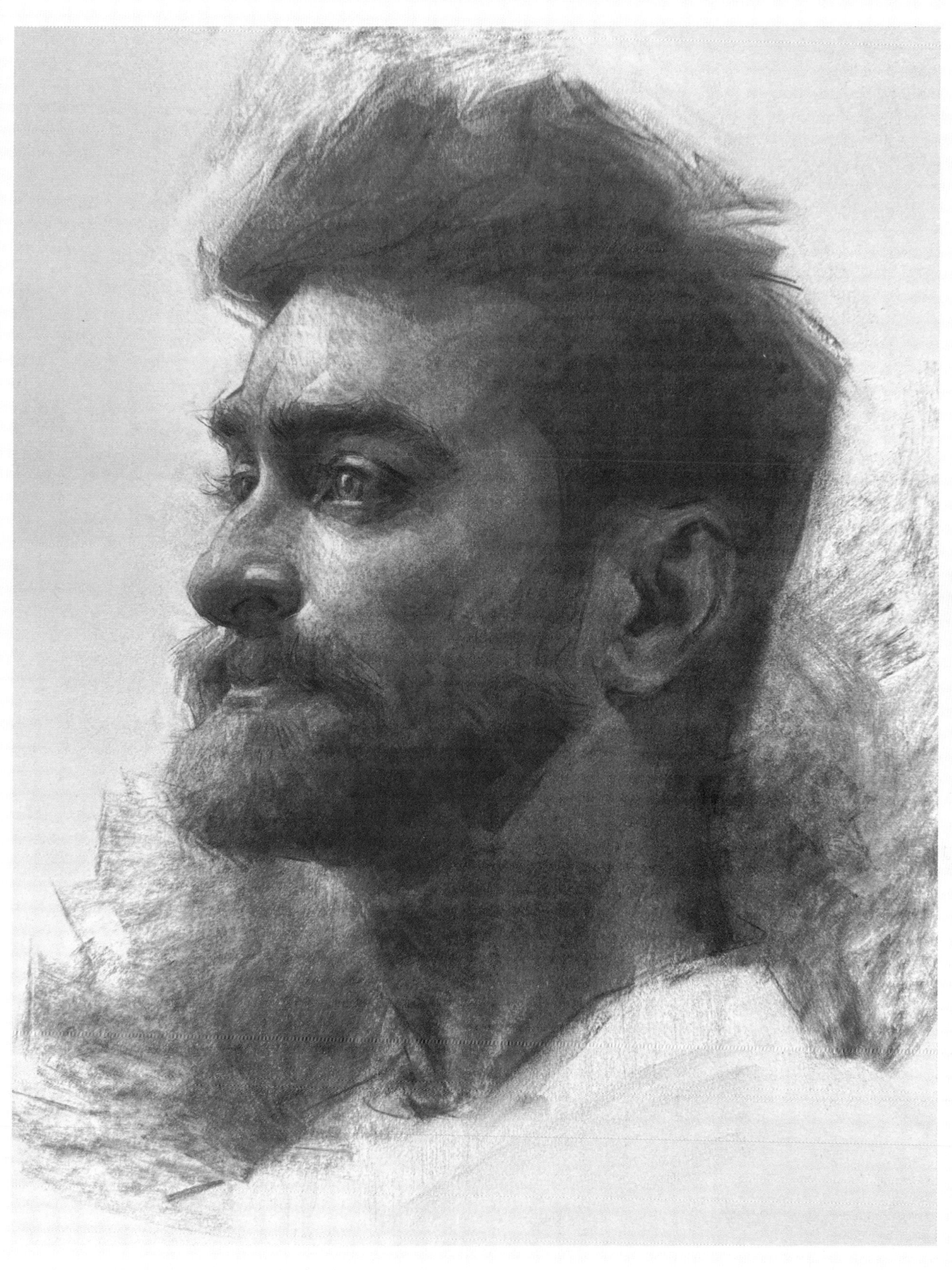

DOUBLE EYELIDS

Eyelids are termed *double eyelids* when they have a visible crease or fold of skin where the eye meets the eye socket, which creates a division in the eyelid, parting it into two sections.

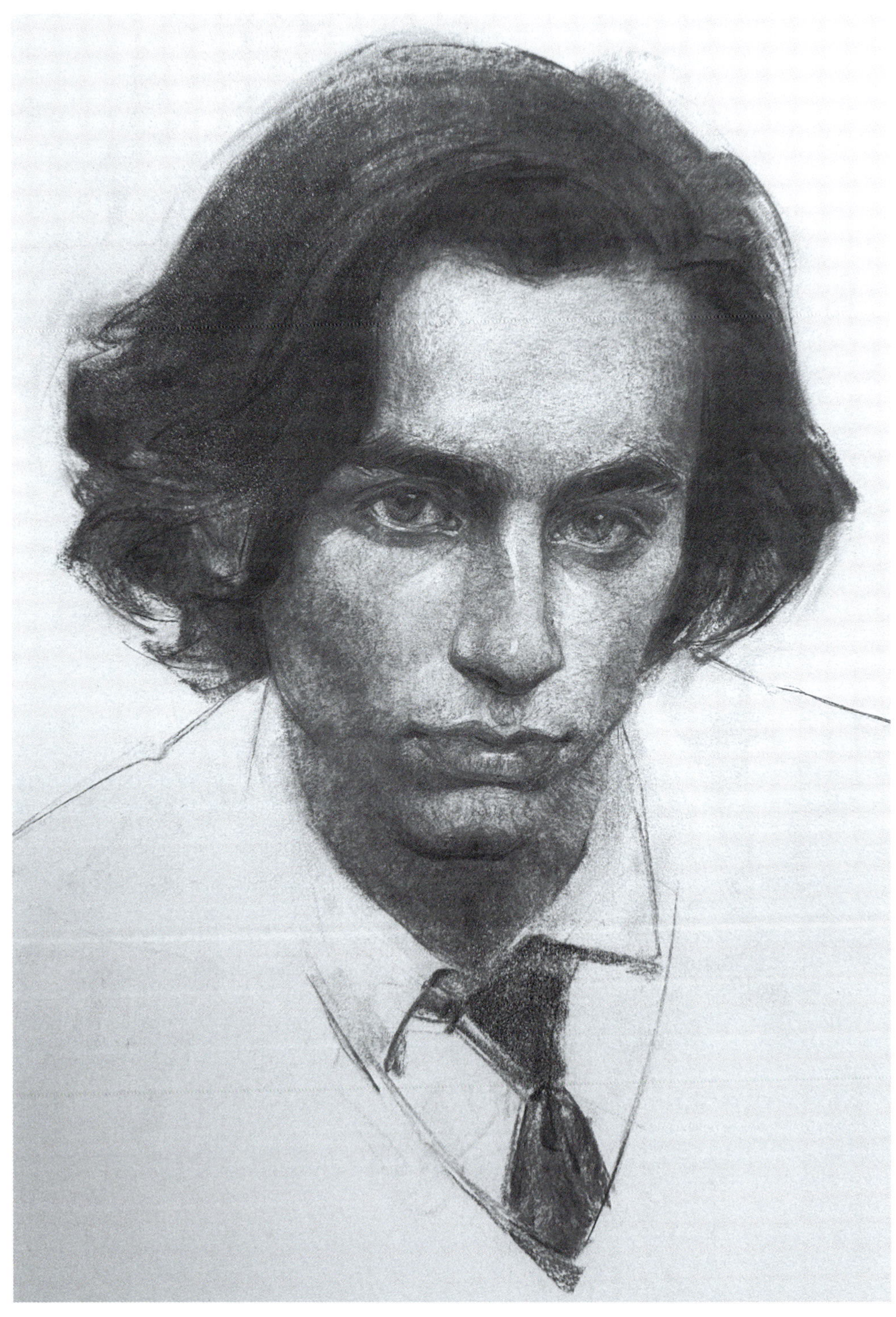

MONOLID EYE (EPICANTHIC FOLD)

Monolids is a common term used to describe eyes that seem to have a single eyelid fold rather than a double lid. Also known as *epicanthic folds* or *single eyelids*, this feature involves an eye cover fold that extends downward, partially or fully covering the upper eyelid and inner corner of the eyes. This gives the eyelid the appearance of having no crease. Monolids are common in people of East Asian, Southeast Asian, Central Asian, and North Asian heritage. These lids are characterized by the eye sitting flush with the brow bone, connected by a stretch of skin without a visible fold. Epicanthic folds may be more noticeable during childhood development stages in any race, especially before the nose bridge fully develops.

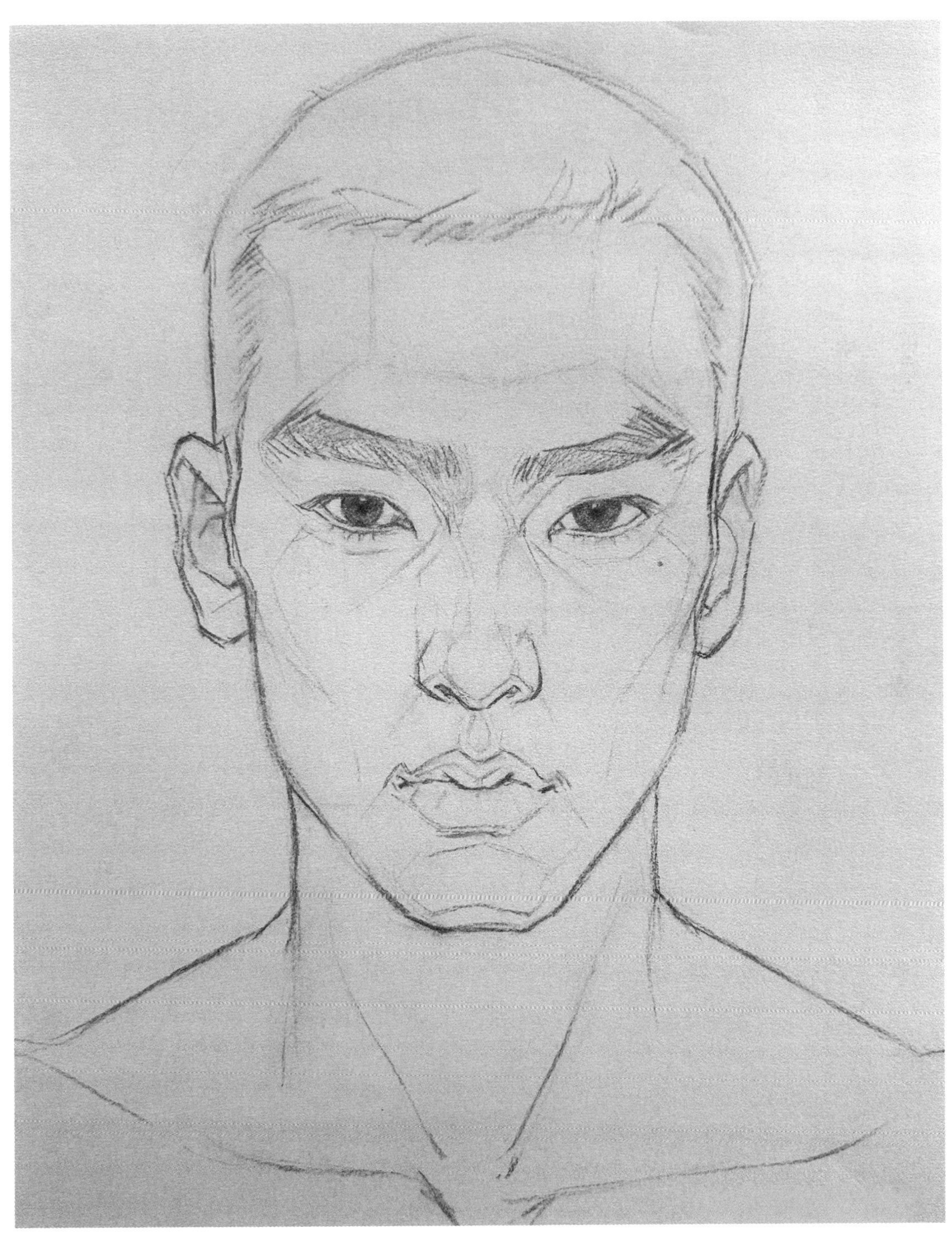

HOODED EYES

Hooded eyes occur when the eyebrow and surrounding soft tissue start to sag, creating a bulge or fold of skin that can partially or completely conceal the upper eyelid.

With hooded lids, the eyelid may not be visible when looking straight into a mirror. Some individuals are born with hooded eyelids, while others develop them as they age (see pages 78–83).

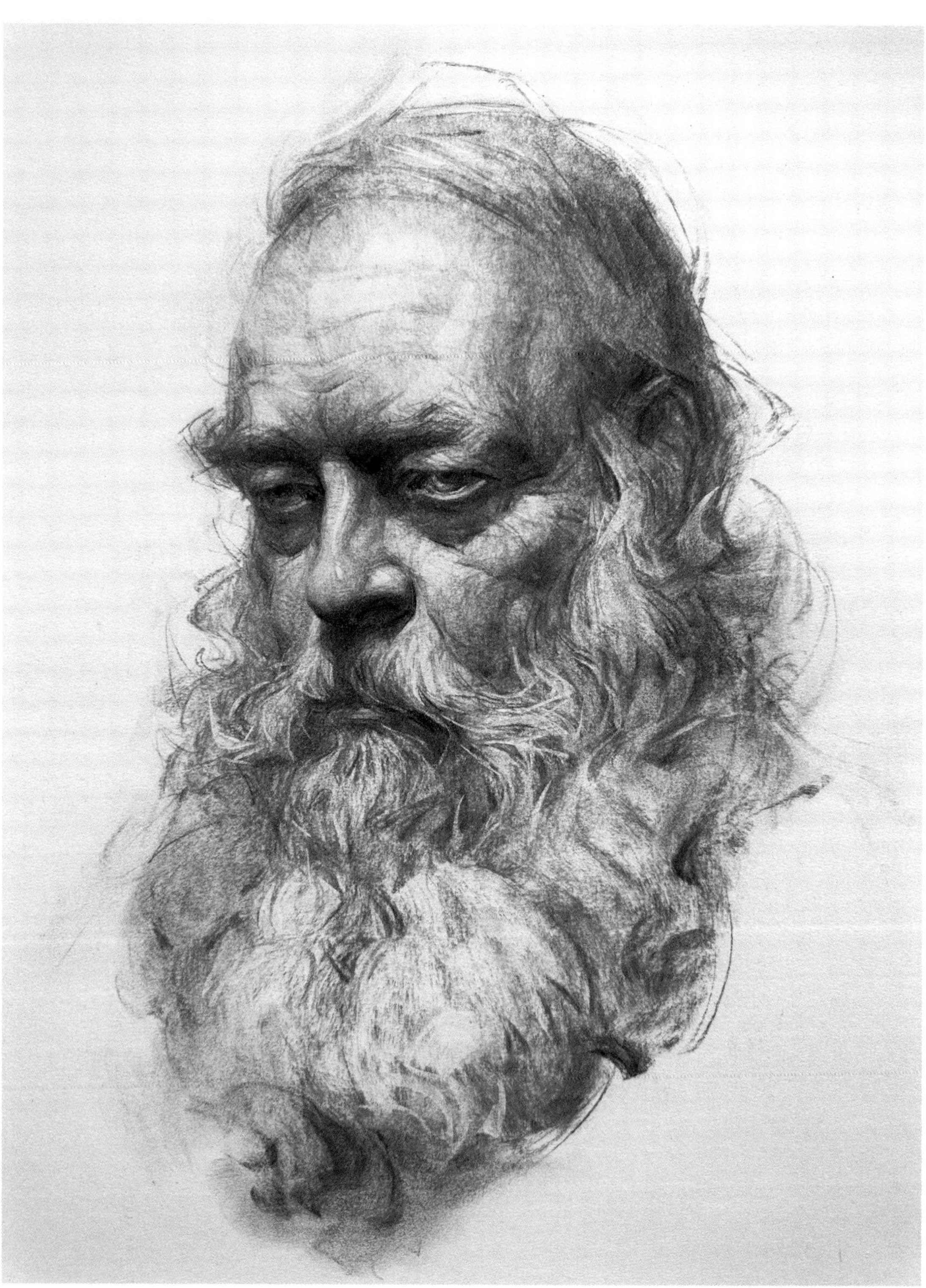

SUNKEN EYES

Sunken eyes are caused by aging, dehydration, or lack of collagen in the skin. Features such as a prominent lower eyelid and the tear trough depression are important characteristics of sunken eyes. This condition is also known by other names, including *tear trough hollows* or *under-eye hollows*, and is often associated with eyelid and mid-face aging.

For more information on the aging face, see pages 78–83.

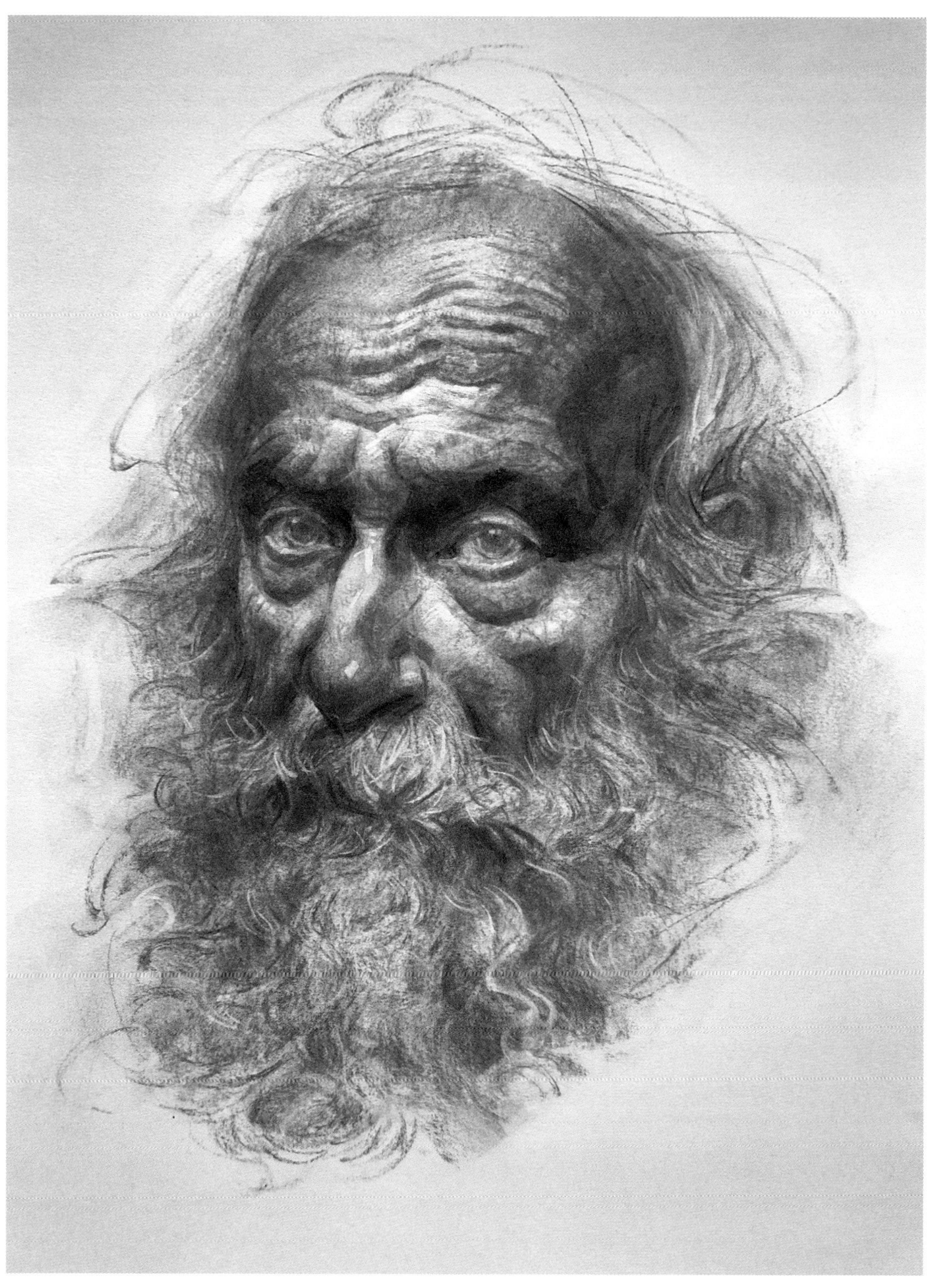

STRUCTURE OF THE EYEBROWS

In humans, eyebrows serve two main functions. First, they allow for communication through facial expression: one raised eyebrow expresses skepticism or interest; two raised eyebrows can express surprise. Second, it's to keep our eyes clear of liquid, such as sweat or rain. The eyebrow is divided into three anatomic parts: head, body, and tail.

The key to drawing eyebrows is to stop viewing them as just eyebrows, or even hair. Instead, think of them as simple shapes first, then consider their values. Simplify and group the eyebrow into one basic general shape. Once the basic shapes and proportions are established, look for more specific groupings of similar eyebrow hairs. First, observe where they overlap. Then, note the similarities in proximity, direction, angle, length, or depth. Identify variations in the eyebrow, such as distinctly different hairs, changes in direction, and noticeable value shifts. Observe in depth to capture the details.

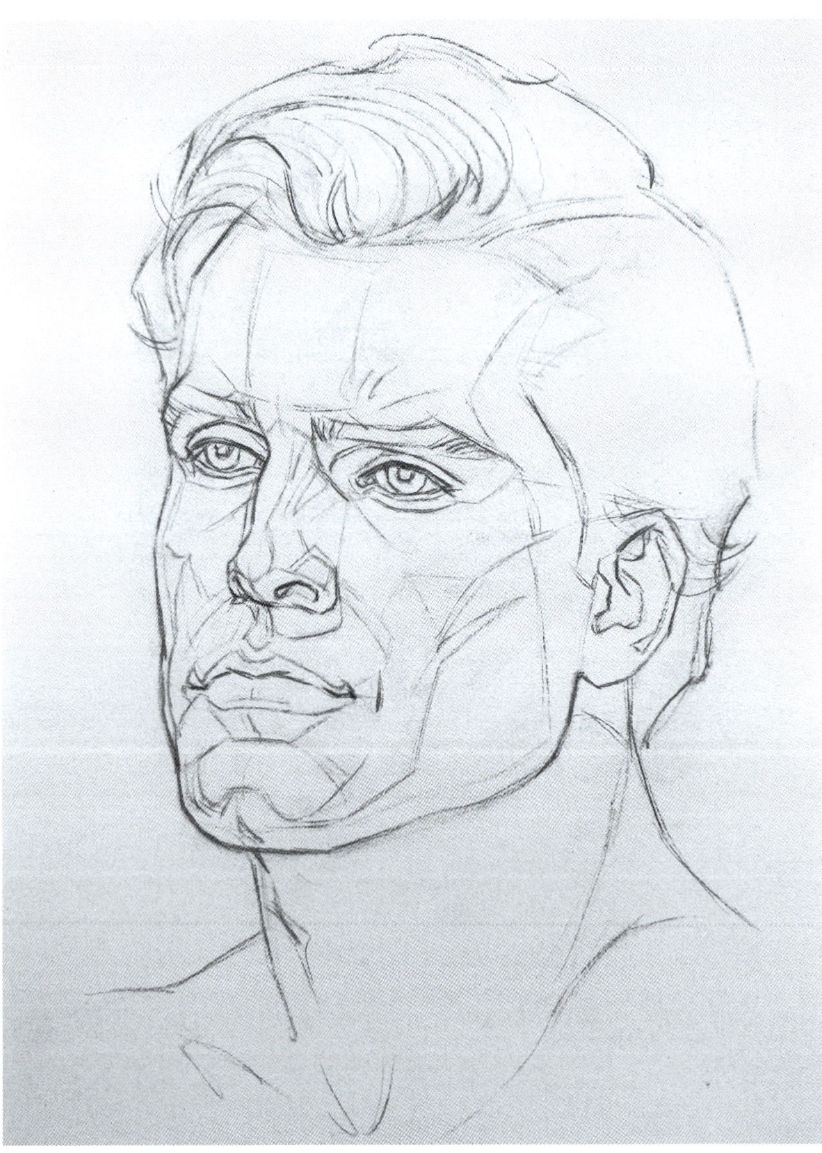

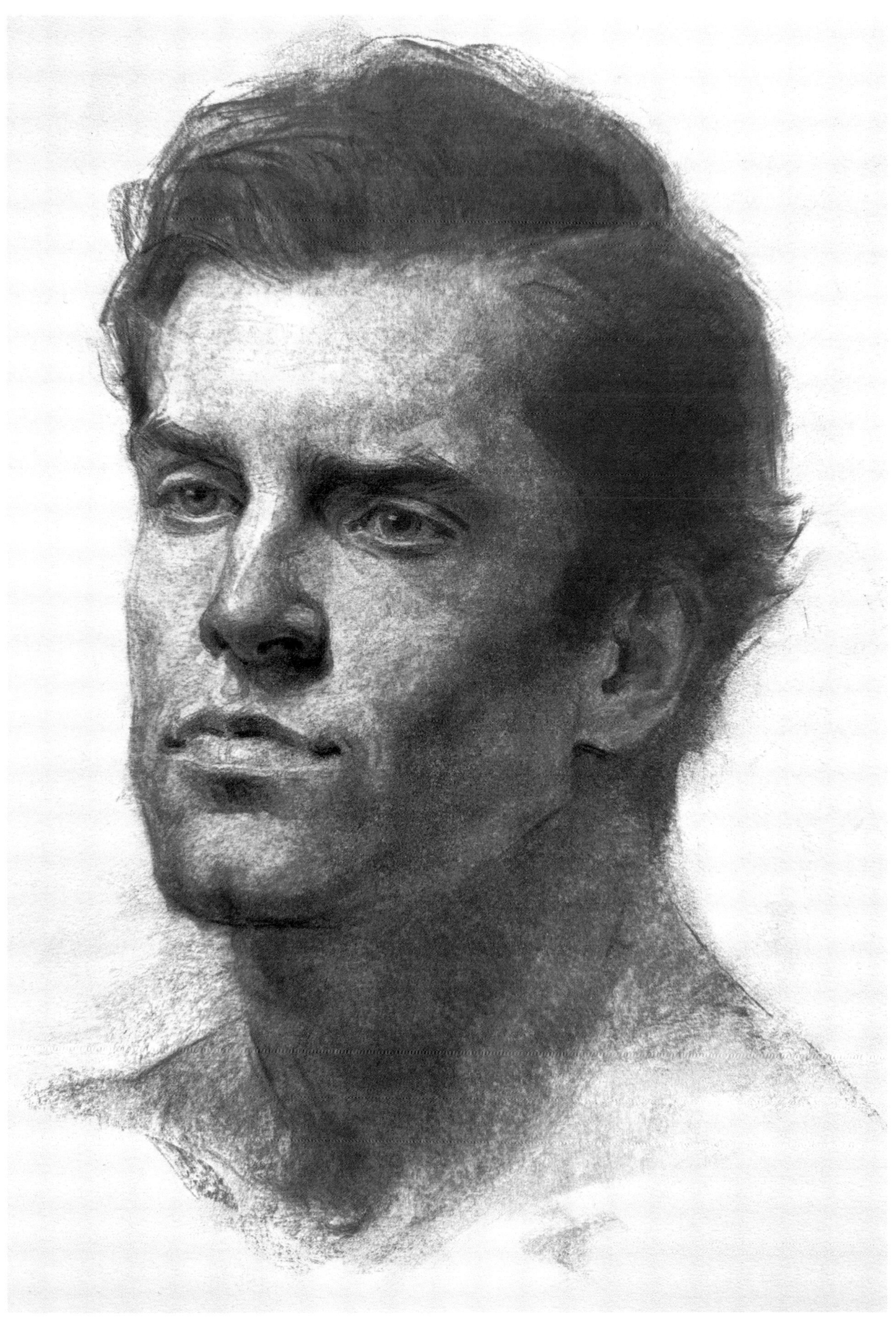

GENDER DIFFERENCES OF THE EYEBROWS

There are a number of differences between males and females. Artists have often followed "ideal" standards designed to make men really "masculine" and women really "feminine." Male and female eyebrows vary in shape, size, and position.

The typical male eyebrow runs over the orbital rim. It tends to be flatter, fuller, heavier, straighter, and closer to the eyes. In contrast, the typical female eyebrow is positioned above the orbital rim. It's thinner, with a pointy tail and upward arch, placing it farther from the eyes.

Eyebrows can have various shapes, such as softly angled, rounded, peaked, curved, or flat, often influenced by fashion trends. The right eyebrow shape can make a female look more alert, rejuvenated, and youthful as well as enhance facial features and help the eyes to stand out.

In summary, while male eyebrows are typically more robust and closer to the eyes, female eyebrows are often narrower, more curved, and positioned higher. The shape and styling of eyebrows, more popular among females, significantly impact the overall facial expression and appearance.

MALE BROWS

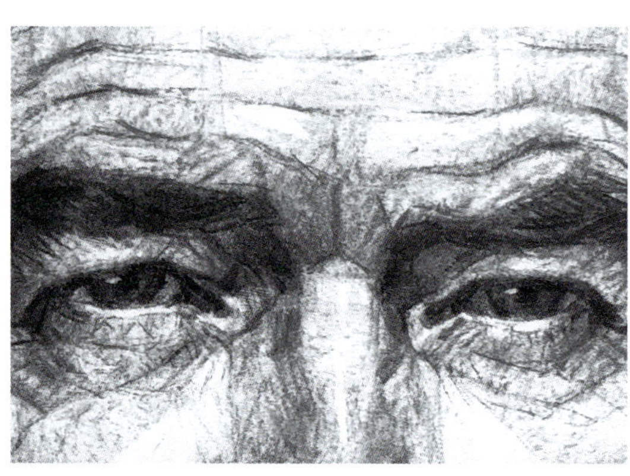

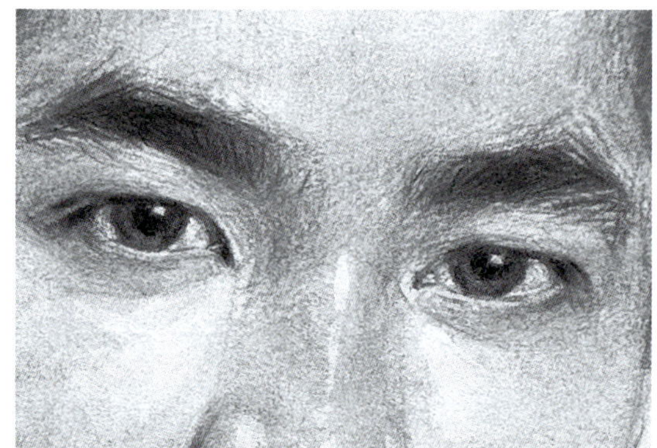

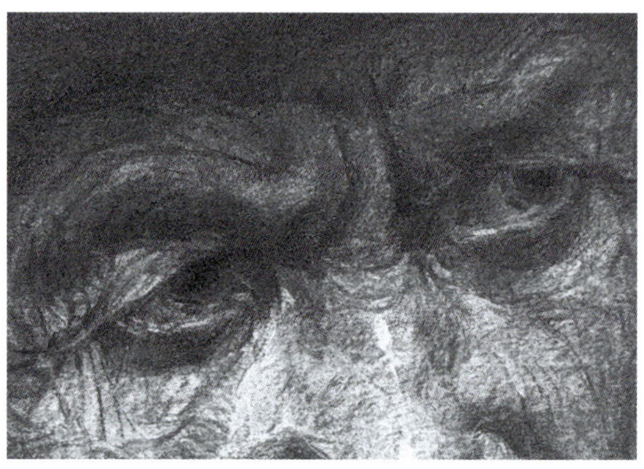

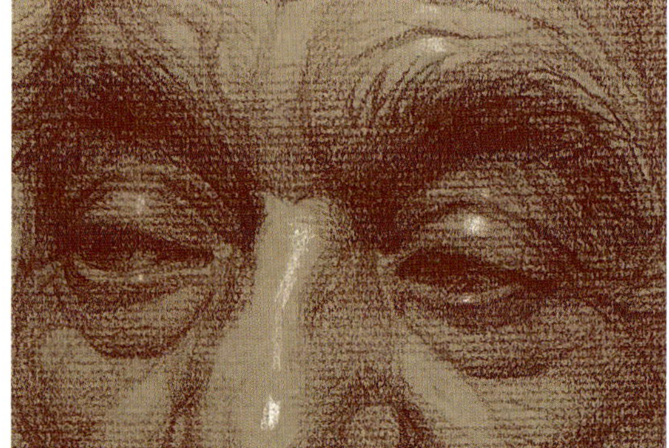

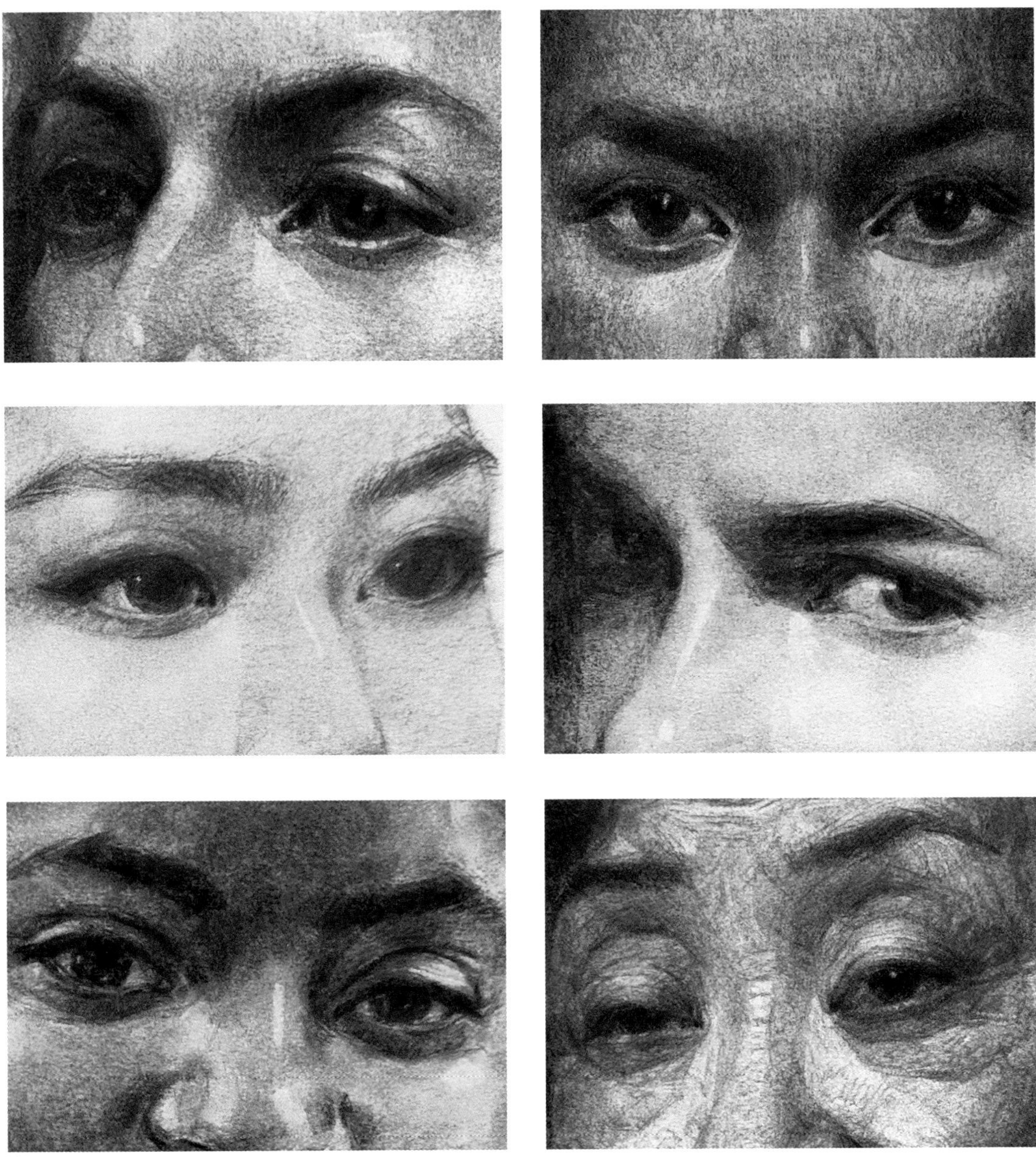

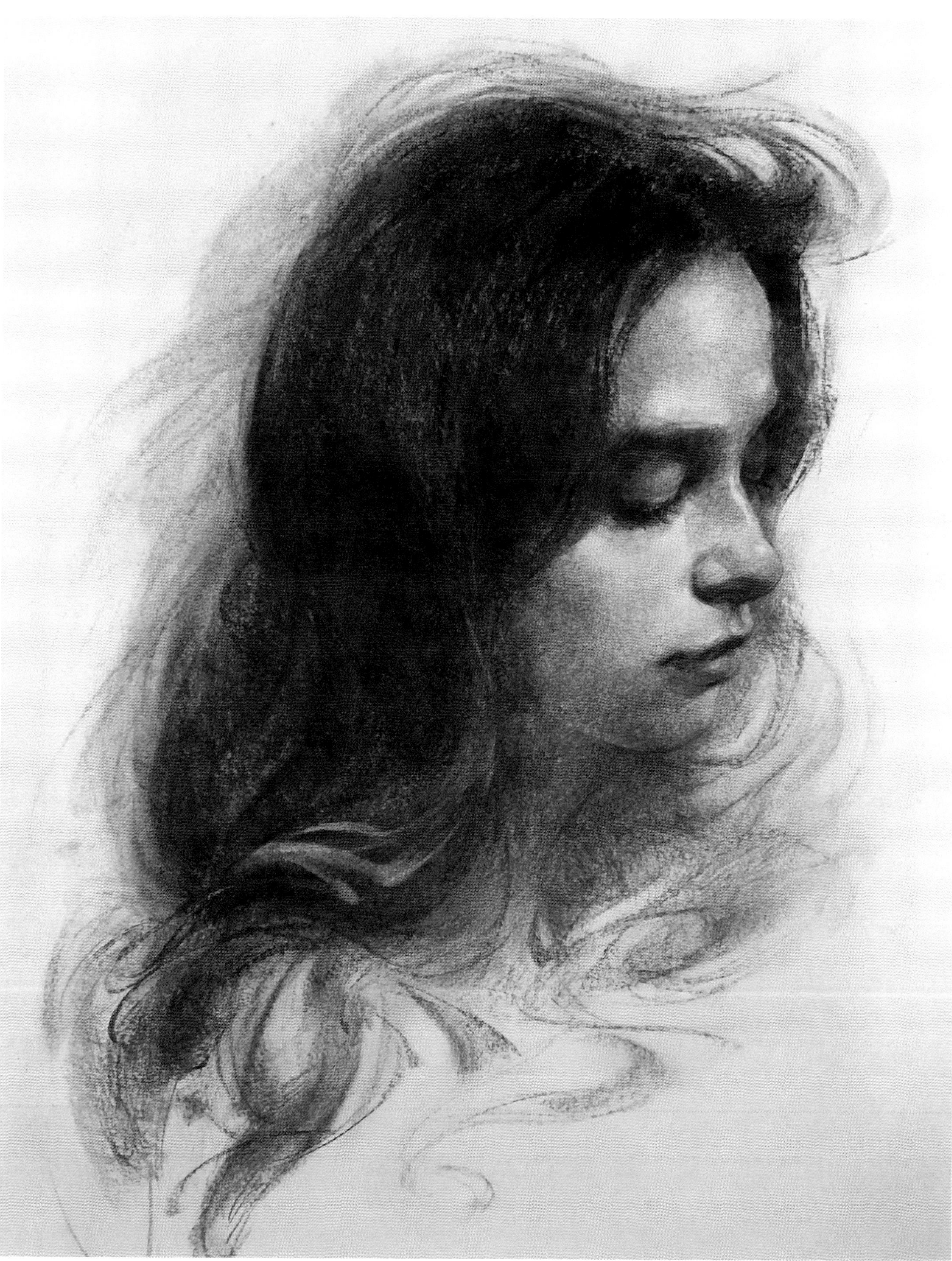

3

ANATOMY OF THE EAR, MOUTH, AND NOSE

ANATOMY OF THE EAR

1. **Helix:** The helix is the curved outer rim of the ear that starts from the skull and ends at the earlobe.
2. **Anti-helix:** The anti-helix runs parallel to the helix and is the innermost section. It splits into two "legs": the upper leg is wide and round, and the lower leg is rounded on the top side but sharp edged at bottom. The anti-helix protrudes more than the outer rim, the tubercle, which is flattened.
3. **Concha:** The concha is the space next to the opening of the ear canal. It directs sound into the ear.
4. **Tragus:** The tragus is a triangular piece of cartilage located on the external ear next to the concha. It usually has two bumps and protects the ear canal.
5. **Anti-tragus:** The anti-tragus is a second, single piece of cartilage that's located opposite of the tragus.
6. **Lobe:** The earlobe, or lobule, is the soft, fleshy tissue located at the very bottom of the outer ear. It can be very minimal on some people.

The ear, irregular in form, is essentially shell-shaped in its general structure. Its outer contour is formed like the letter *C*. It's wider at the top and narrower at the base, giving it a top-heavy shape. In the center, it has a bowl-like depression, large enough to admit the curve of the thumb. Pay attention to the angle of the ear as it's not straight up and down but tips slightly backward at a 10- to 15-degree angle. The line of the ear toward the face aligns with the upper angle of the lower jaw. The ear attaches directly to the head at its front edge but is held away from the head by the cartilage of the wedge-shaped bowl of the concha. The ear casts a shadow downward underneath it, near the jaw.

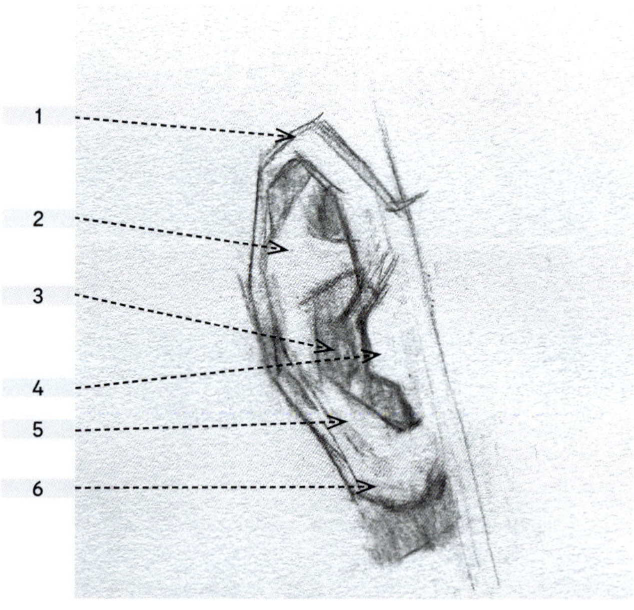

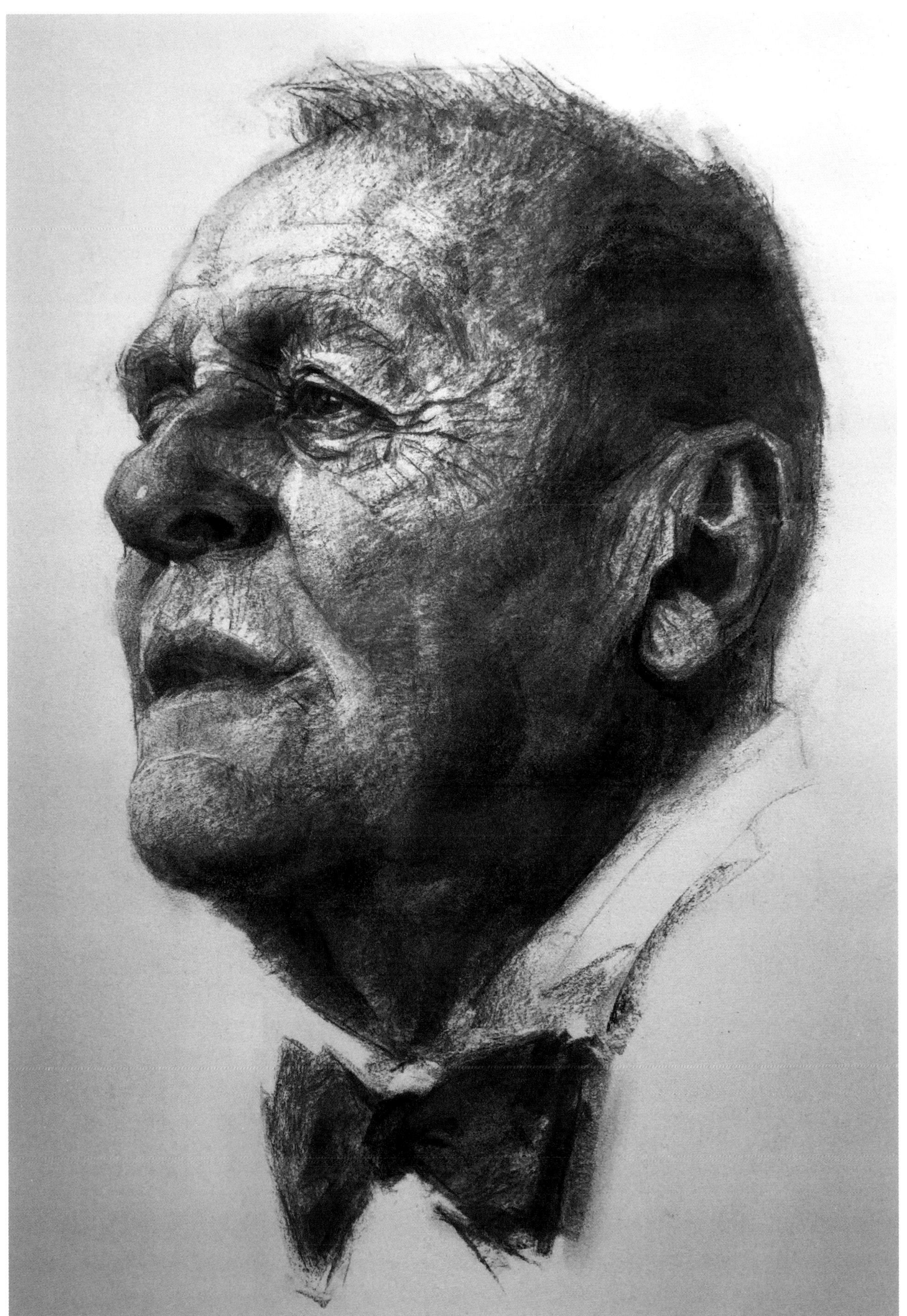

DRAWING THE EAR

The ear has two main roles: hearing and balance. Drawing the ear can be tricky because it's made up of many interlocking shapes. To make it easier, think of the ear as a collection of contours, not just an ear.

When drawing the human ear, it's crucial to place it in the right spot and at the correct angle. The ear is positioned at the outer edge of the jawbone, and its angle runs parallel to the length of the nose. The axis of the ears is always perpendicular to the center axis of the face. Generally, a human ear has lost practically all movement.

Avoid drawing all models in the same pose or angle. Instead, approach each ear as though you've never drawn one before. Step out of your comfort zone and explore new positions and perspectives. Pay attention to changes in angle and shadows and take the time to draw them well. Try drawing ears from every viewpoint until you are completely familiar with their placement in any head pose. A well-drawn ear is an intricate thing of beauty.

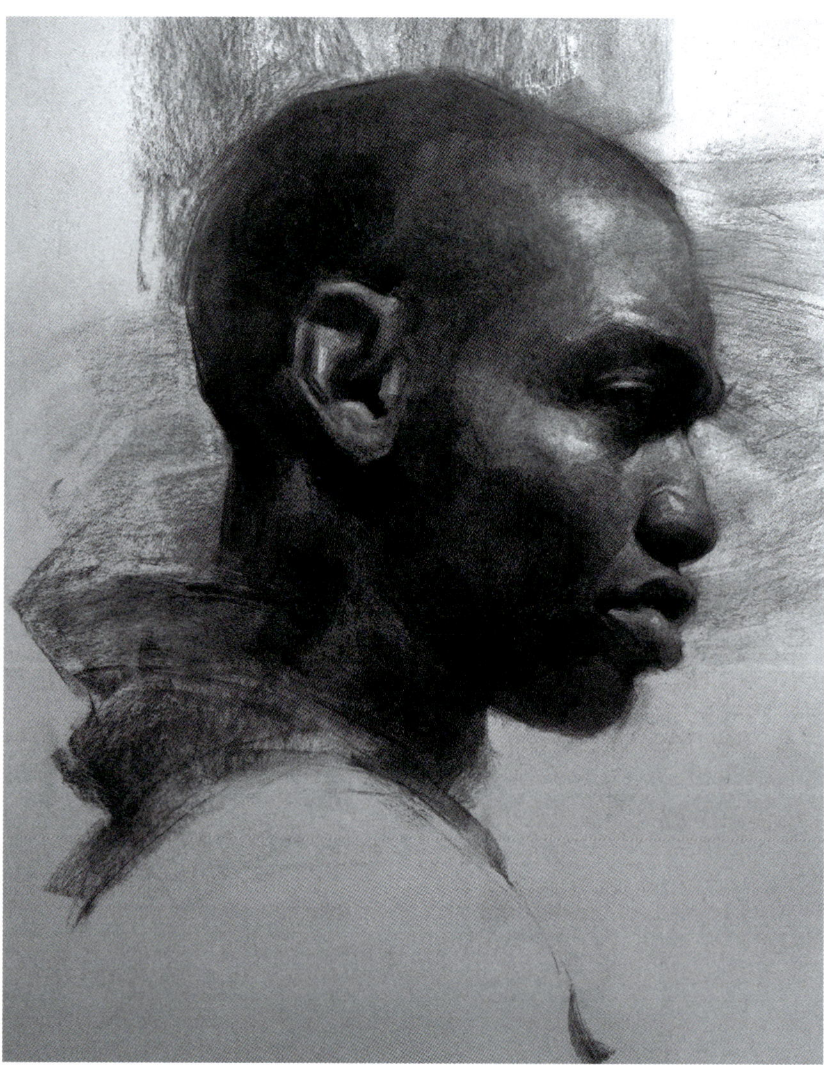

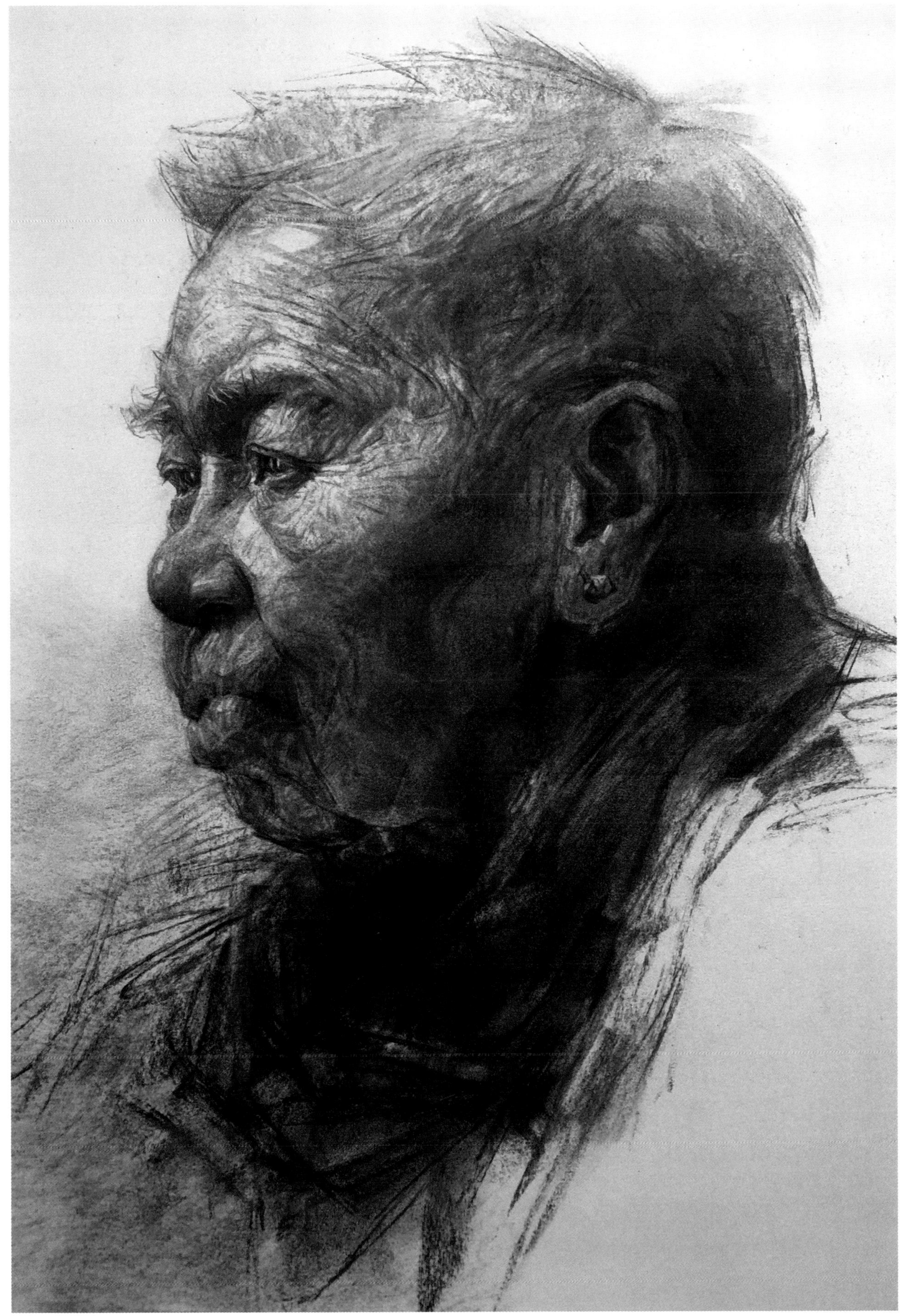

EAR COMPARISONS

As we age, an ear's structure deteriorates—the eardrum often thickens and the inner ear bones and other structures are affected as well. The shape changes, and the ears can appear larger. Also, the skin on our ears may droop, sag, or stretch out. Years of wearing earrings may cause longer lobes and there may be more hair growing inside. The earlobe can become less smooth and wrinkles on the earlobe, or "earlobe creases," and vertical wrinkles in front of tragus might also appear as we age.

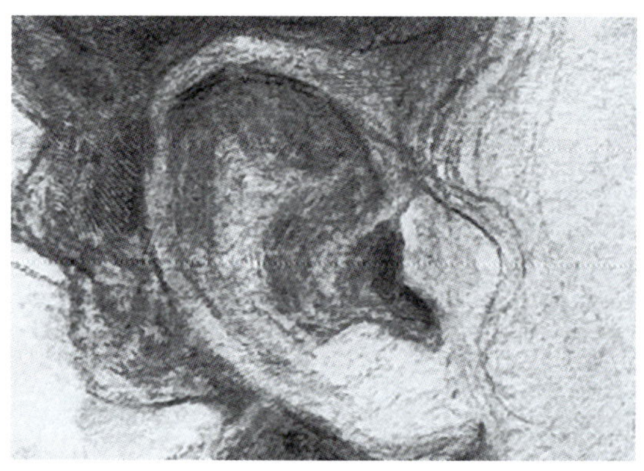
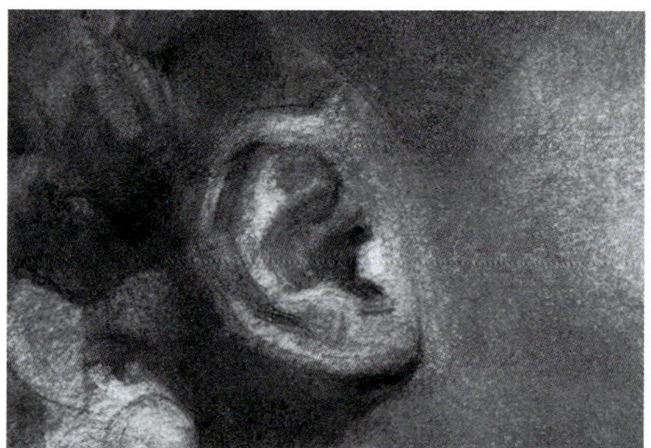
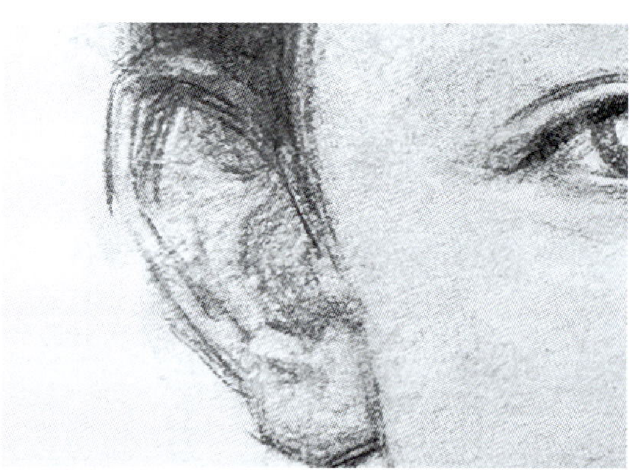
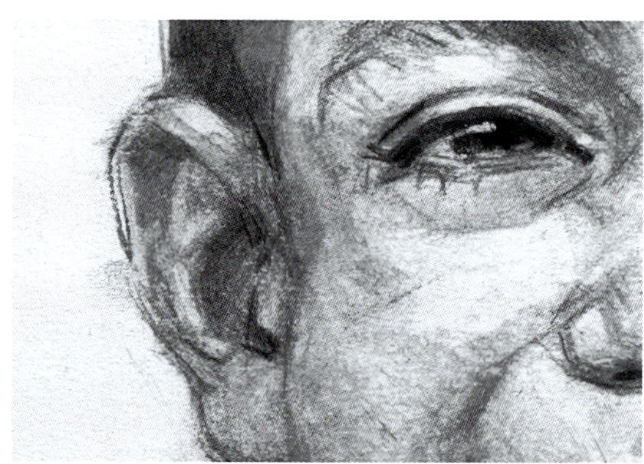
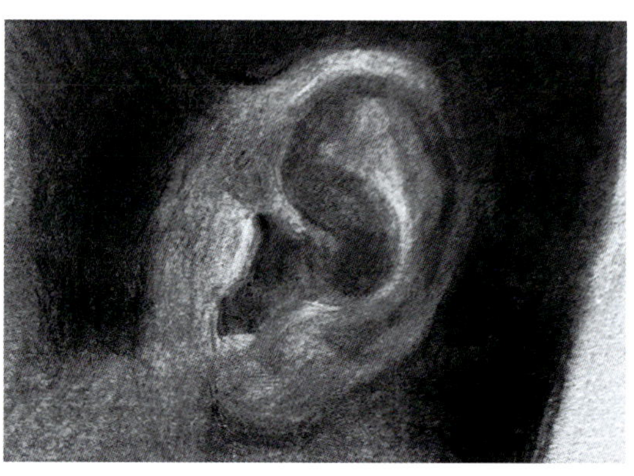
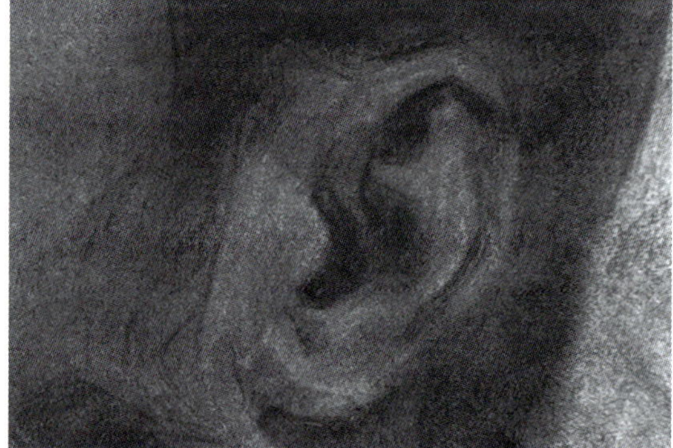

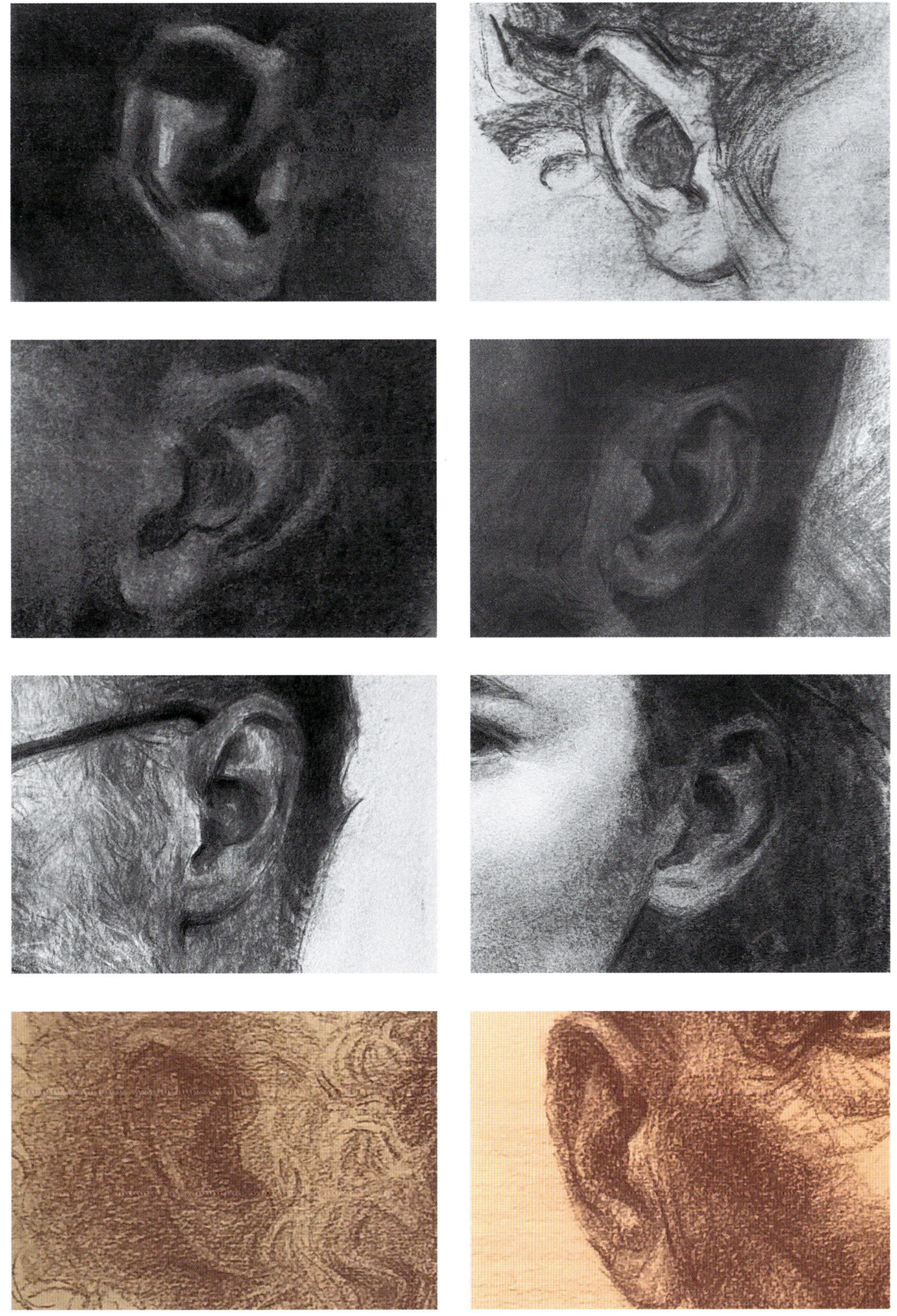

ANATOMY OF THE MOUTH

The mouth is arguably the most important feature of the face for conveying mood or emotion. It's the primary indicator of expression, often more direct and less subtle than the eyes. The corners of the mouth alone can communicate volumes.

To draw the upper lip of a female mouth, use curving lines to suggest its bow shape and softness. Use a single curve to depict the full lower lip. On the egg-shaped head, the mouth's placement is usually marked by a horizontal line between the lips.

There's often a depression beneath the lower lip. Remember that the lips are composed of soft, toned shapes rather than harsh outlines. Blend the edges into the lip to maintain a soft appearance.

1. **Roof:** The roof of the mouth is formed by the palate and separates the oral cavity from the nasal cavity.
2. **Philtrum:** The philtrum is the vertical indentation in the middle of your upper lip that extends from the top of the lip to the nose.
3. **Mouth:** The mouth, also called the oral cavity, is the opening to the digestive system that also helps you to speak, eat, and breathe. The upper lip tubercle and the lower lip body are each made up of two fused tubercles, similar to peanuts in the shell.
4. **Pillar of mouth:** This area is located in the center of the lower lip region and is usually cast in shadow.
5. **Chin:** The chin, also known as the *mental protuberance*, is the midline protrusion located on the front of the lower jaw.

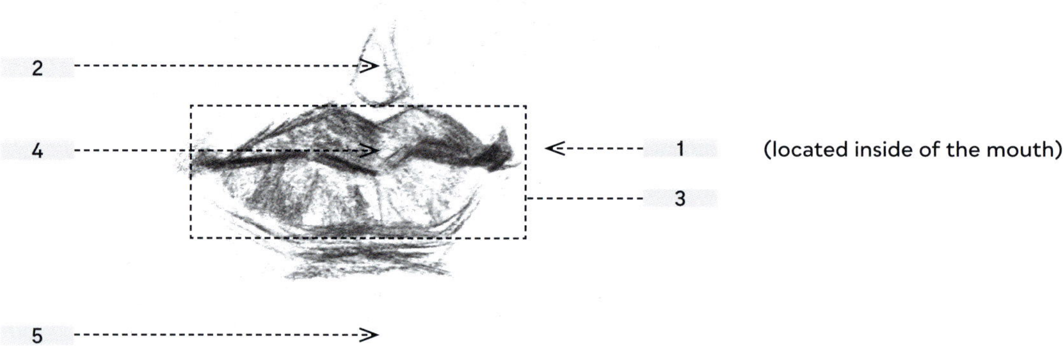

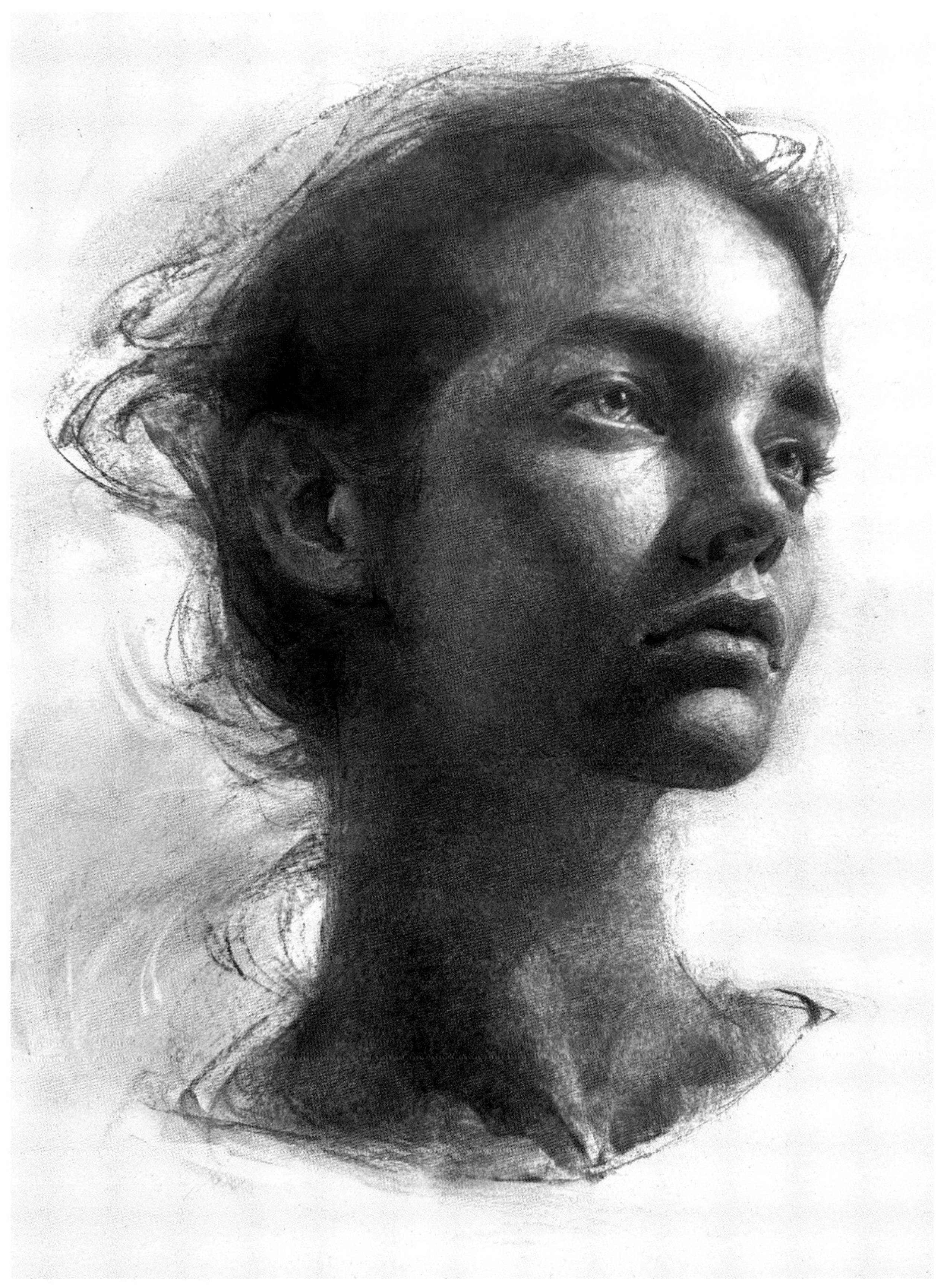

DRAWING THE MOUTH

The mouth has two main functions: eating and speaking. In art, the mouth can reveal a lot about mood and emotion. The mouth is extremely mobile and seldom lacks expression. It's capable of smiling, pouting, expressing grimness, anger, pain, or pleasure, as well as laughing, shouting, speaking, whistling, and more. Because the mouth can appear simple, especially when closed, there's a tendency to oversimplify it in drawings. Avoid outlining the mouth with hard, definable edges. The best way to study and draw the mouth with diverse expressions is to use a mirror and model your own physical appearance.

Move your lips and tilt your head at various angles. Try not to overemphasize the details of the teeth, as they can easily appear exaggerated and spoil an otherwise good head drawing.

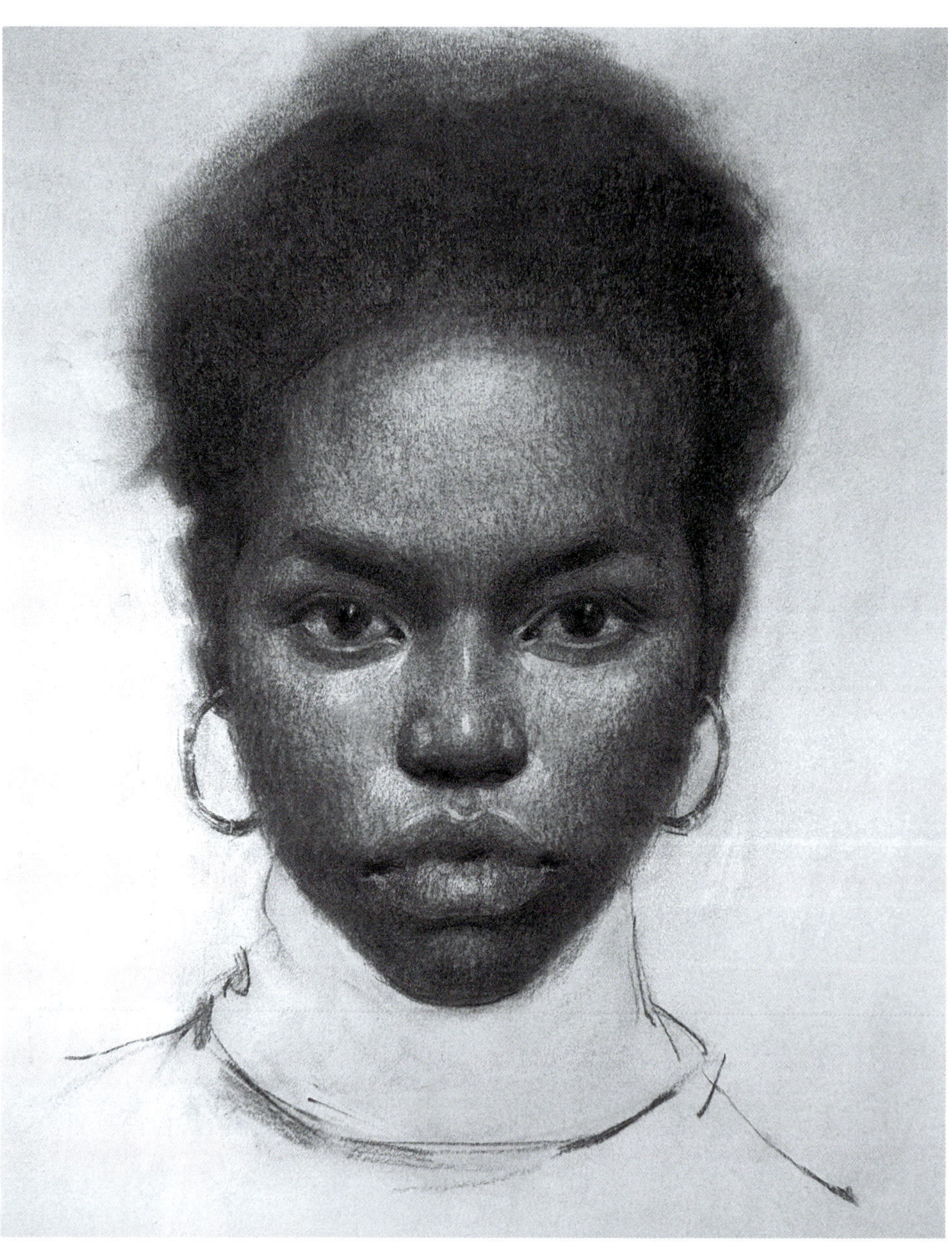

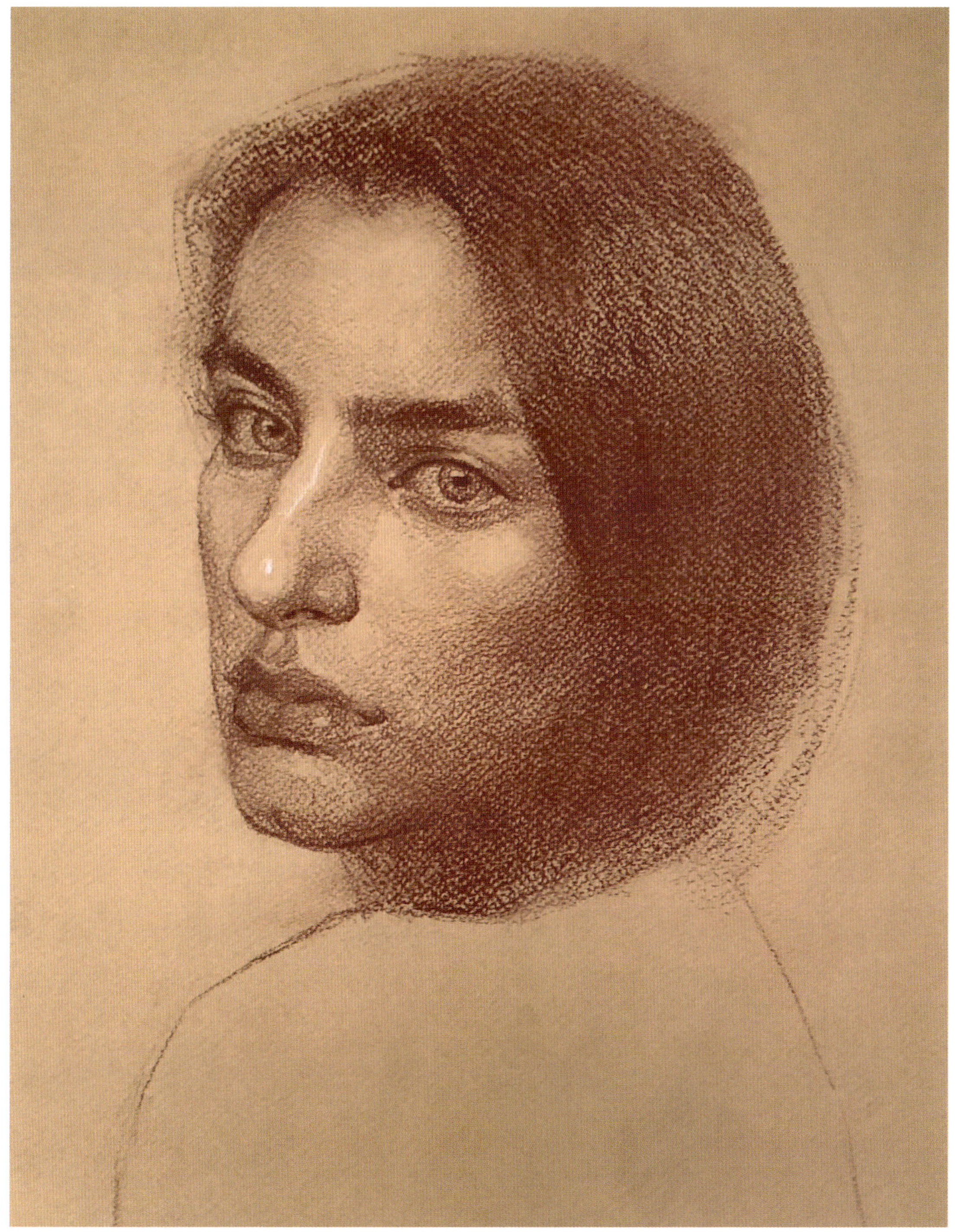

PROPORTIONS OF THE MOUTH

There are some proportional guidelines for drawing mouths:

- In a frontal view, the corners of the mouth typically align with the pupils of the eyes.
- Generally, the bottom lip is thicker than the top lip.
- Because most light sources come from above, the top lip often appears darker in shading.

MOUTH COMPARISONS

The mouth is singularly the most important feature of the face for conveying the mood. It is the number one indicator of facial expression. With aging, the lips get thinner and vertical wrinkles appear above and below the mouth. Flesh sags around the chin and the sides of the jaw, producing jowls. A downward fold shows up at the corners of the mouth as we age, giving a bit of a wry expression. The philtrum on the upper lip flattens out, losing its delicate curve. Lines around the mouth, known as commissure lines, which are created by innumerable widening of the mouth, fall from the corners of the mouth, making the mouth droop.

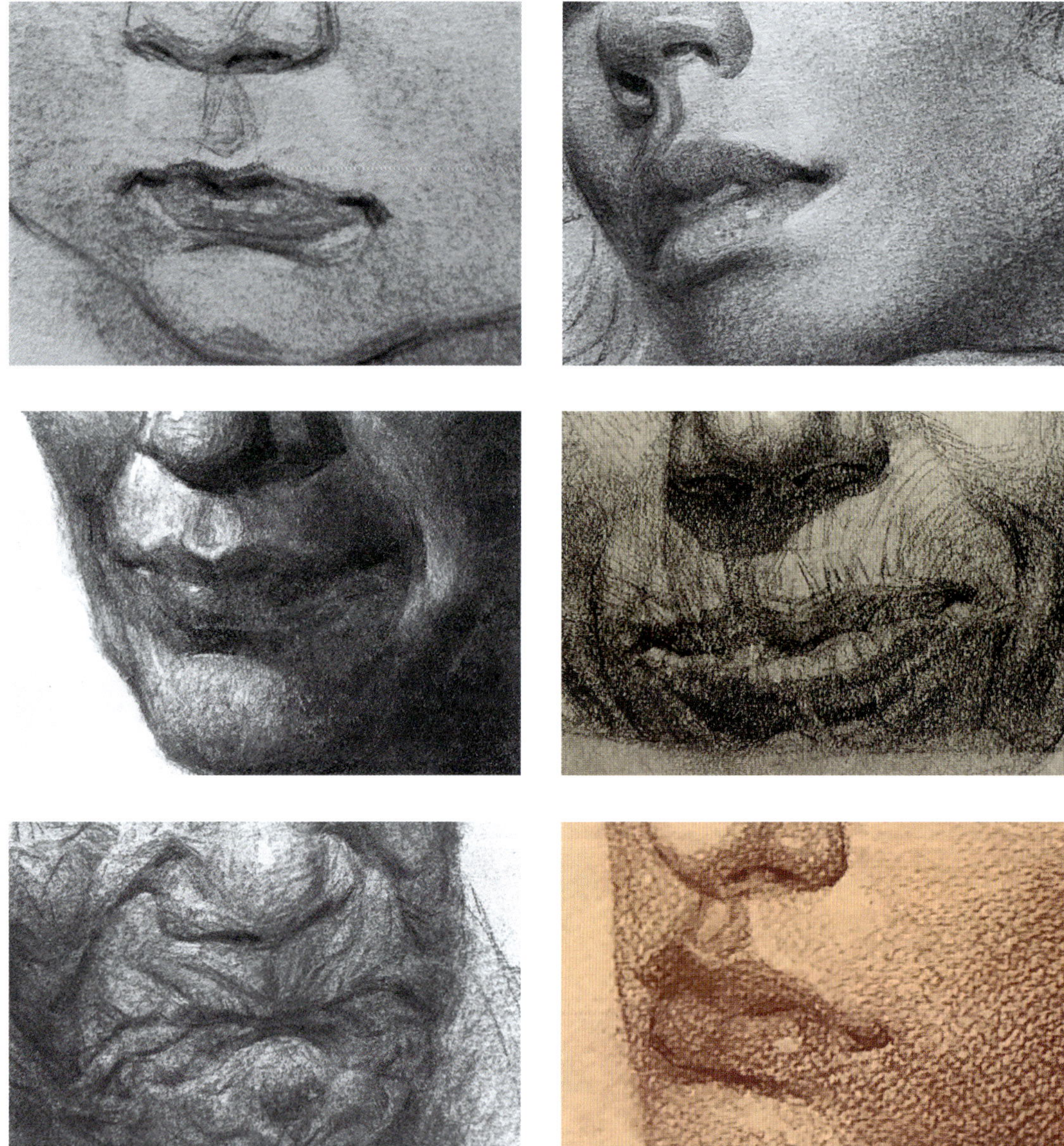

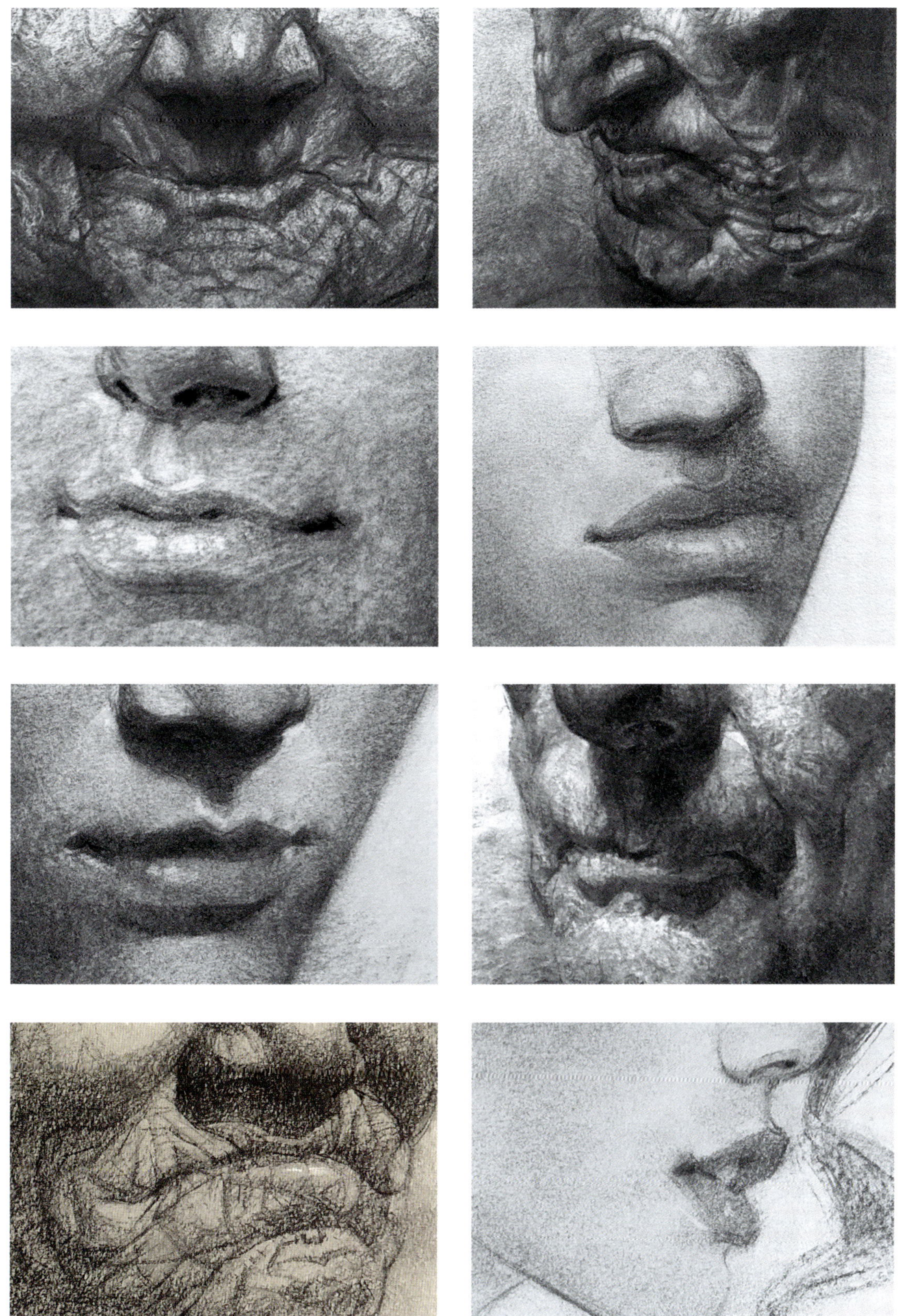

ANATOMY OF THE NOSE

1. **Nasal bone:** The nasal bone is a small, flat, rectangle-shaped bone made up of two bones that connect midface to form the bridge of the nose.
2. **Cartilages:** The external part of the nose is made up of five different types of cartilage. The cartilages are responsible for maintaining the shape of the nose as well as providing support.
    a. **Glabella:** The glabella is the slightly elevated region located between the eyebrows.
    b. **Upper lateral:** The upper lateral cartilages are a paired set of cartilages located in the middle third of the nose.
    c. **Lower lateral:** The lower lateral cartilages are a paired set of cartilages located in the lower third of the nose.
    d. **Ala:** The ala, or the wing of the nose, provides the structure around the nostrils.
    e. **Septum:** Consisting of both cartilage and bone, the septum divides the nasal cavity into the left and right halves.

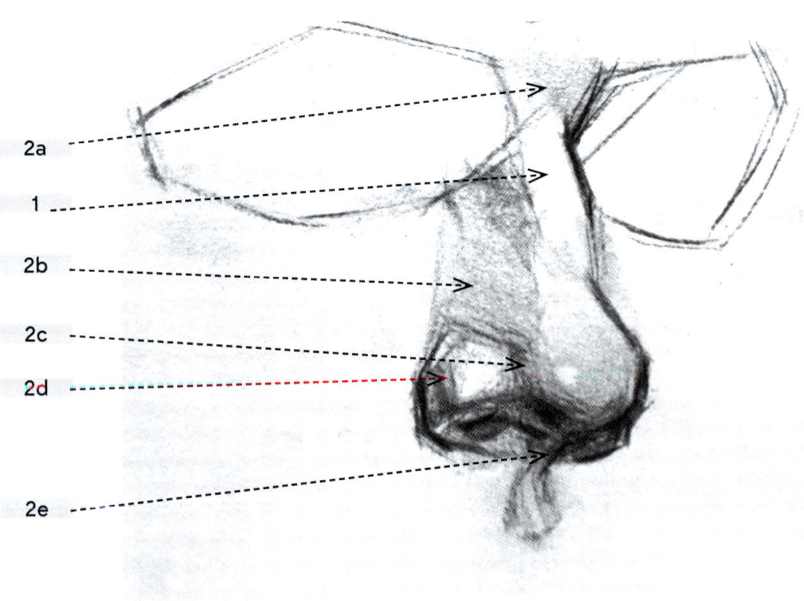

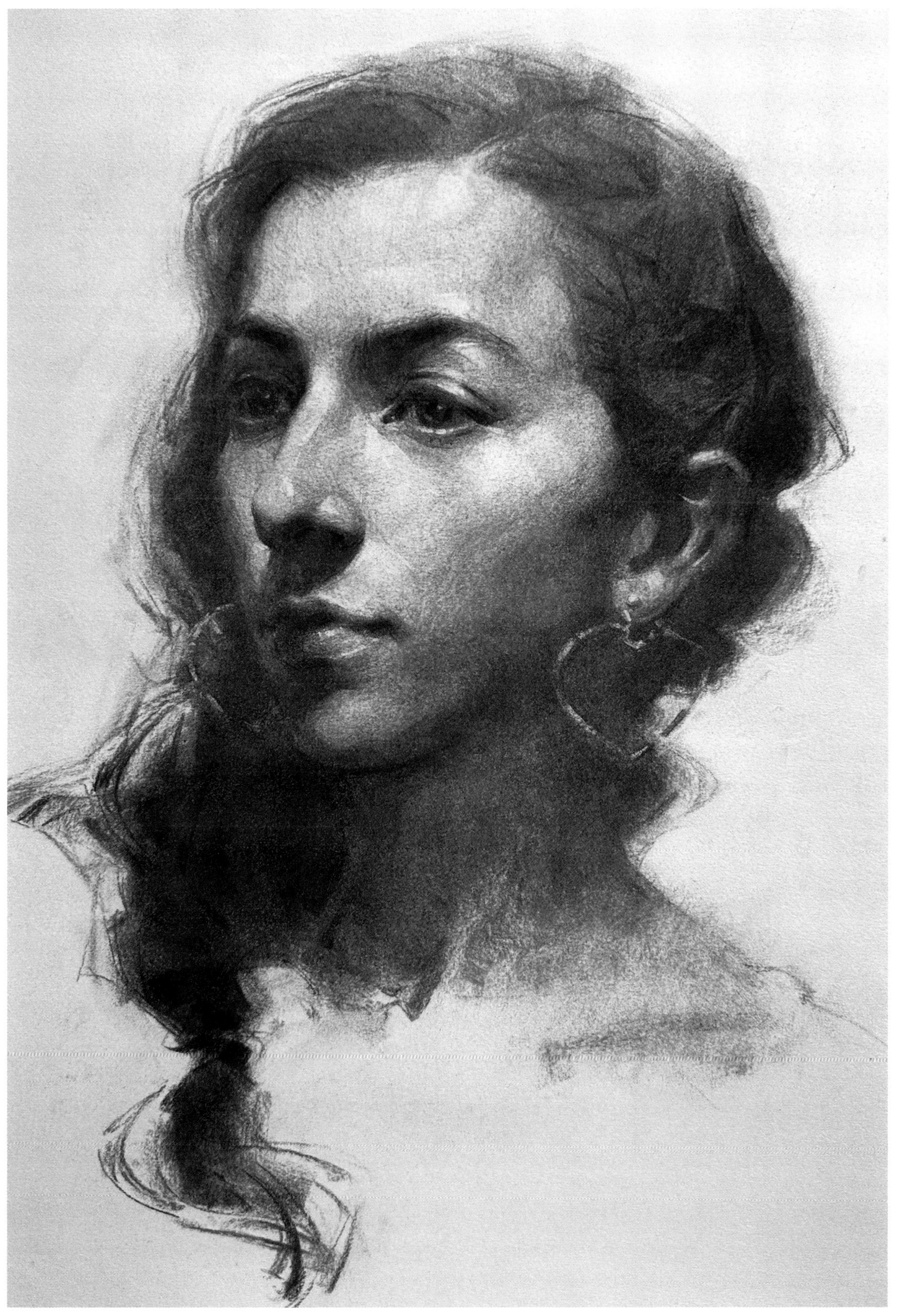

DRAWING THE NOSE

Noses come in various shapes and sizes. The shape and proportions of the nose are crucial characteristics of every face. To draw a good likeness, it's important to draw the nose accurately. Generally, the nose has a triangular, wedge-shaped form, narrow and depressed at its root under the brow ridge and broad and prominent at its base in the mid-region of the face. The nose consists of top, front, bottom, and side planes. The under plane of the nose is distinctly triangular, with its broad base gently curving on the upper region of the mouth barrel.

The nose, with its spherical similarities, is an excellent feature for learning the elements of shading and how they apply to all the facial features. Practice shading and blending principles when drawing the nose. Its size and shape are in direct proportion to the eyes, mouth, and ears, making it crucial to the overall size and scale of all of the other facial features. The nose is composed of soft edges where it gently curves and hard edges where the planes overlap. An inaccurately drawn nose will affect the total outcome of the portrait and ruin the likeness.

Look for the reflected light around the edge of the nostrils. If you can draw a really good nose, you're on your way to creating excellent portrait drawings!

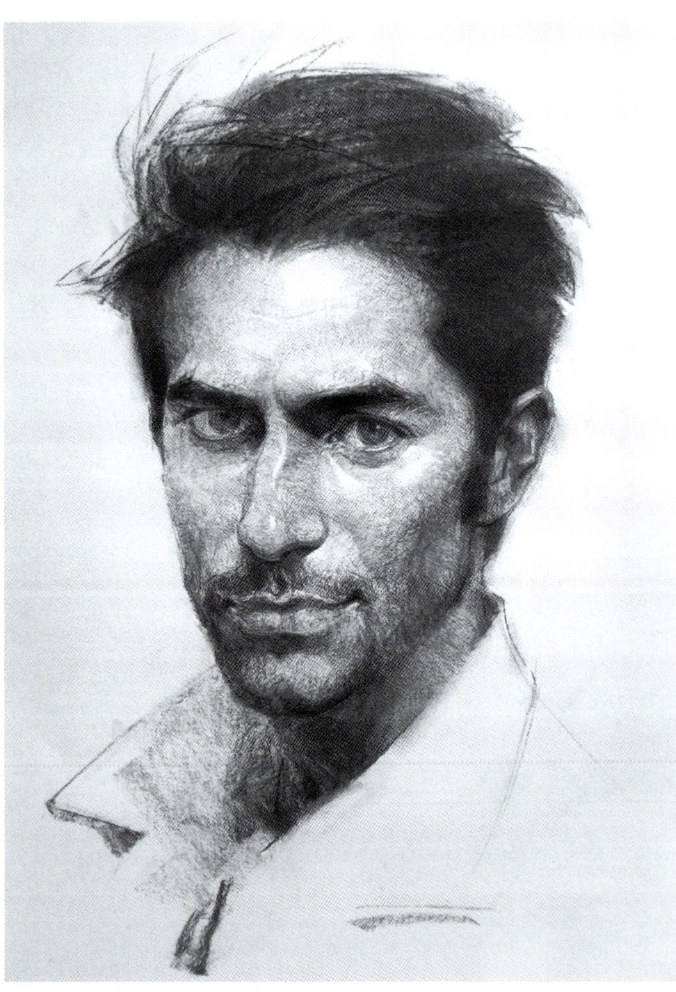

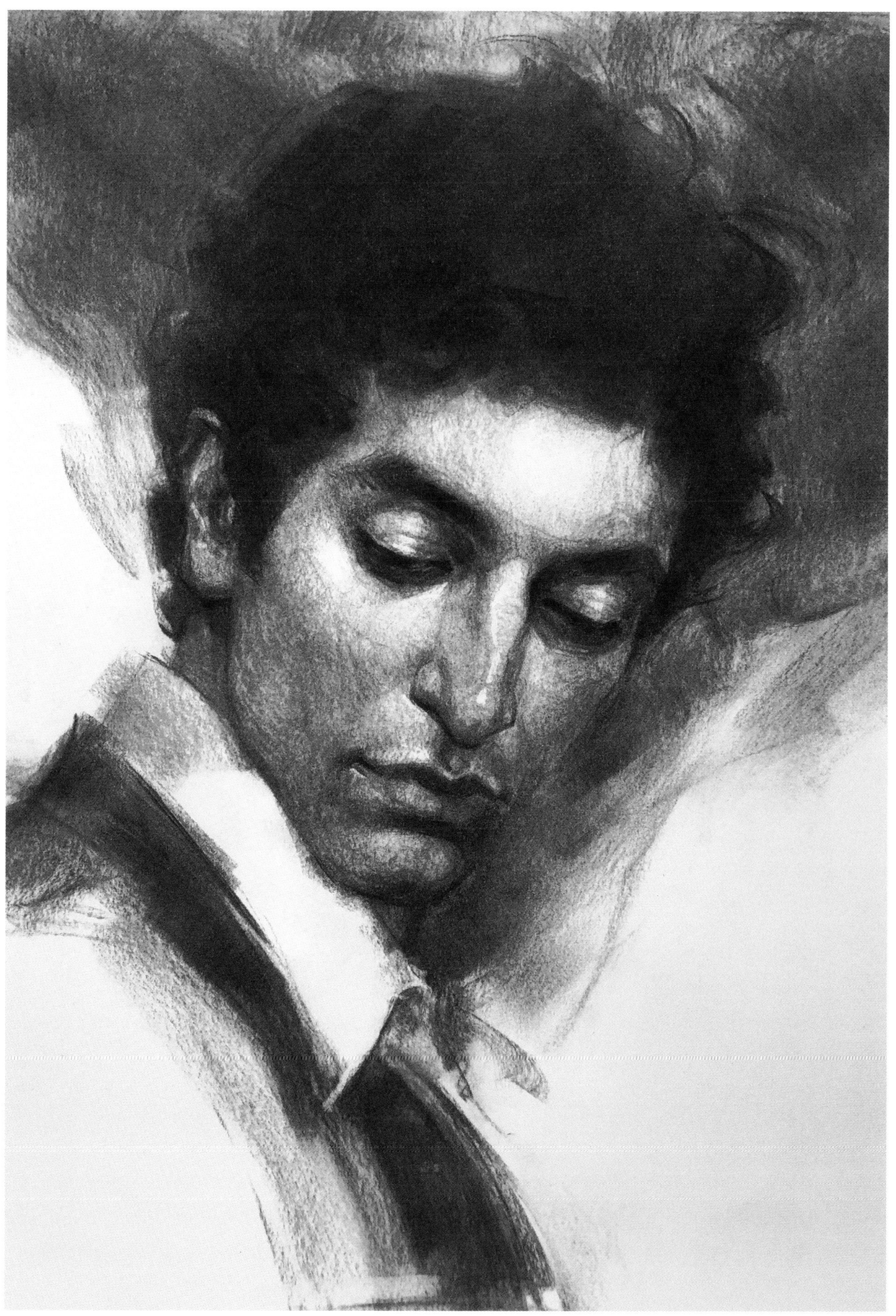

NOSE COMPARISONS

The nose is a prominent and important feature of every face. To learn the variations in noses, it's helpful to divide them into categories: small, large, or very large; concave or convex; hooked, Roman, or straight. The tips of noses can be elevated, horizontal, depressed, flattened, tapering, or twisted. The wings of the nose, the alae, may be delicate or puffy, round or flat, triangular, square, or almond-shaped.

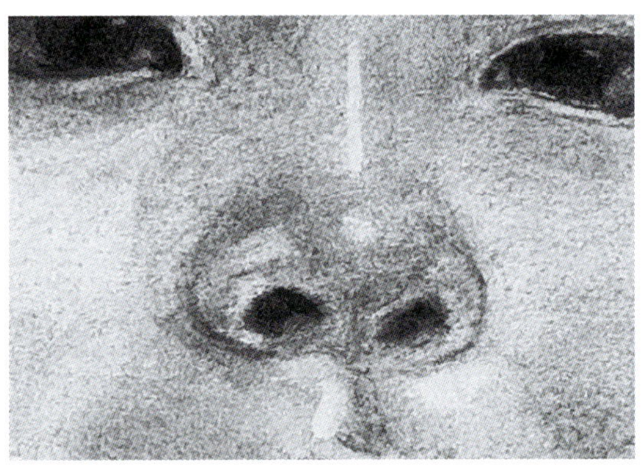
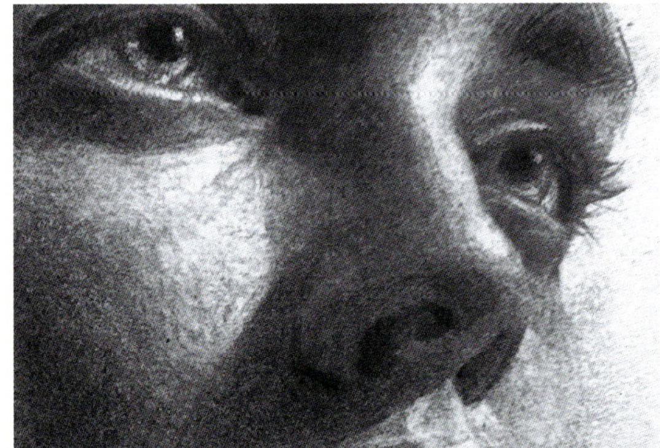
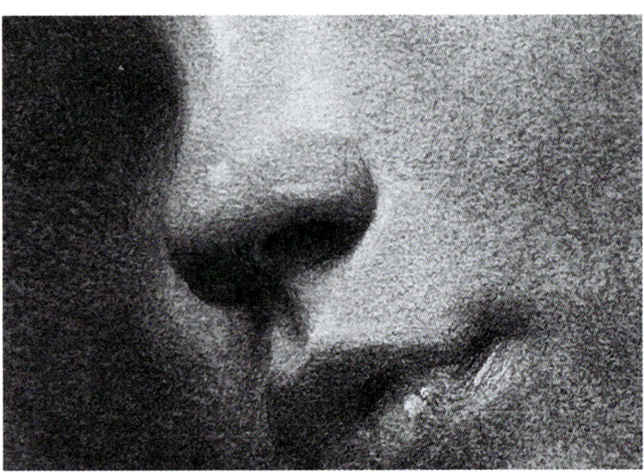
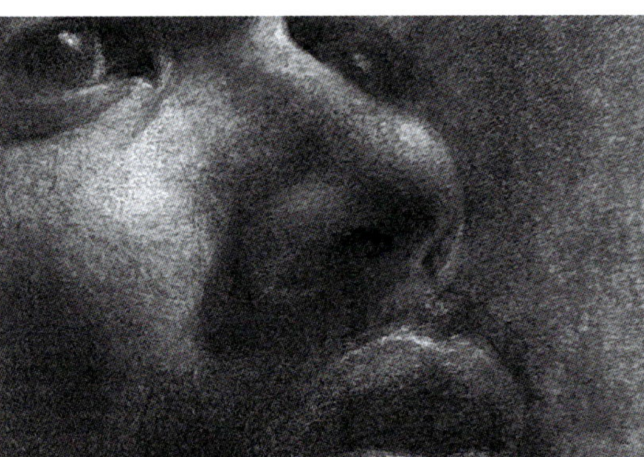

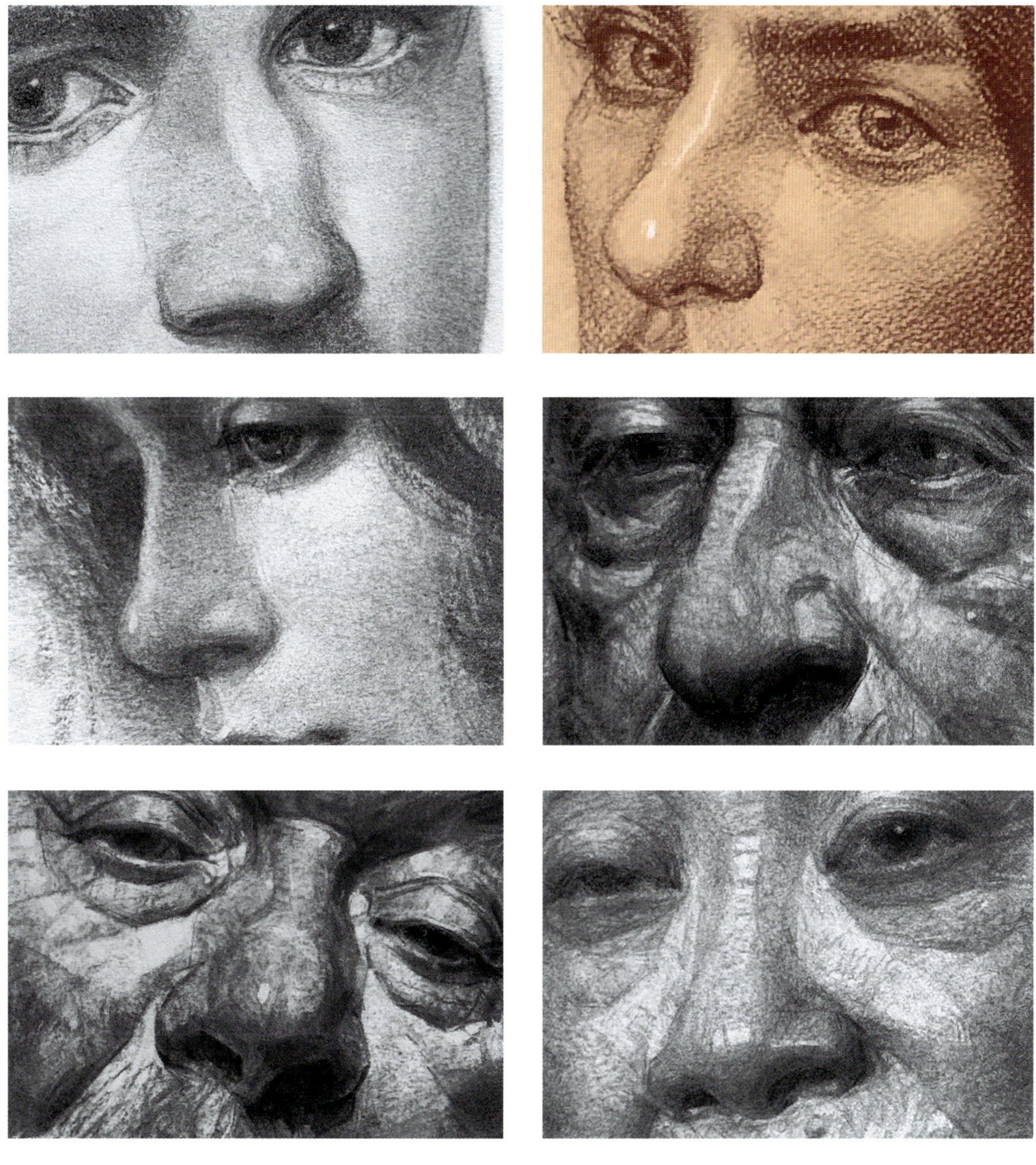

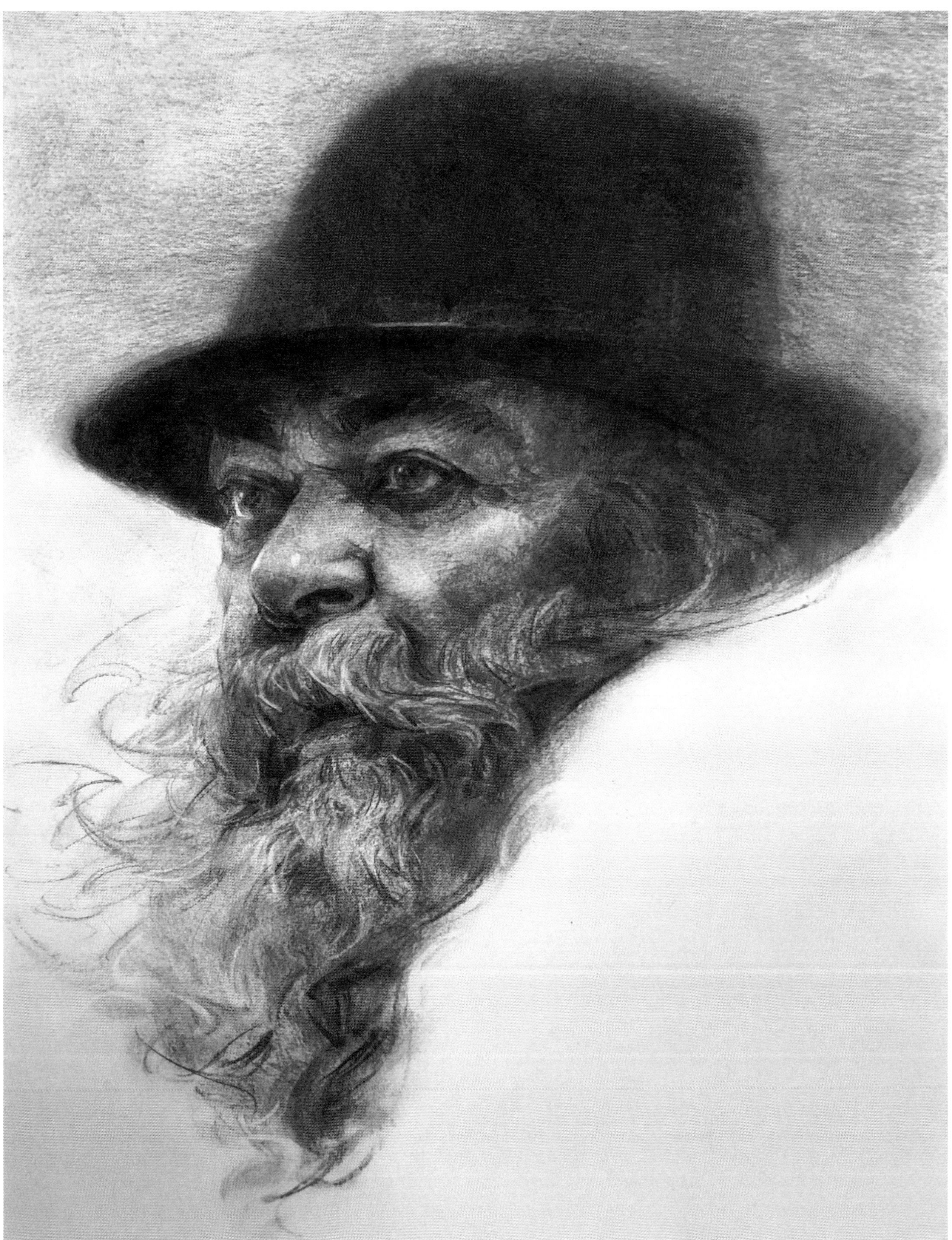

4

EXPRESSIONS AND THE AGING FACE

REGIONS OF THE AGING HEAD

1. FRONTAL REGION
2. GLABELLAR REGION
3. ORBITAL REGION
4. TEMPORAL REGION
5. NASAL REGION
6. INFRAORBITAL REGION
7. ZYGOMATIC REGION

8. ORAL REGION
9. BUCCAL REGION
10. PAROTIDEOMASSETERIC REGION
11. MENTAL REGION
12. SUBMANDIBULAR TRIANGLE
13. PARIETAL REGION
14. AURICULAR REGION

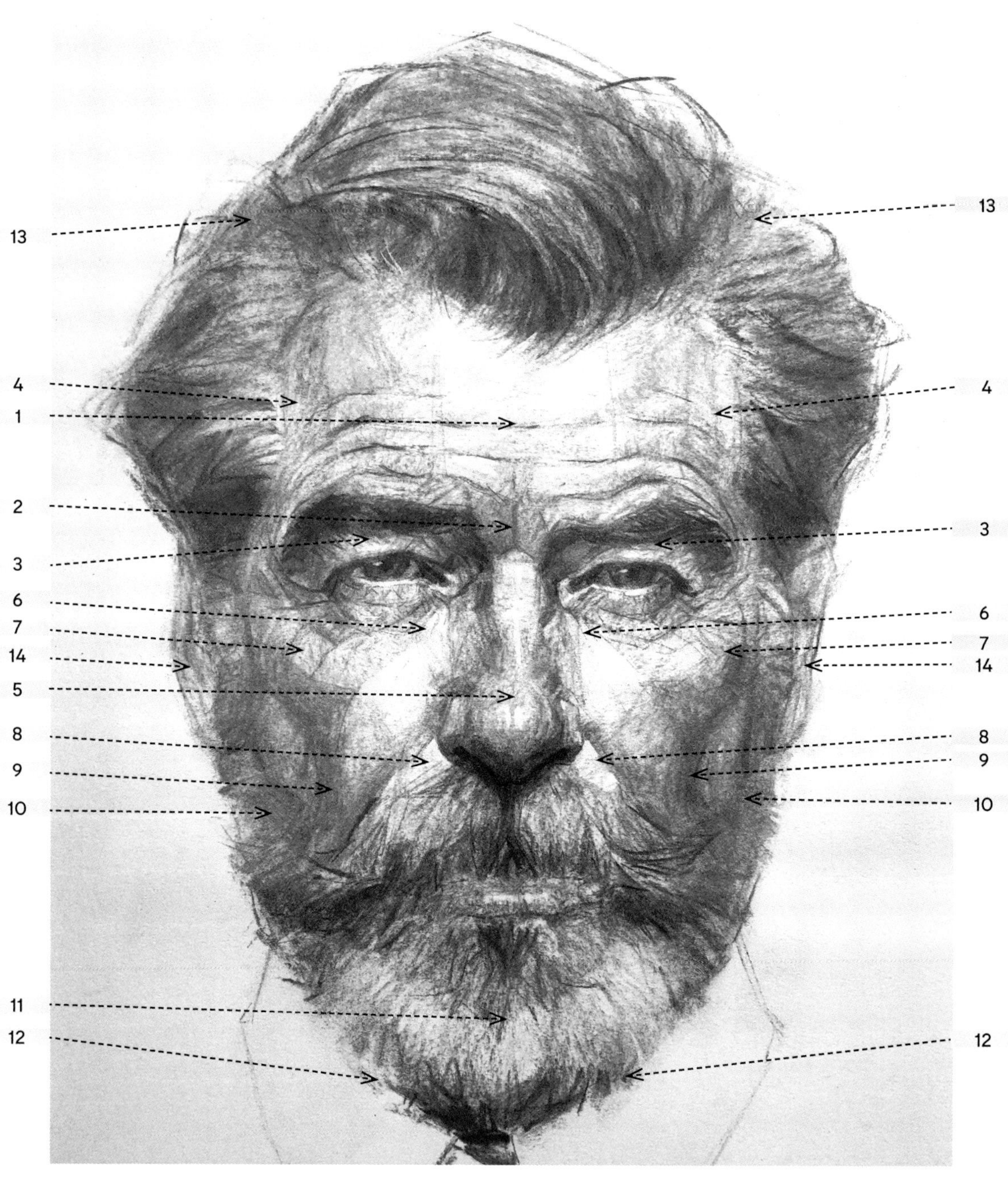

REGIONS OF THE AGING FACE

1. CHEEK REGION
2. SUPRAORBITAL REGION
3. UPPER EYELID
4. LOWER EYELID
5. INFRAORBITAL AREA
6. INFRAORBITAL SULCUS
7. TEAR TROUGH
8. INFRAORBITAL FURROW
9. MODIOLUS
10. PHILTRUM
11. NASOLABIAL FOLD

12. LABIAL FISSURE
13. PILLAR OF MOUTH
14. CHIN
15. TUBERCLE
16. VERMILION BORDER
17. GLABELLA
18. ROOT OF NOSE
19. BRIDGE OF NOSE
20. TIP OF NOSE
21. WING OF NOSE (ALA)

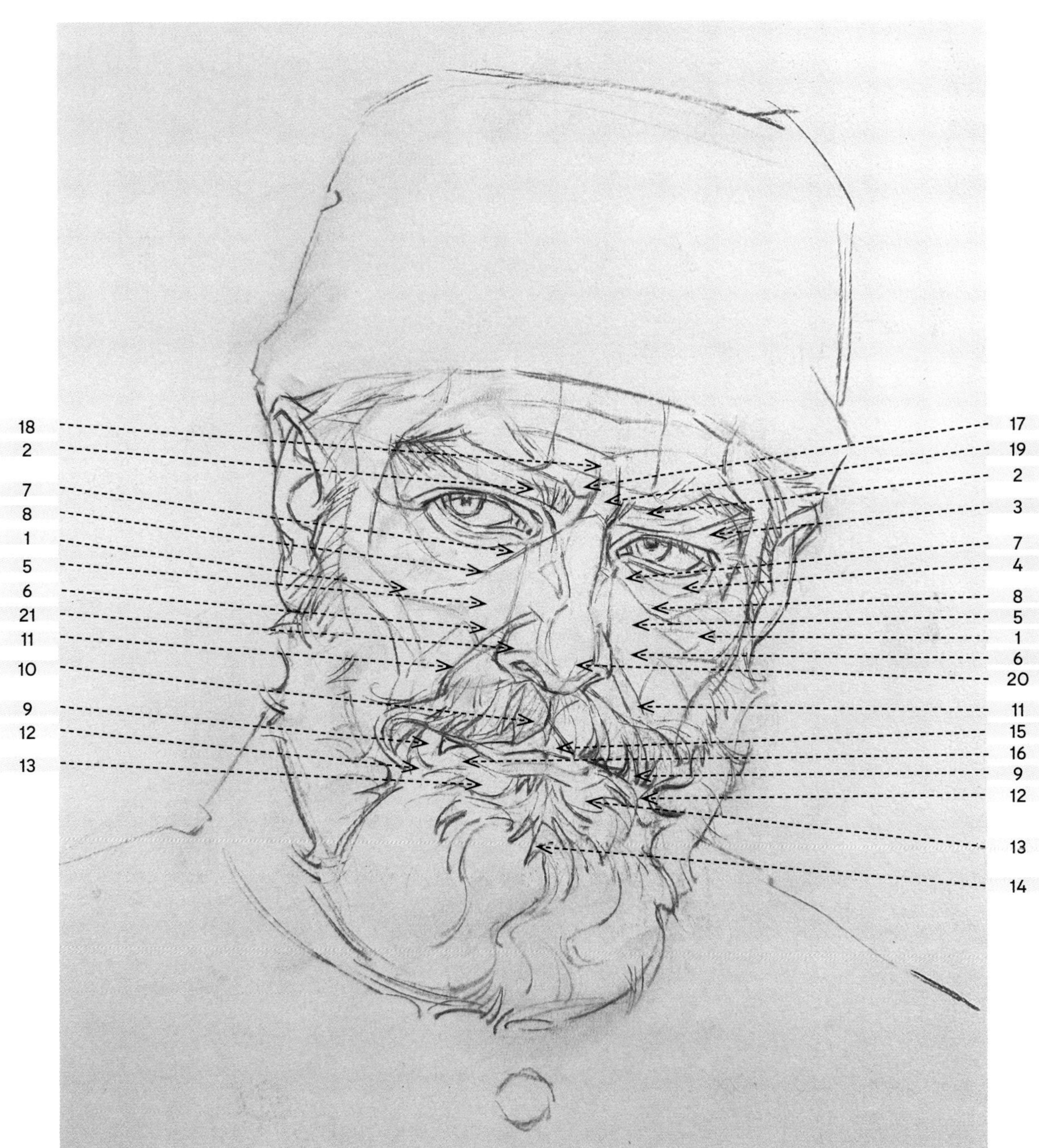

ANALYSIS OF FACIAL MARKINGS

Once you've memorized the size, shape, and placement of the general facial muscles, you can then proceed to identify the lines, humps, and bumps in the face. Older people, with more lines and wrinkles, are preferable to younger ones to look for this information.

As our culture constantly reminds us, wrinkles are obvious signs of aging. With practiced observation, you can learn to eliminate most of the wrinkles and instead focus on the lines, bones, and soft arrangements of the flesh beneath the surface. Small wrinkles are distracting and don't help define the form. Instead, try to detect the subtler characteristics that will give the impression of age and capture an accurate likeness. Remember, wrinkles are not actual lines on the face, just deep skin creases of light and shadow.

Older faces are treasure troves for artists, providing an endless resource of characters and configurations. Approach drawing an aging face by skimming over the network of wrinkles and go straight to focusing on the underlying forms.

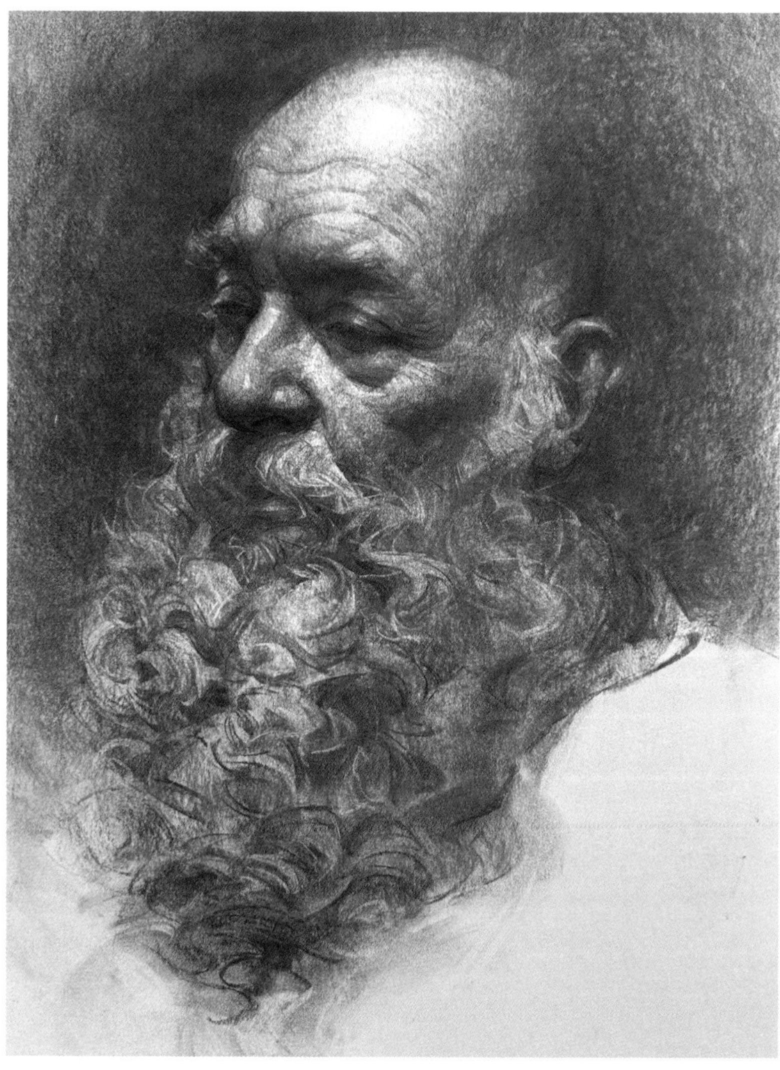

1. HORIZONTAL FOREHEAD FURROWS
2. VERTICAL FROWN FURROWS
3. CROW'S-FEET
4. OBLIQUE NOSE FURROWS
5. TEAR TROUGH
6. ALAR FURROW
7. NASOLABIAL FOLD
8. JUGAL FURROW
9. RADIATING MOUTH FURROWS
10. COMMISSURAL FURROW
11. MARIONETTE LINES
12. MENTAL CREASE
13. NECK FURROWS
14. STRANDS OF PLATYSMA

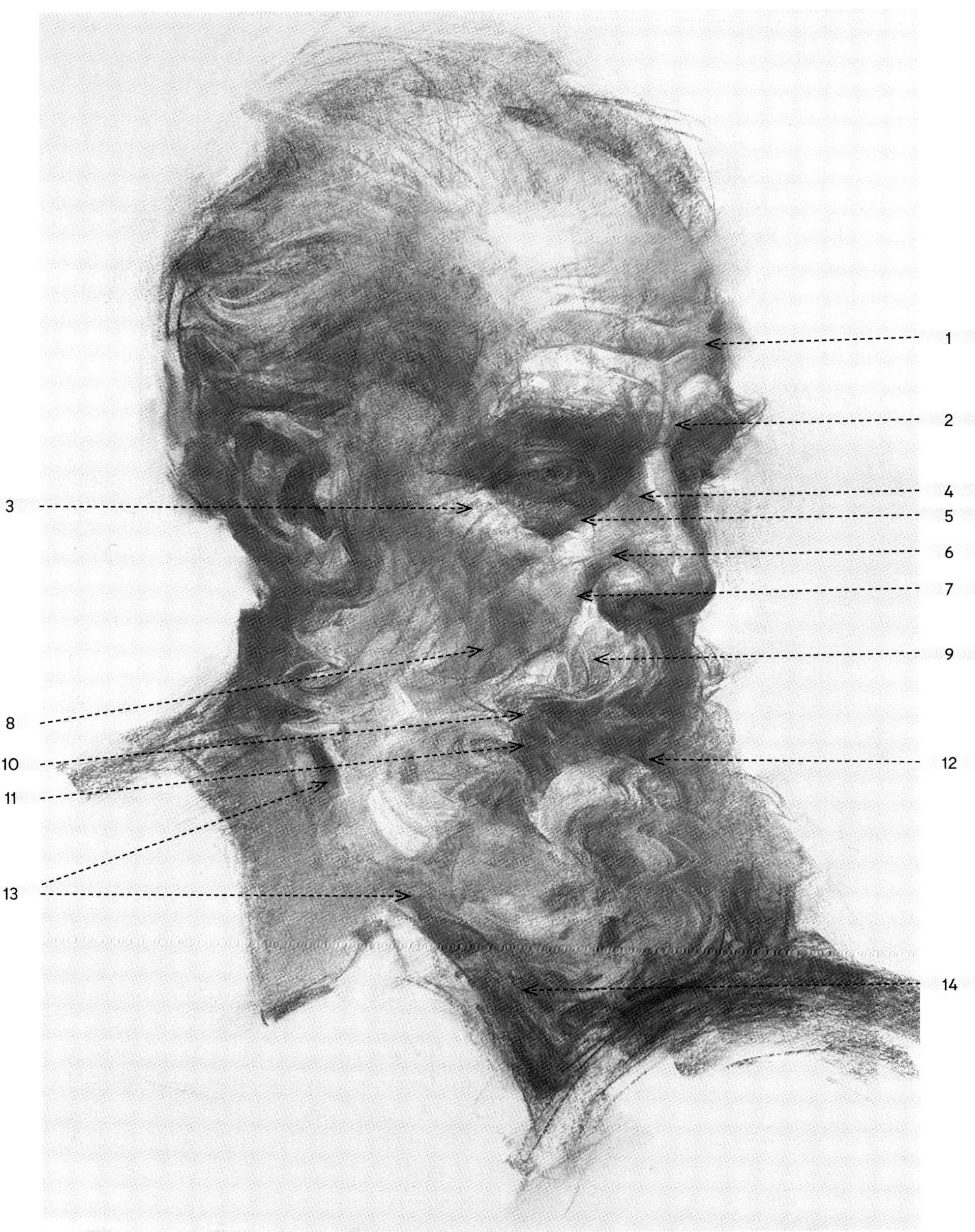

CAPTURING THE SUBTLETIES OF AGE

Learn to age a face by focusing on the changes in its forms. As people age, the cheekbones, the jaw, and the chin become more prominent. Gravity causes the cartilages of the nose and ears to appear larger and more saggy. Both the skin and underlying structures lose strength and elasticity, causing them to stretch out and sink downward. The nasal tip often looks enlarged, wider, and heavier. Overall, the changes to the ears and nose are the most noticeable.

The main changes with aging occur in the cheeks and around the eyes and mouth. The flesh droops at the sides of the chin and along the jawline. Bags form under the eyes, and crow's-feet develop at the corners of the eyes. The eye sockets grow larger, making the eyes appear more deep set, and loss of mass in the jaw may make the lower face look smaller relative to the rest of the head. The lips get thinner and move inward, creating a straighter line. Creases develop from the corners of the mouth down the sides of the chin. The skin above the eyelids droops, and the brows drop inward toward the nose bridge. A few deeper lines form across the forehead and between the eyebrows. The hairline moves up and back, and the hair at the top of the head thins significantly.

Aging is an extraordinary process that goes beyond the idea of merely losing one's youth. As people age, they gain wisdom, develop new perspectives, and accumulate rich memories.

Young people's beauty is often seen as a natural, effortless occurrence. In contrast, the beauty of older individuals is likened to a work of art, shaped by a lifetime of experiences, resilience, and personal growth. This perception celebrates the unique and profound beauty that comes with age, emphasizing that aging brings its own remarkable and dignified form of attractiveness.

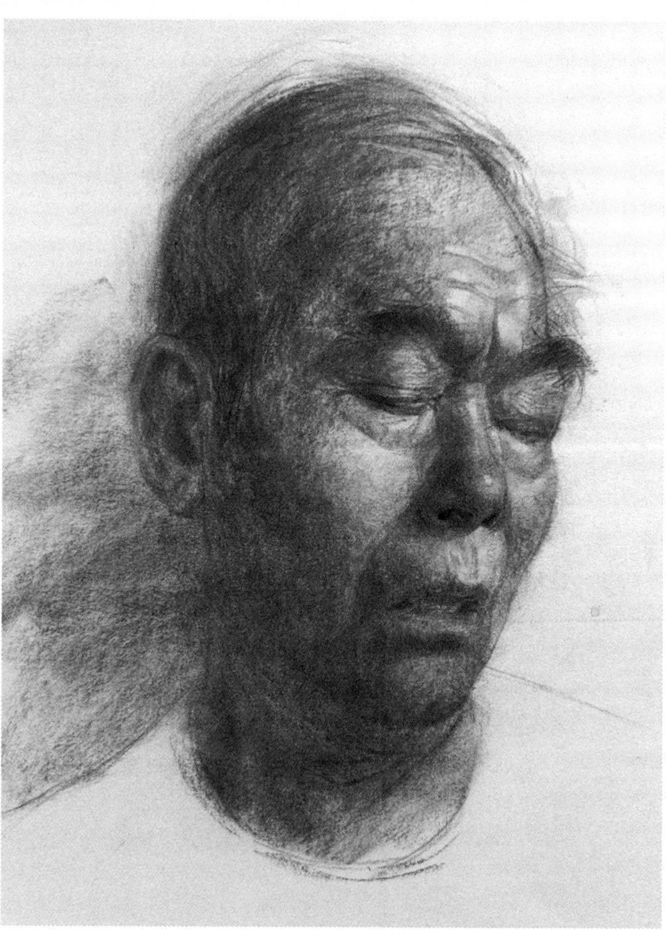

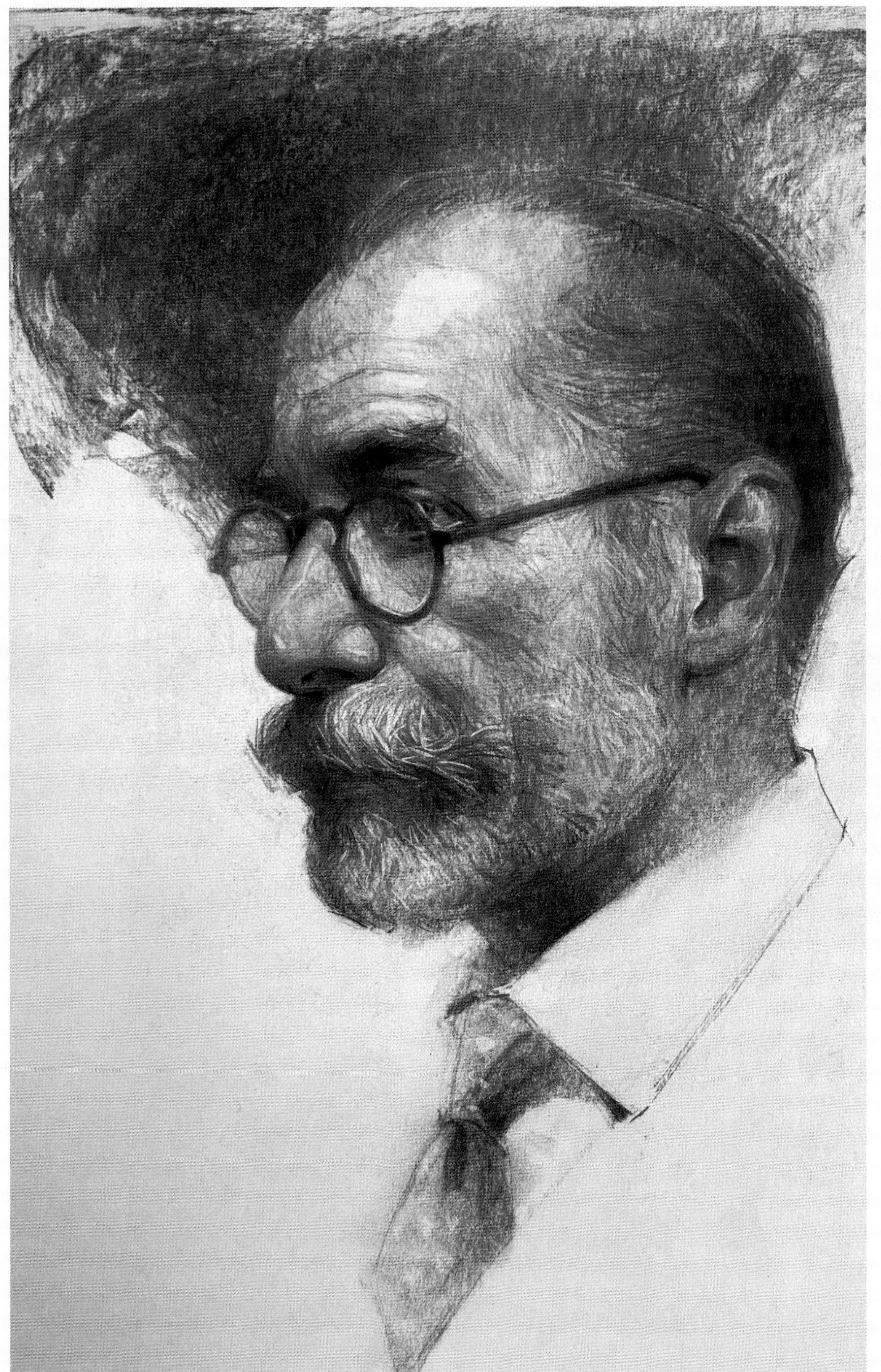

AGING OF THE EYES AND ORBITAL AREA

TEAR TROUGH

The tear trough, otherwise known as the *nasojugal groove*, is a 1-inch (2- or 3-centimeter) depression that begins under the inner portion of the lower eyelid. As we age, the fatty tissue under the lower eyelid and upper cheek naturally decreases. The skin and muscles of the lower eyelid slowly lose elasticity and become less tight. These changes can make the tear trough area puffy or cause it to bulge away from the face.

When the tissue under the eye pushes outward, "bags" develop. This unevenness of these areas can create shadows, making "dark circles" appear under the eyes.

SUNKEN EYES

Sunken eyes and tear troughs can be caused by a decrease in orbital fatty tissue, making the upper and lower orbital rims more visible. Most people begin to develop sunken and dark eyes by their late 30s and early 40s.

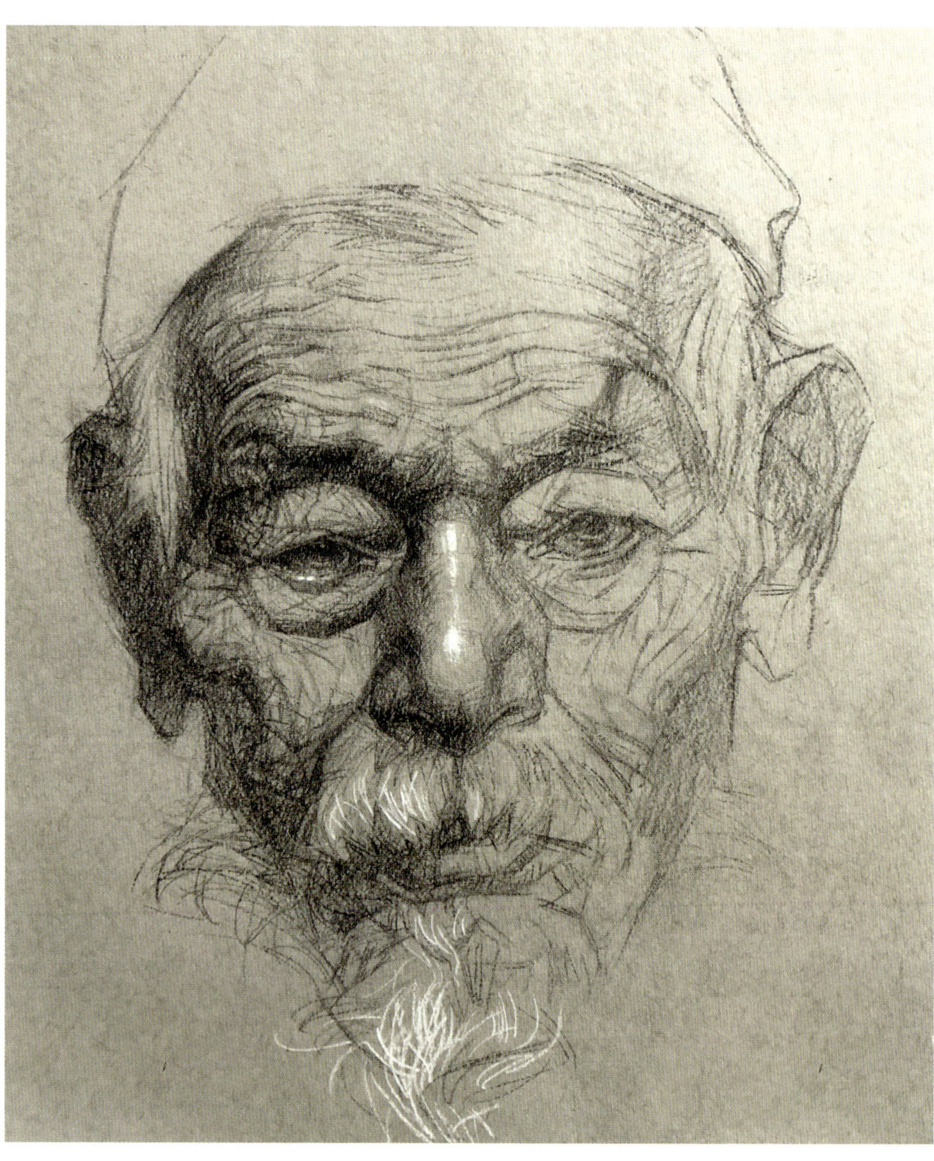

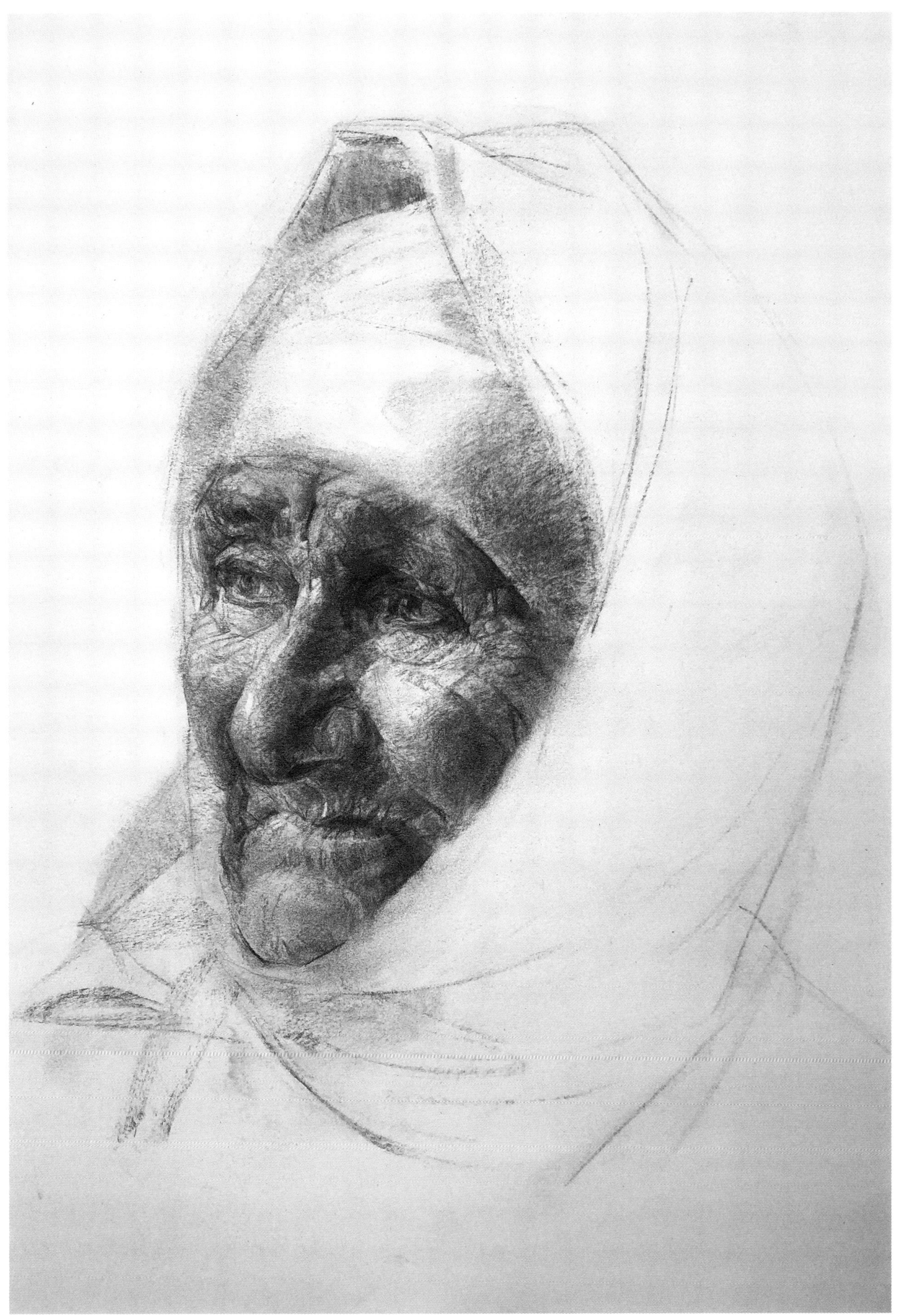

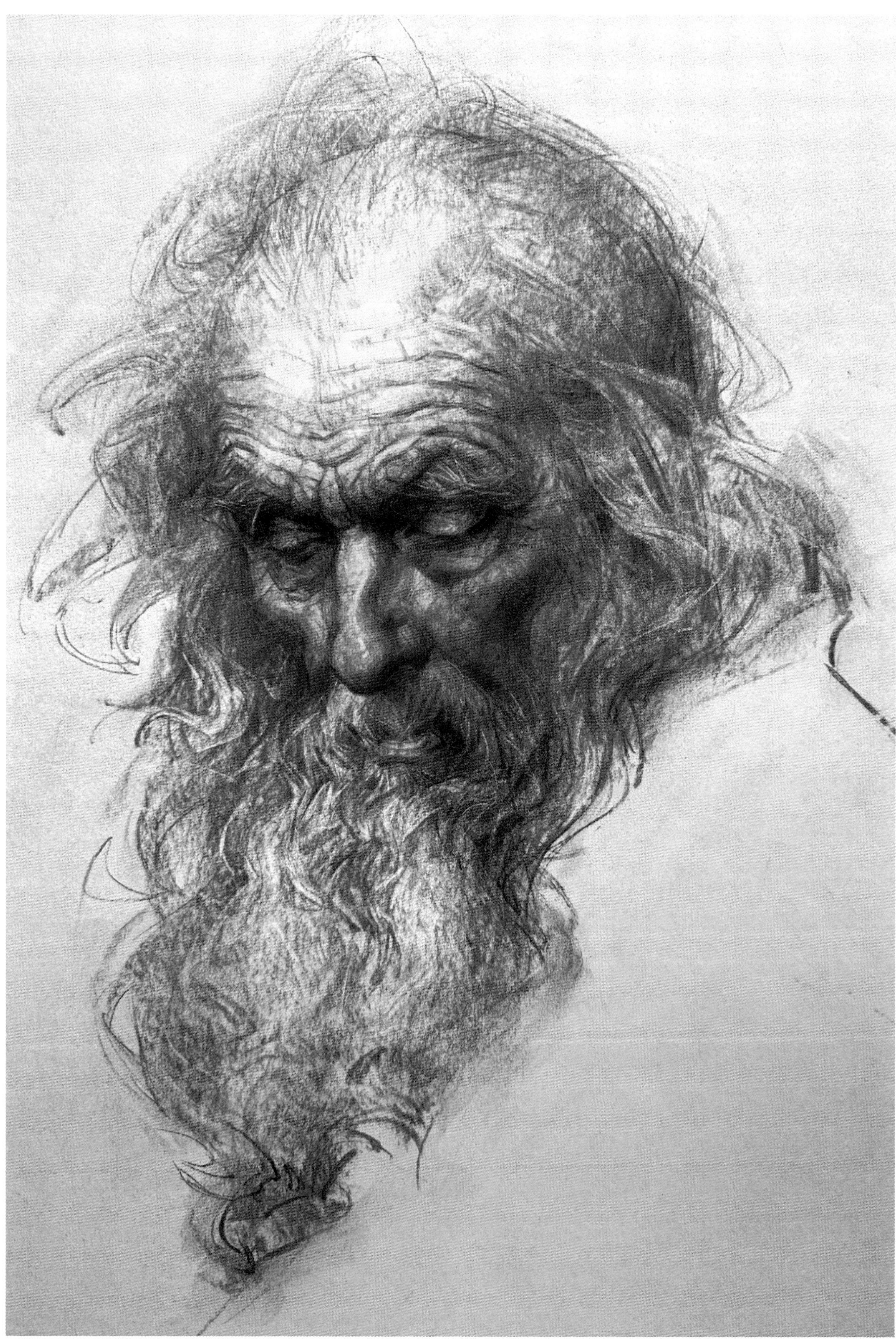

UNDER-EYE BAGS

Under-eye bags can appear due to the weakening of the orbicularis oculi muscle, loss of fat, and aging skin.

CROW'S-FEET

Crow's-feet, also known as *literal canthal lines* or *laugh lines*, are fine lines that form at the outer corners of eyes. These wrinkles develop from tiny muscles contracting in response to various emotions such as happiness, excitement, sorrow, and melancholy. Crow's-feet often begin as noticeable lines that form when you smile and your eyes naturally squint.

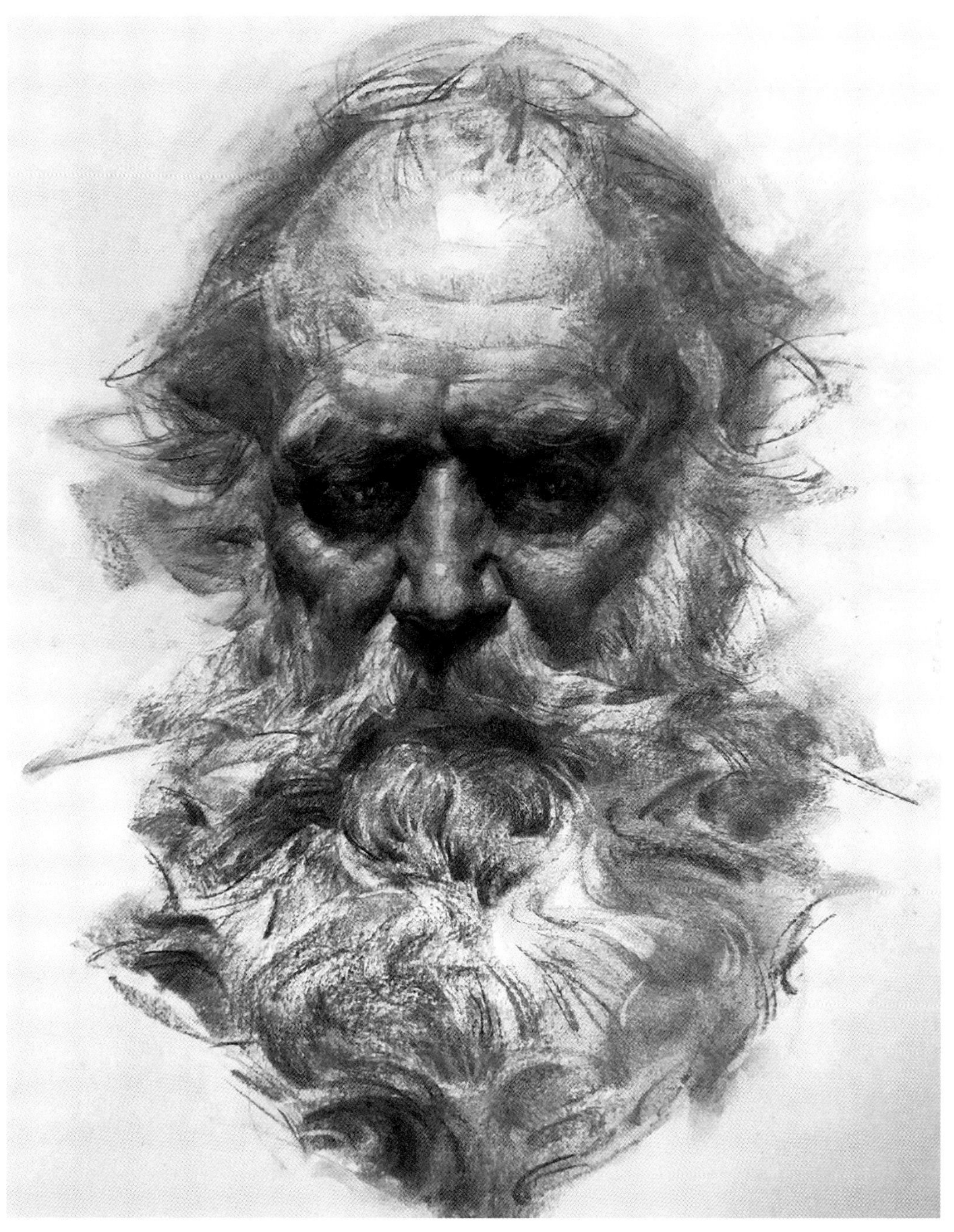

FROWN LINES

Besides crow's-feet, there are vertical frown lines that appear between the eyebrows and nose when you frown. These lines form due to the contraction and movement of paired facial muscles called *corrugator supercilii muscles*. Horizontal lines, or deep grooves, also develop on the forehead from similar muscle activity.

RECEDING ORBITAL RIM

Bone tissue along the orbital rim recedes with increasing age, while the central orbital parts remain relatively stable. This causes an excess of upper eyelid skin and makes the visible areas of the eyes smaller. Sometimes, lower lids weaken and droop, revealing more of the white part of the eye, called the *sclera*. This change can make a person look tired and years older.

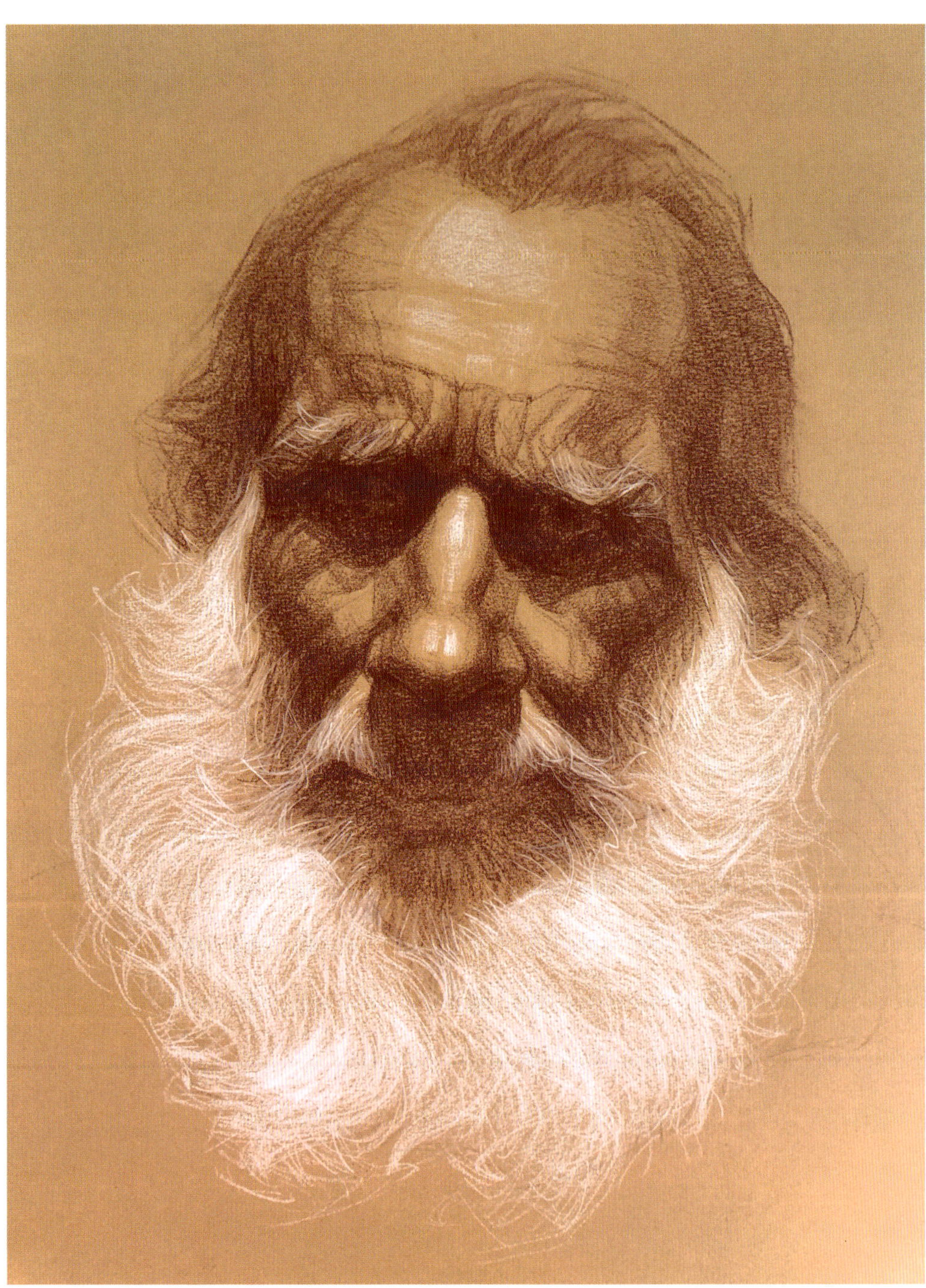

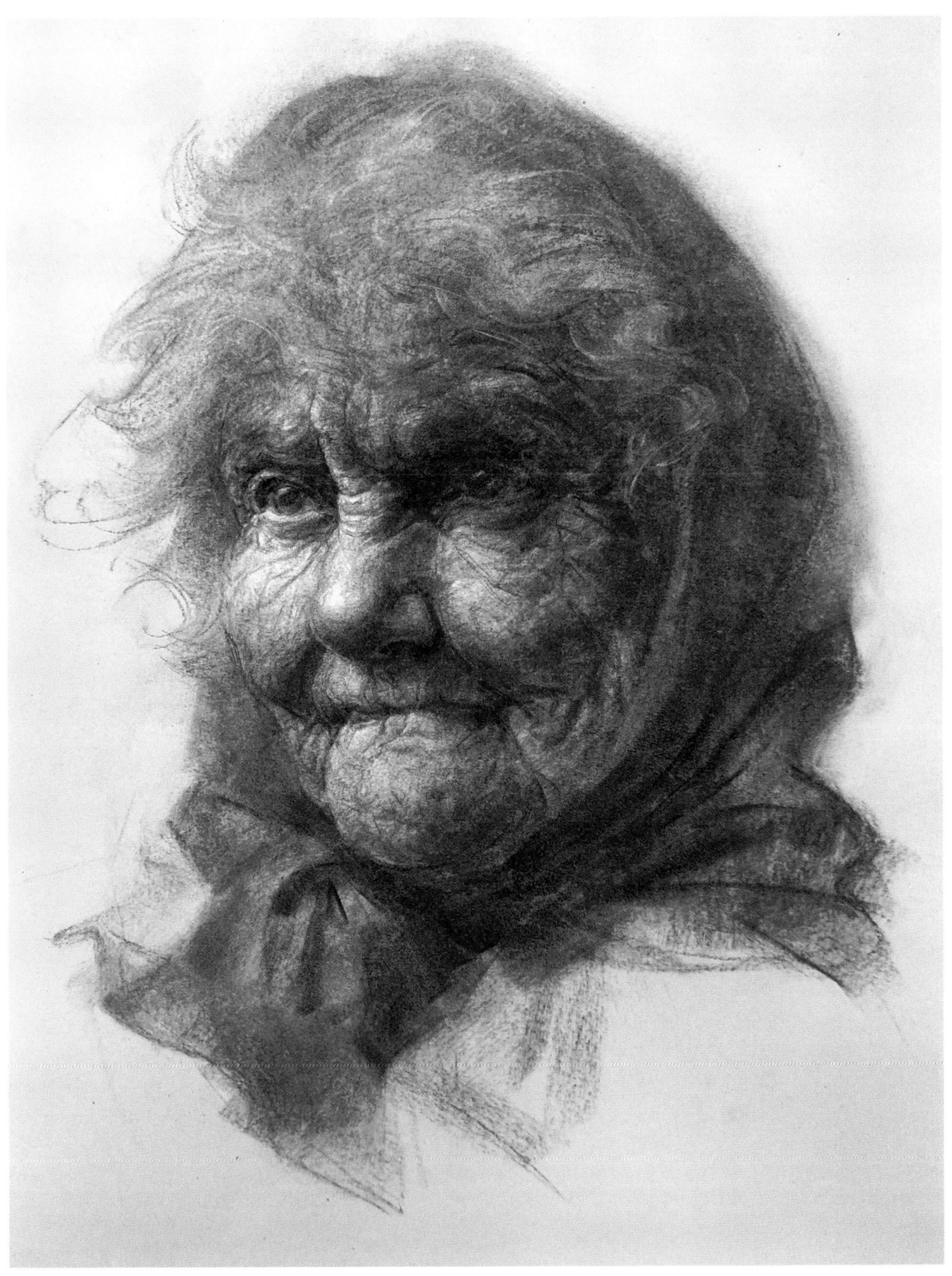

AGING OF THE MOUTH AND ORAL AREA

THINNER LIPS

Human lips change throughout adulthood. Dryness increases with age, more so on the lower lip than the upper. Starting at around age 45, lips slowly lose their volume, becoming thinner and rolling inward.

NASOLABIAL FOLDS

Nasolabial folds, also called *smile lines* or *laugh lines*, are also regarded as facial features. These are the two skin creases that extend from either side of the nose to the corners of the mouth. These folds can become more pronounced and permanent with age.

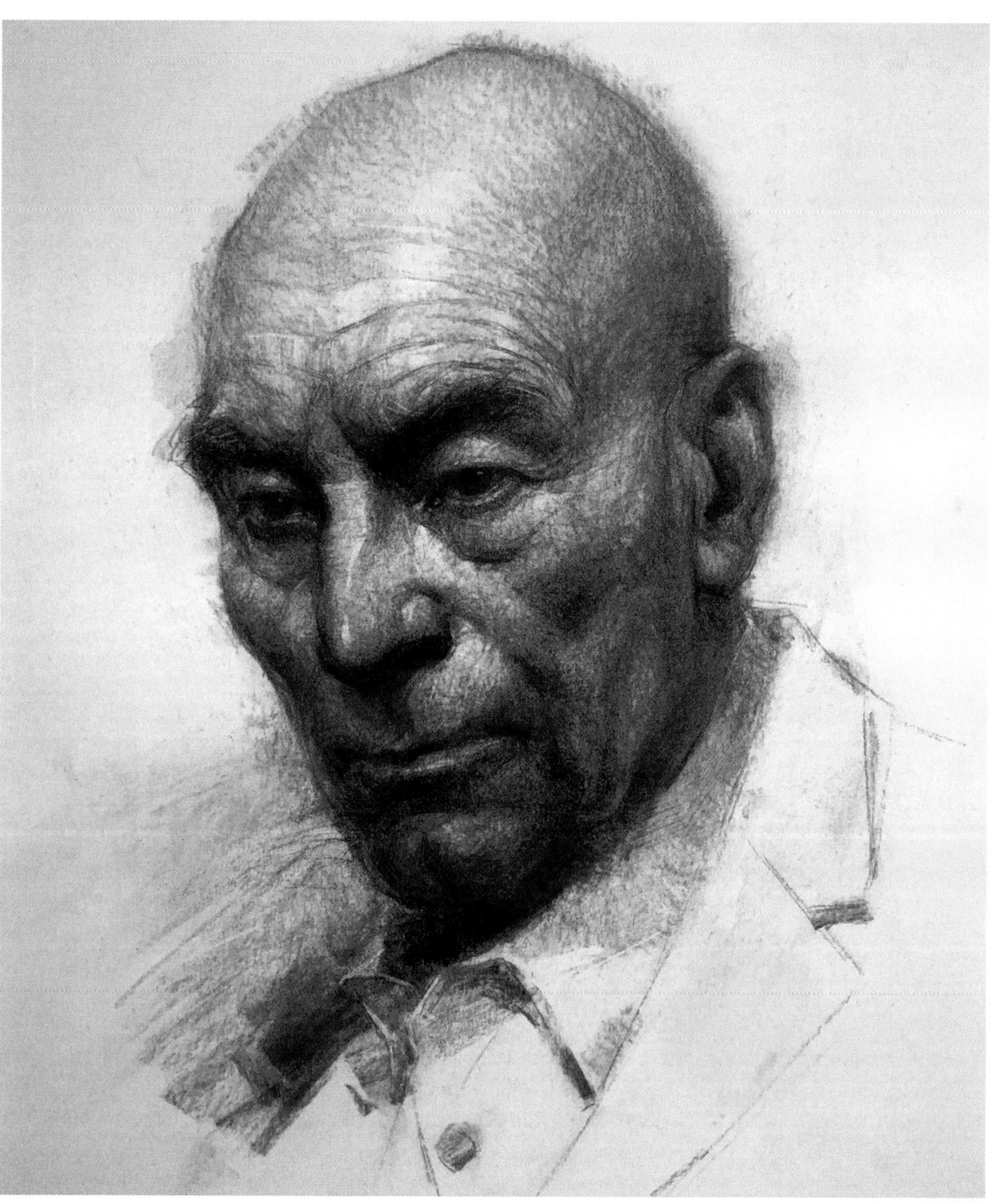

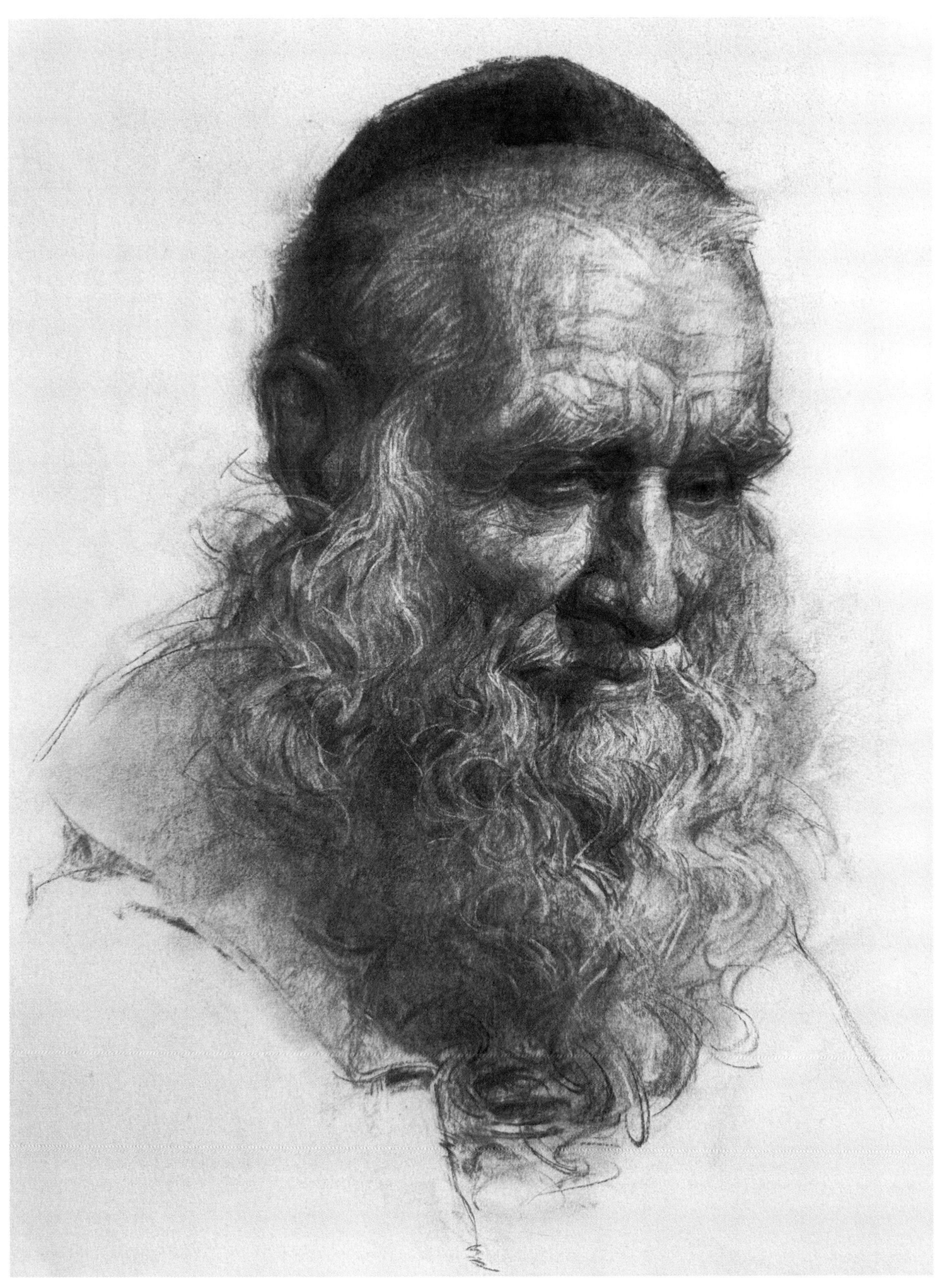

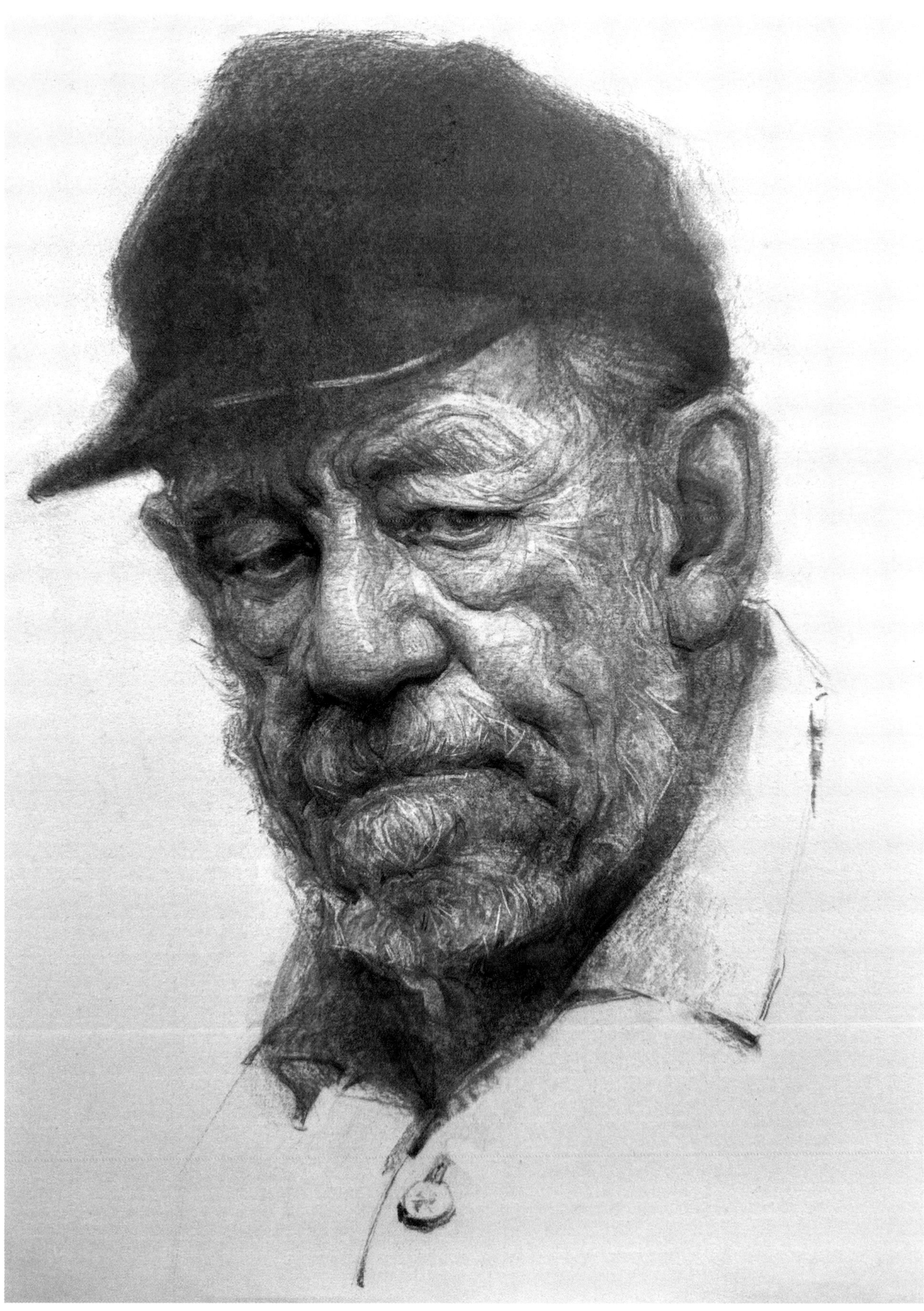

MARIONETTE LINES

Marionette lines, also called *puppet lines* or *mentolabial folds*, are lines that run from the corners of the mouth downward toward the chin. These lines can create sagging in the lower half of the face. As the face ages, soft tissues lose their volume and elasticity and face muscles droop, often sliding down due to gravity. Marionette lines can deepen into marionette folds as we get older.

DROOPY MOUTH CORNERS

As the face ages, soft tissues lose their volume and elasticity and facial muscles slacken. This can lead to droopy mouth corners, also known as an *inverted smile*, which results from a reduction of cheek volume, skin elasticity, and high contraction of one or both depressor anguli oris muscles, also called the *triangularis muscle*.

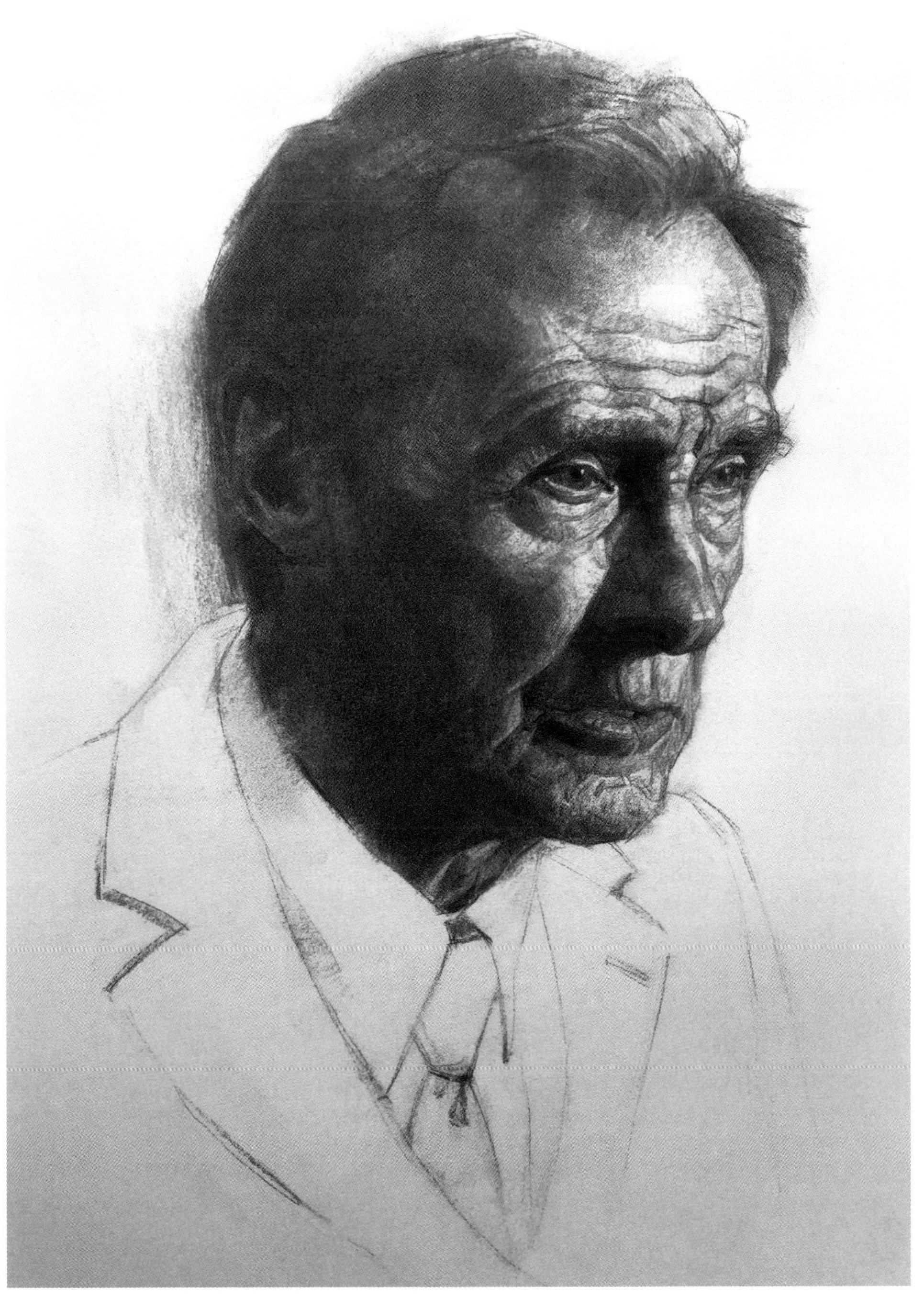

CHIN WIDENING

The loss of volume in the sides (lateral) and lower (inferior) portion of the chin results in a relative protrusion of the central chin, making the chin appear wider when viewed from the front.

LESS DEFINED JAWLINE

In addition to wrinkles, a less defined and a more obscured jawline is a telltale sign of aging. A flaccid jawline forms due to the aging of the superior and inferior jowl fat plus the addition of loose skin, which may create the look of a double chin. Losing teeth can also diminish the jawline, contributing to the slackness.

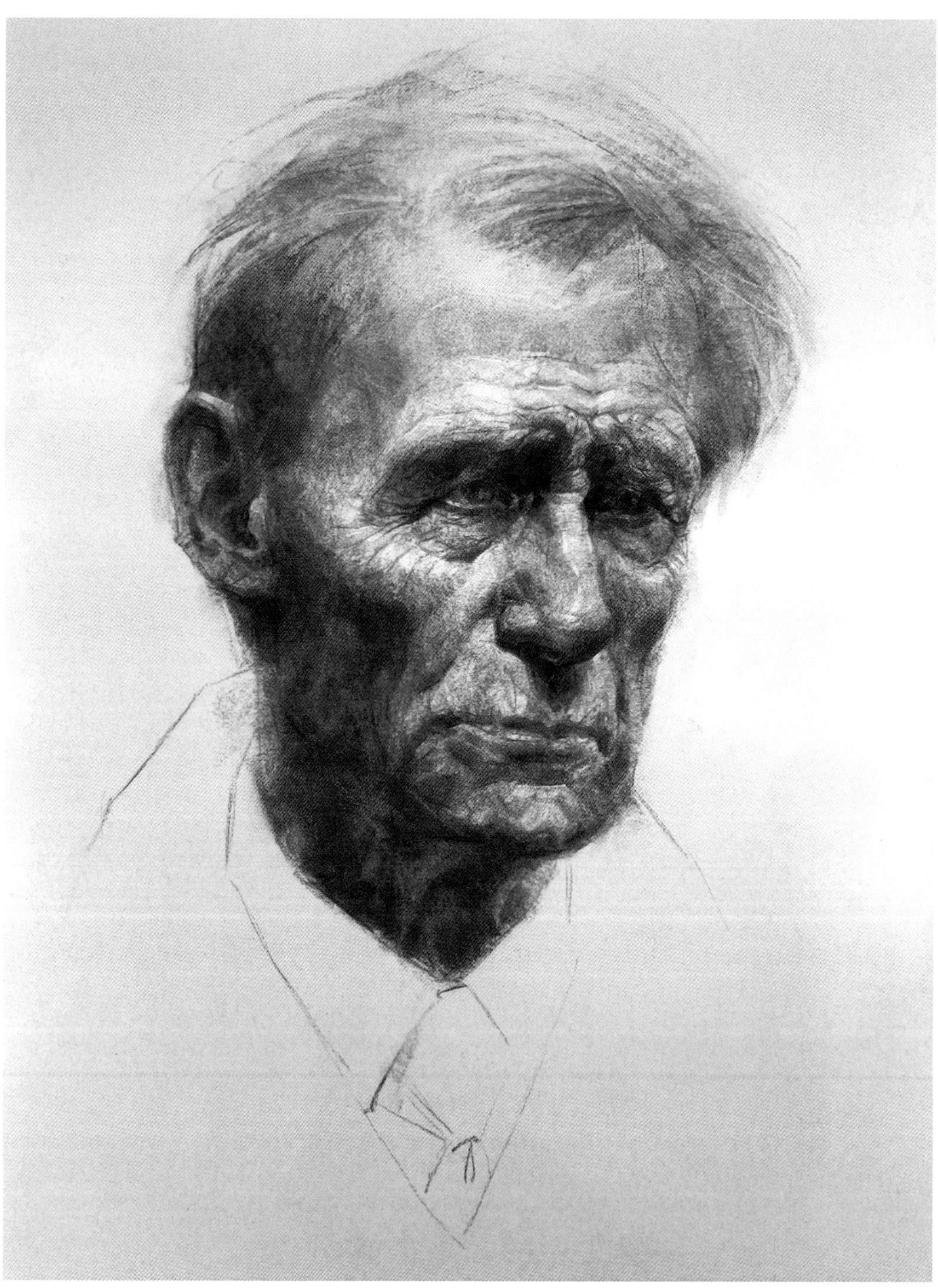

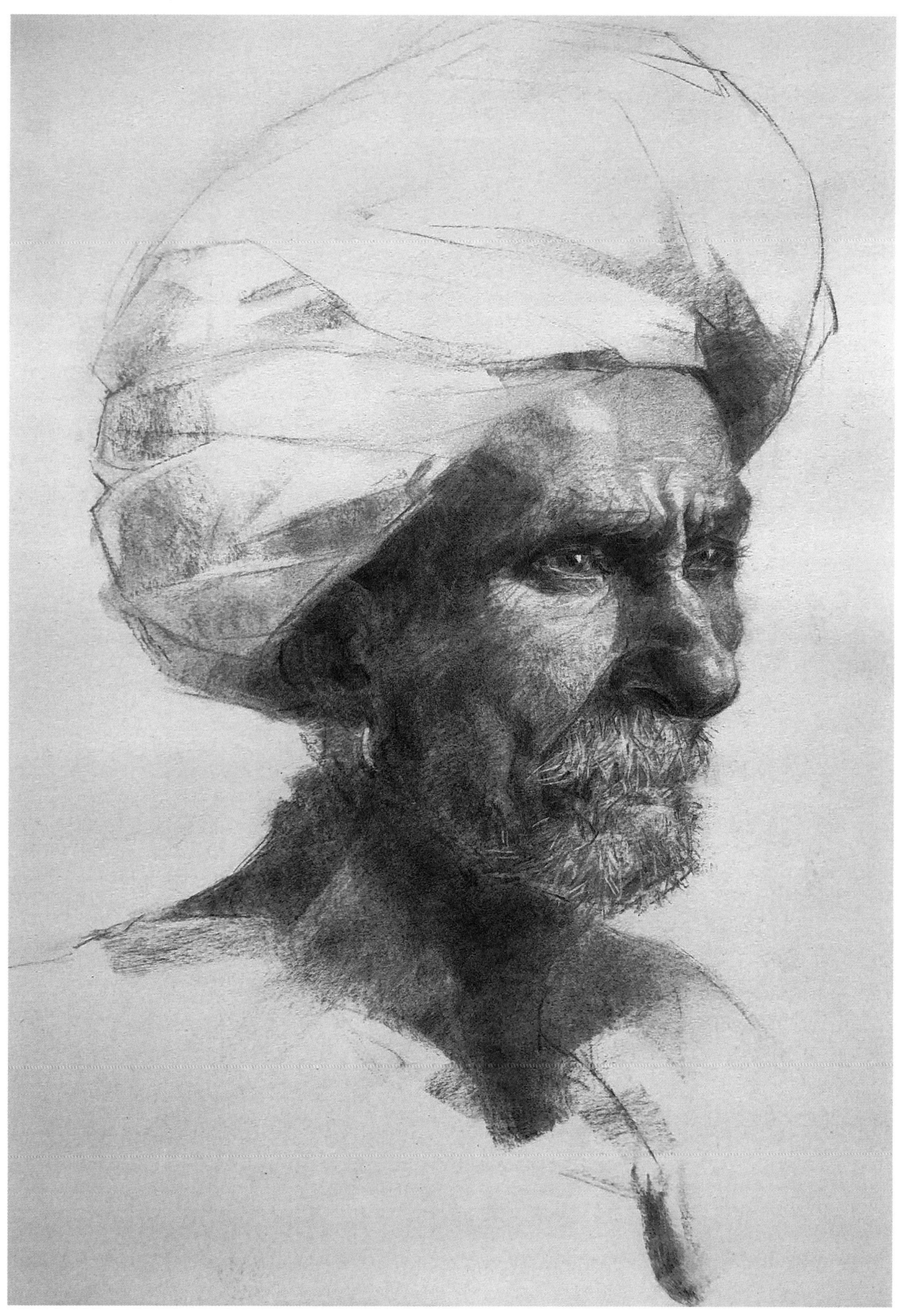

MENTAL CREASE AND PEAU D'ORANGE

The mental crease, or labiodental sulcus, is
the horizontal crease below the lower lip and
above the chin. The mentalis muscle, which
originates on the mandible, elevates, everts,
and protrudes the lower lip, creating wrinkles
in the chin. Over time, repeated actions of this
muscle can lead to a mental crease, giving an
expression of doubt. This crease can appear
as a single groove of varying depths or as
multiple wrinkles or folds.

Peau d'orange, the French term meaning
"skin of an orange," describes dimpling on
the chin caused by visible attachments with
the mentalis muscle, seen through aging thin
skin. This uneven, textured chin, resembling
an orange peel, results from the loss of skin
elasticity. This leads to puckering, lines,
bumps, and divots on the surface.

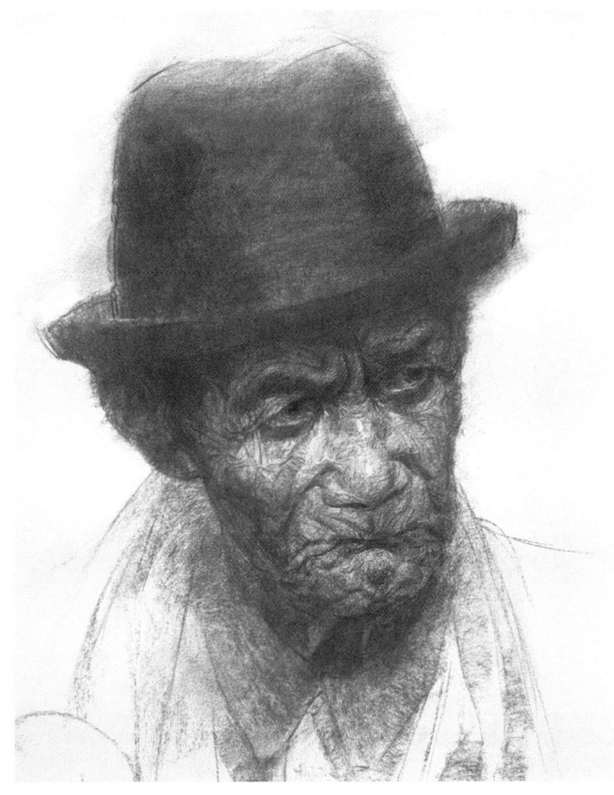

Mental crease.

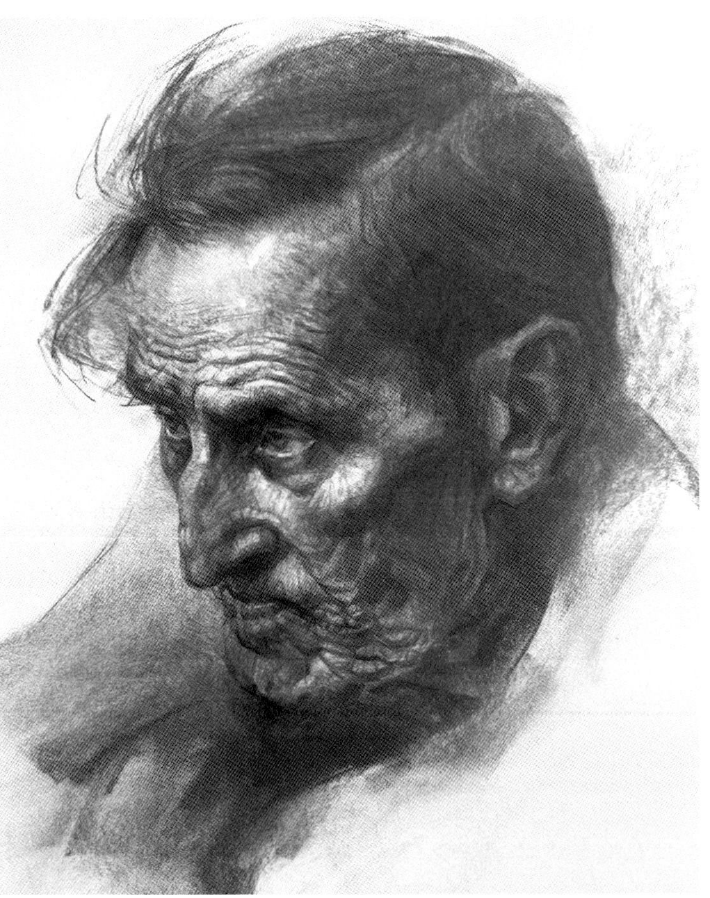

Peau d'orange.

AGING OF THE NOSE

NOSE HUMP

With age, thinning and loss of elasticity of the nasal skin often leads to a pseudo hump on the bridge of the nose. The skin over the dome is thin and lacks subcutaneous tissue, making bony irregularities more noticeable.

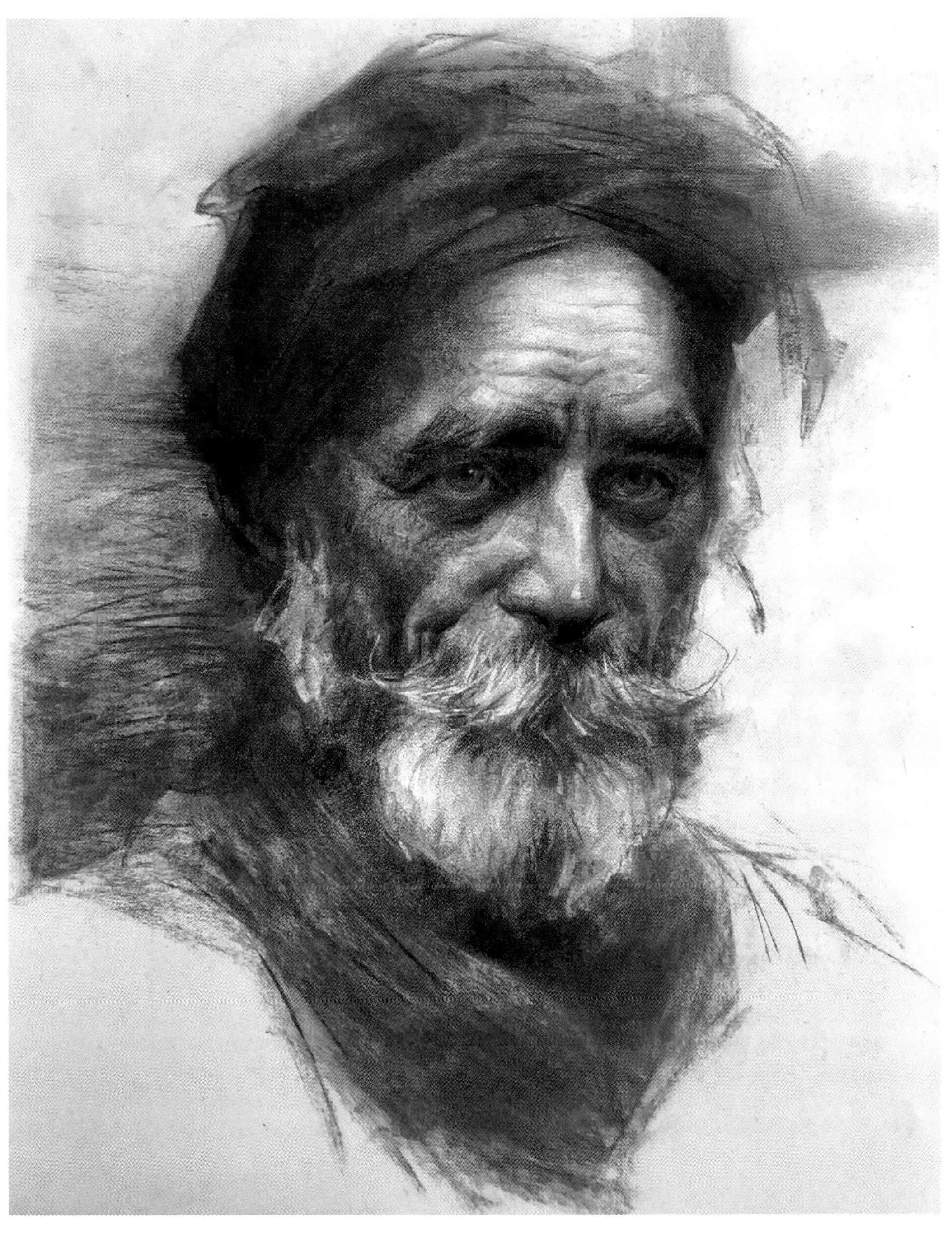

DROOPY NOSE TIP (NASAL TIP PTOSIS)

Facial sagging and a droopy nose tip result from changes in the nasal skin and the weakening of the cartilage framework and nasal bones that once offered strong support. As we age, the skin of the nose becomes thinner, and the sebaceous glands of the nose increase in activity. This causes the skin to become thicker, more glandular, and more vascular, which contributes to nasal tip ptosis.

LARGER NOSE

As the nasal tip progressively descends, it pulls on and separates the connective tissues between the cartilages at the end of the nose, resulting in its lengthening and enlargement. Over time, your skin loses elasticity and firmness, leading to sagging. Loose, slack skin over a weaker cartilage frame makes the nose appear longer.

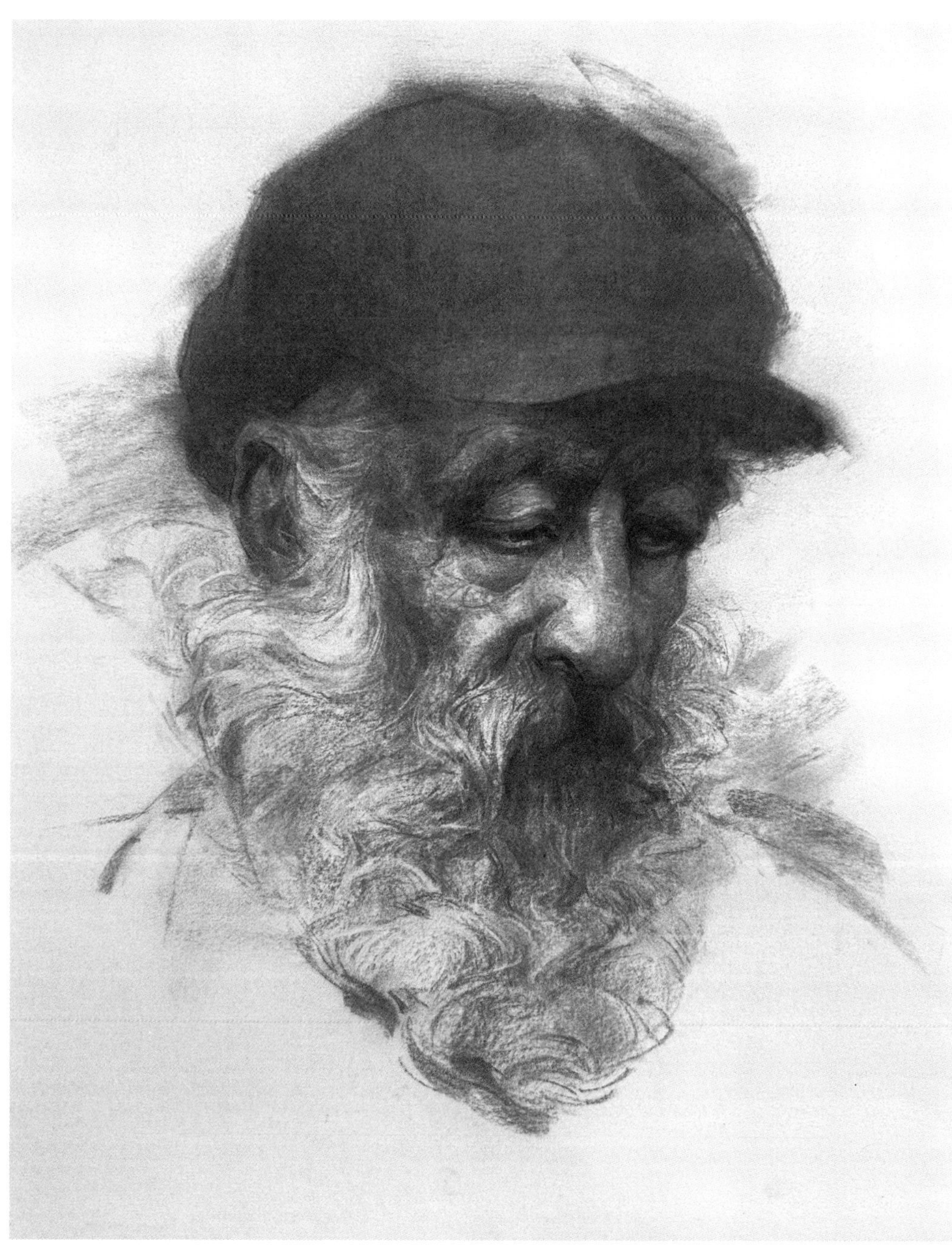

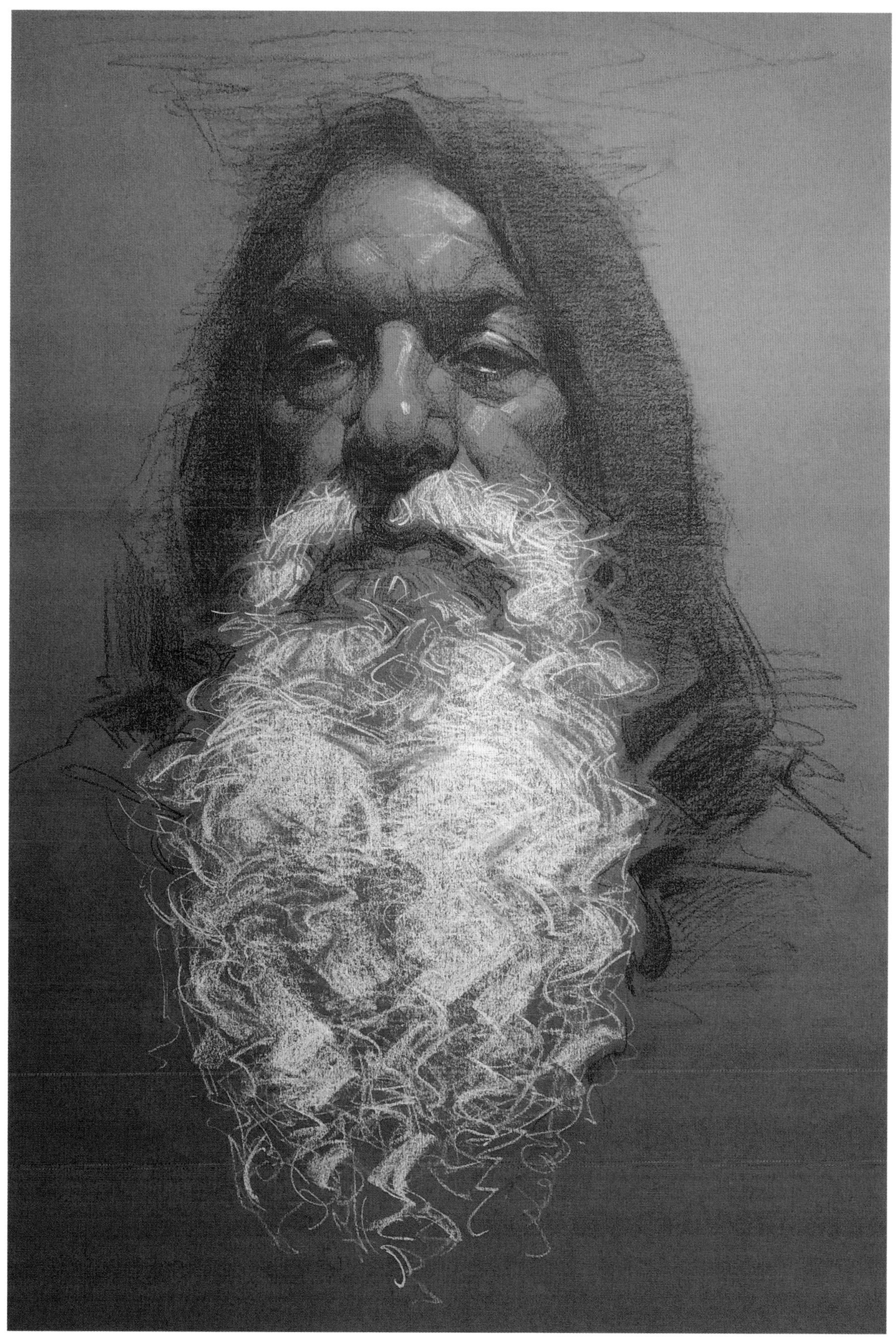

AGING OF THE EARS

LARGER EARS

The enlargement of the ear is associated with aging changes in collagen. Collagen, a protein, is one of the major building blocks of bones, skin, muscles, tendons, and ligaments. As with the nose, the loss of suppleness in the skin around the ears also causes the ears to appear larger.

EARLOBE SAGGING

As people age, their earlobes undergo noticeable changes. They can become droopy, floppy, larger, or even deflate due to alterations in the cartilage of the external ear and the earlobe itself. Over time, earlobes may develop folds and take on a "collapsed" appearance.

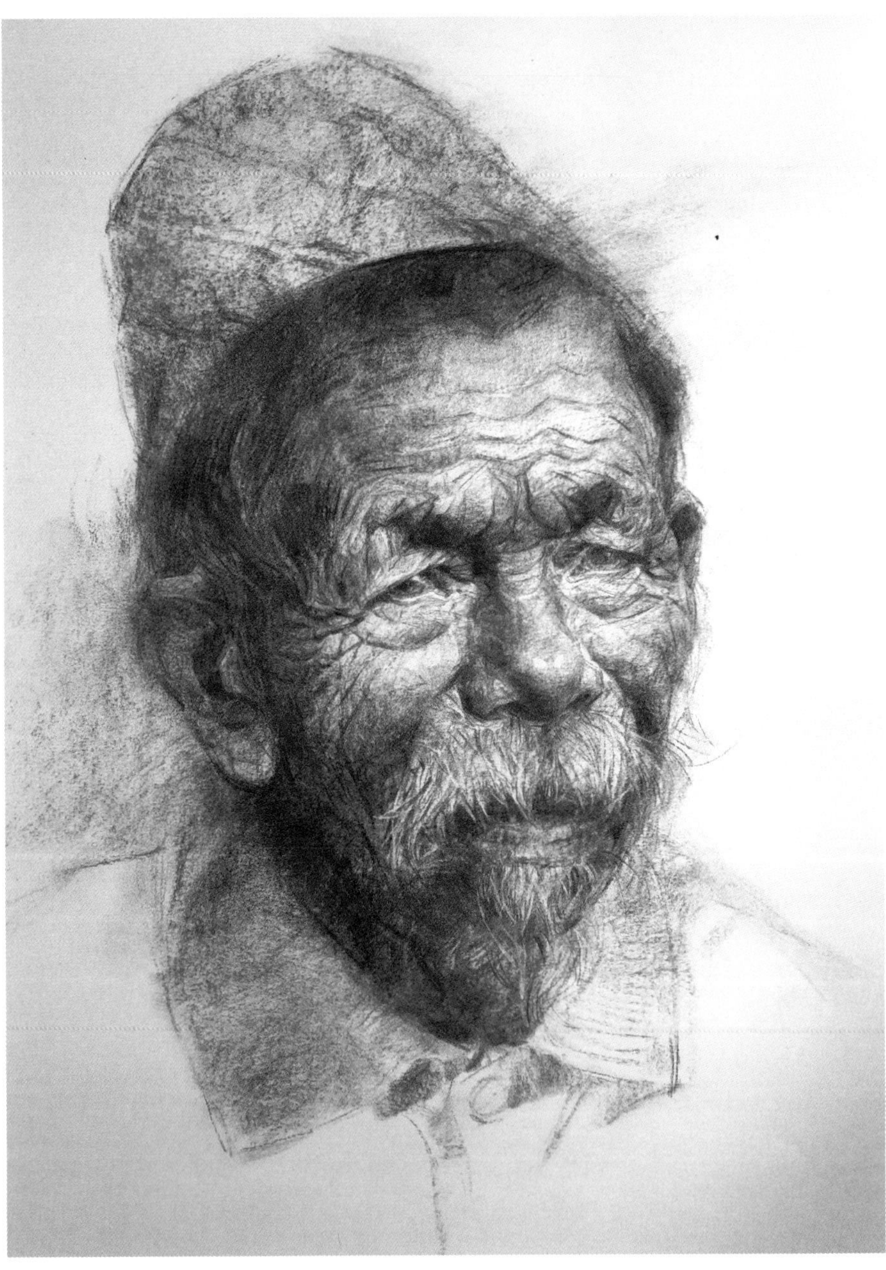

A significant factor in these changes is the reduction of collagen levels in the skin and cartilage. Collagen provides strength and elasticity to these tissues. With age, the decrease in collagen leads to stretching and changes in the soft tissues of the earlobes, causing them to lose their firmness and shape. This process contributes to the sagging and other age-related changes observed in earlobes.

EAR HAIR

With age, ear hair begins to protrude from the external auditory meatus, the ear canal. The fine vellus hair, often called *peach fuzz*, can grow on the outer ear, anti-tragus, helix, and earlobe. The hair inside your ear, called *cilia*, helps protect your inner ear from debris. As you age, you may notice an increase in ear-hair growth that wasn't there before.

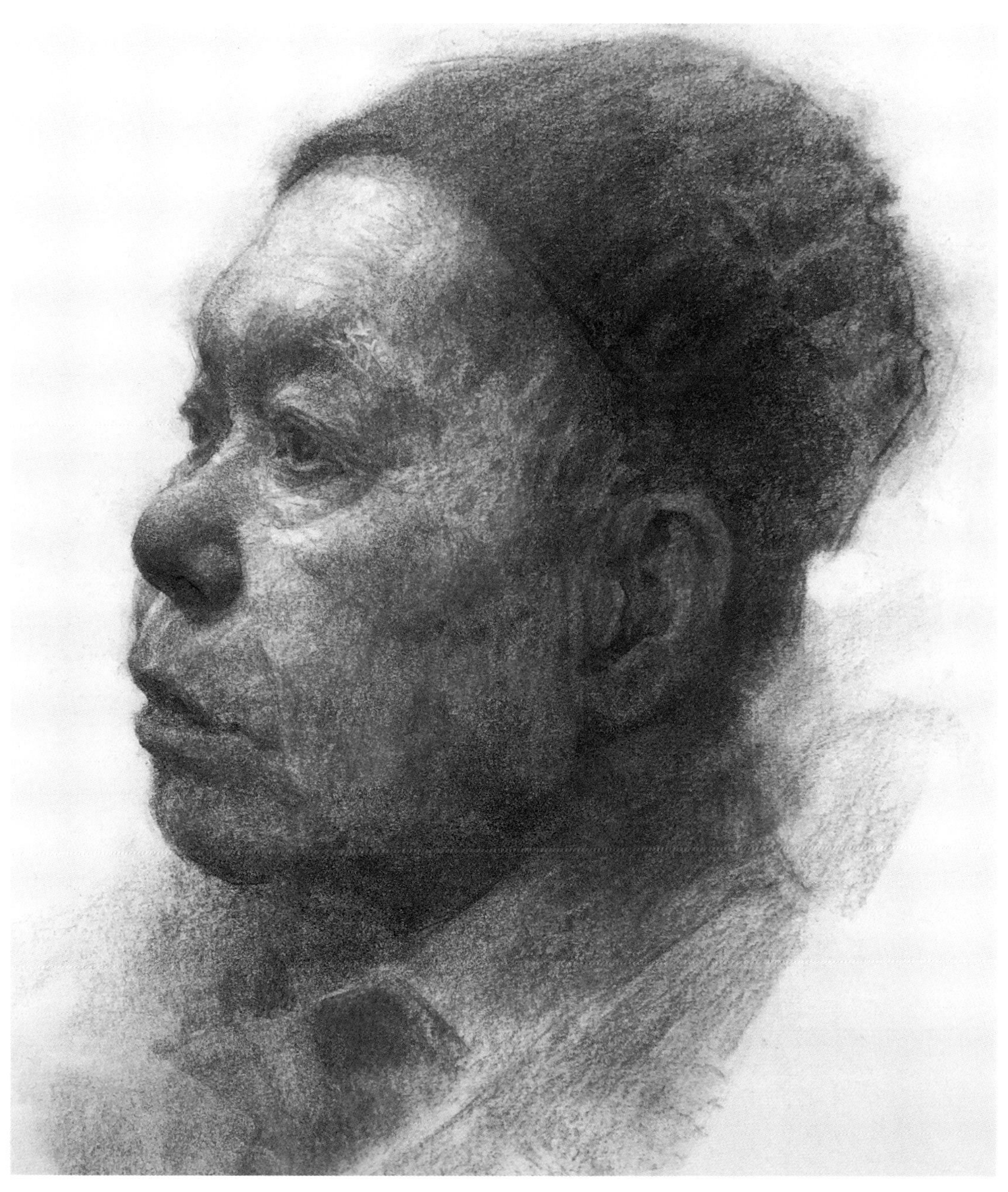

AGING OF THE NECK

NECKLACE LINES

Necklace lines, or wrinkles on the neck, are ringlike lines that run horizontally across the neck. These wrinkles develop due to reduced collagen and elastin production in the skin, which can be attributed to aging, fluctuations in weight and hormones, sun damage, and smoking. The amount of necklace lines varies from person to person, but usually two to three are inevitable.

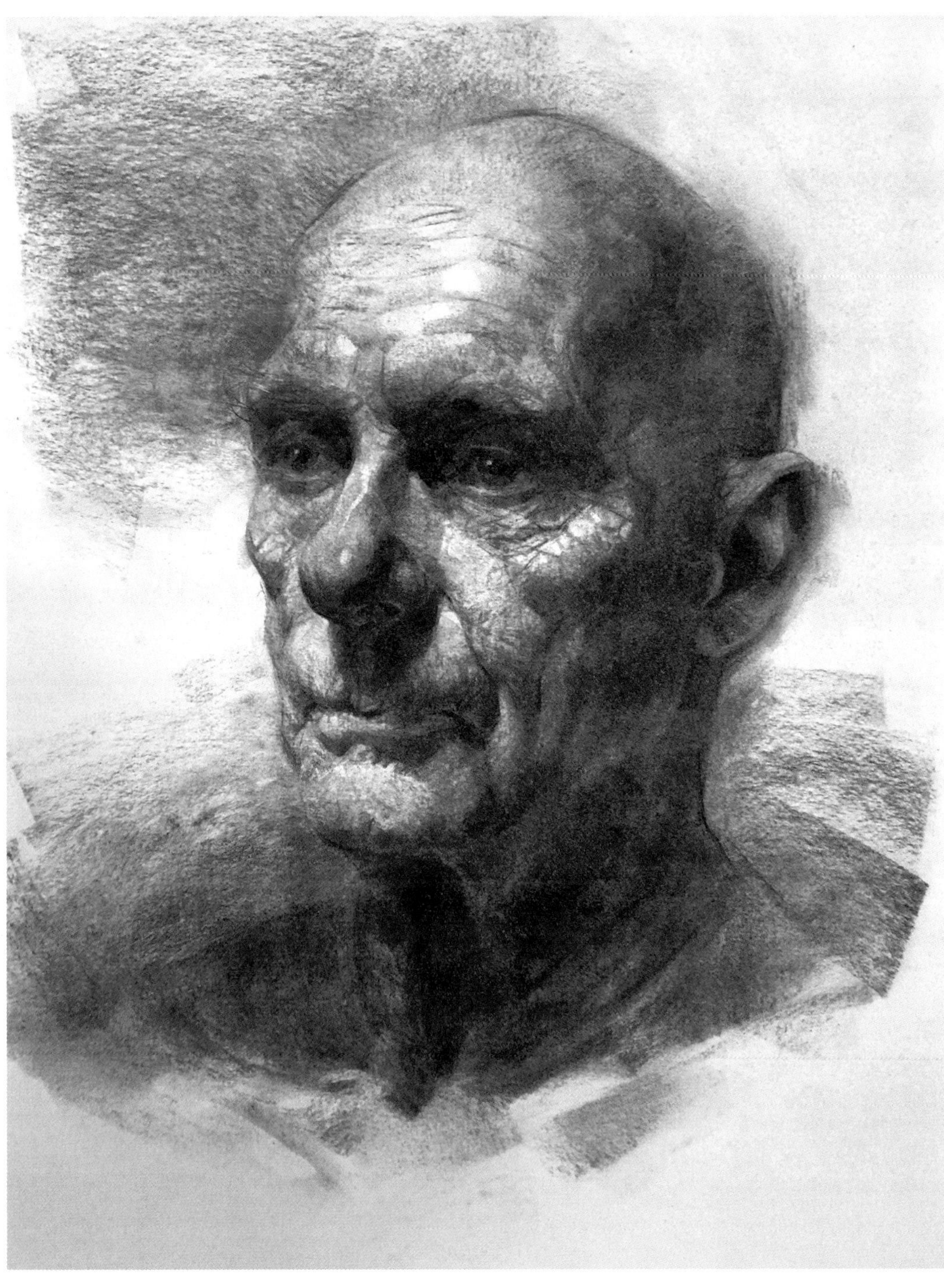

NECK CORDS

The most noticeable signs of an aging neck include the formation of vertical muscle bands, loose and sagging skin, and the accumulation of excess fat. These muscle bands form due to the regular use of the platysma muscle, with vertical lines indicating the two muscle edges. The platysma is a thin superficial muscle just under the skin of the neck that extends from the chest and shoulders up to the jaw. As you age, the skin and muscles of the neck become loose, and the platysma can form very visible ropelike bands that when combined with weakened neck muscles and loss of skin elasticity, creates a "turkey neck" appearance. The loose skin can become droopy and wrinkled, often compared to the neck of a turkey. Age and sun exposure are the two main culprits.

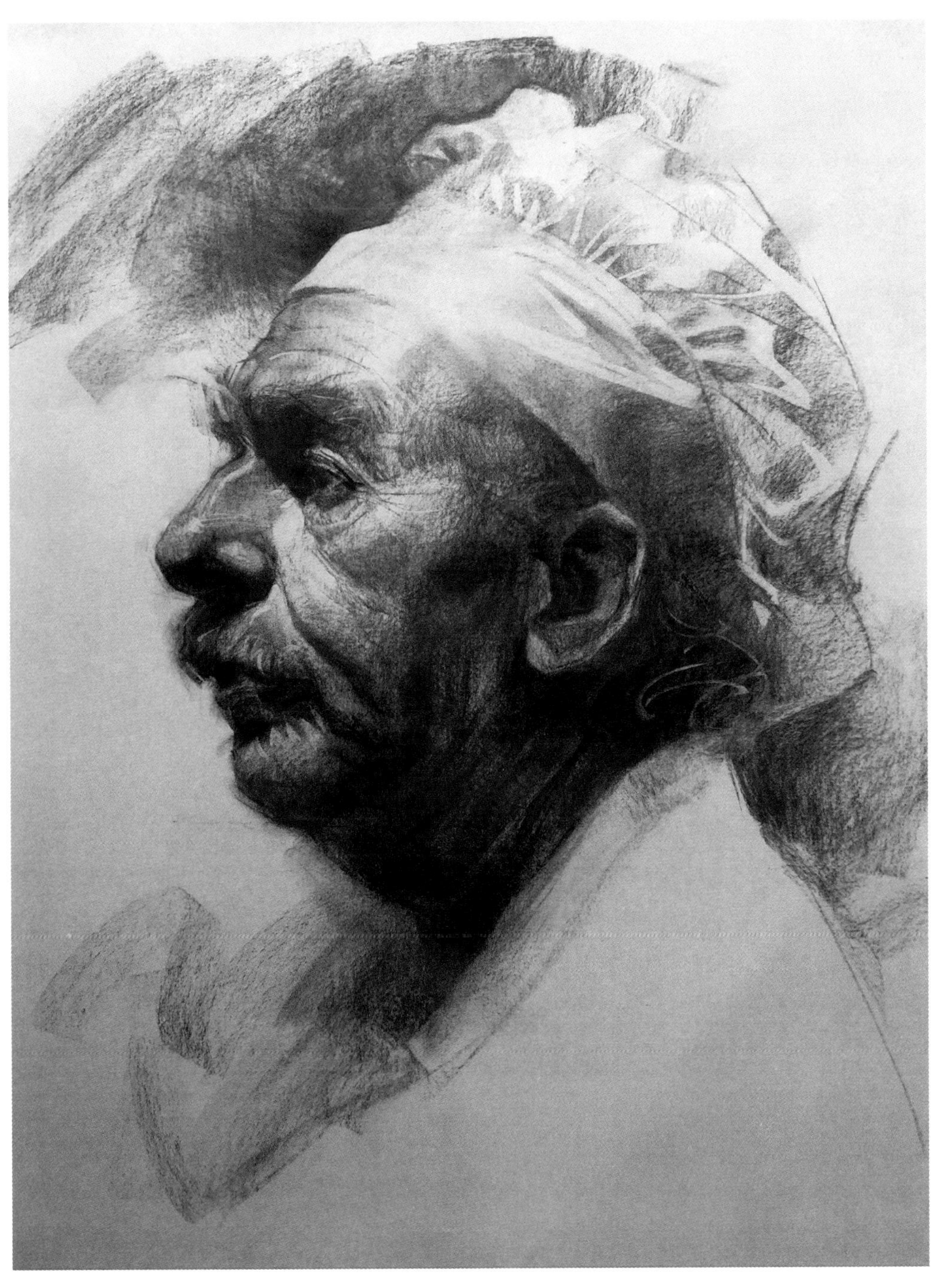

FOREHEAD WRINKLES

Forehead wrinkles are the horizontal lines
that form on your forehead. They appear
over time due to repeated facial expressions,
aging, and factors like sun exposure and
genetics. As skin loses elasticity, these lines
become more noticeable.

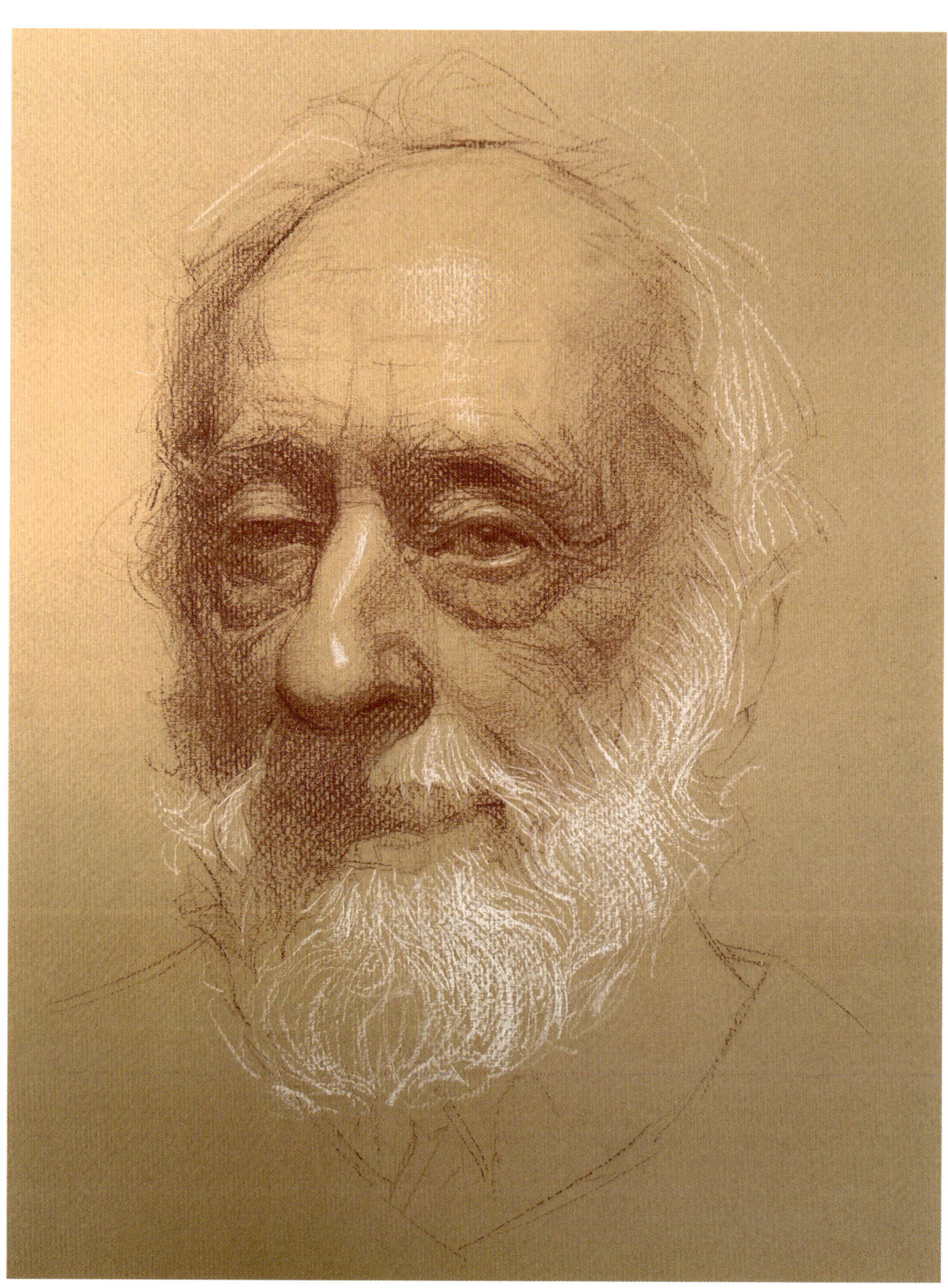

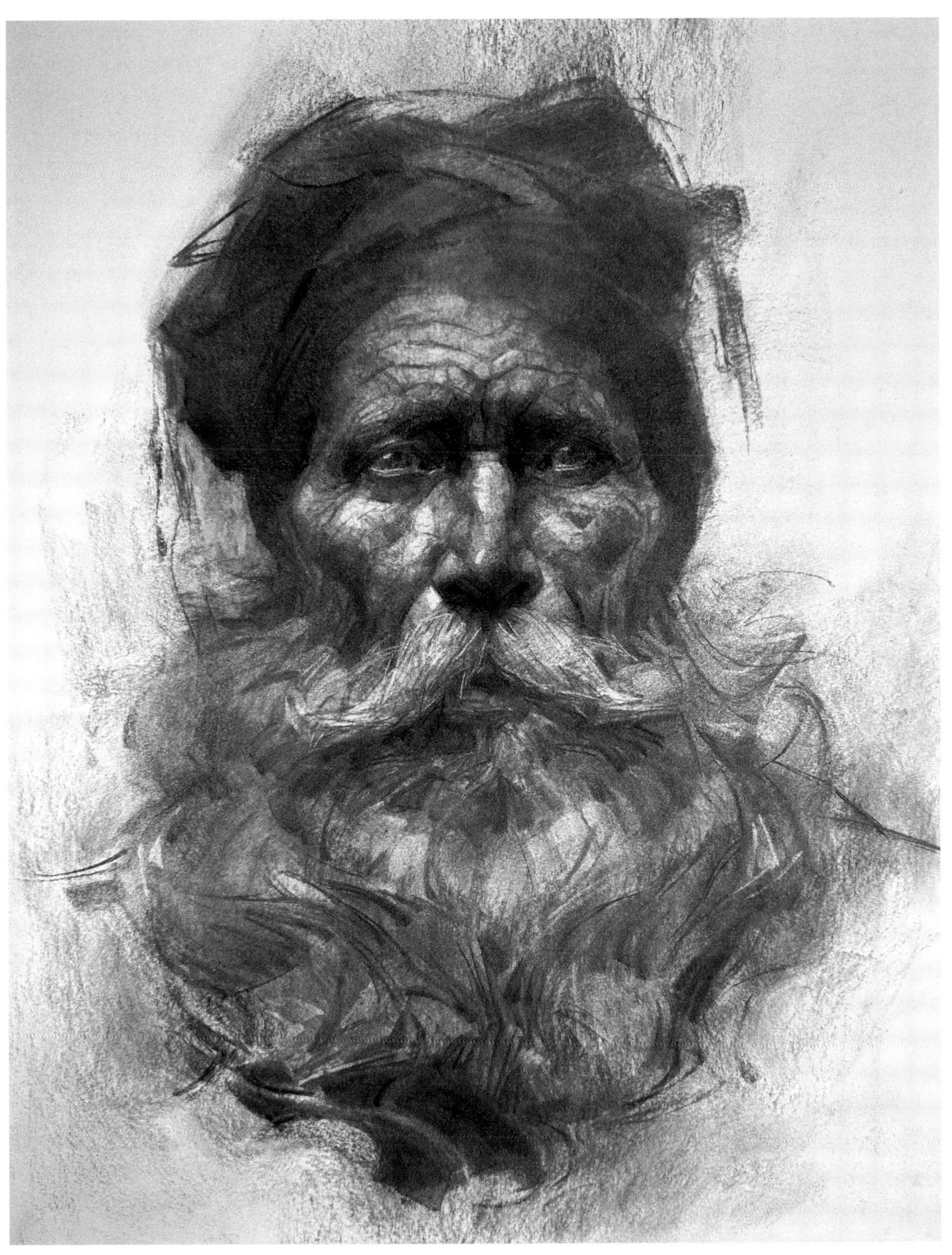

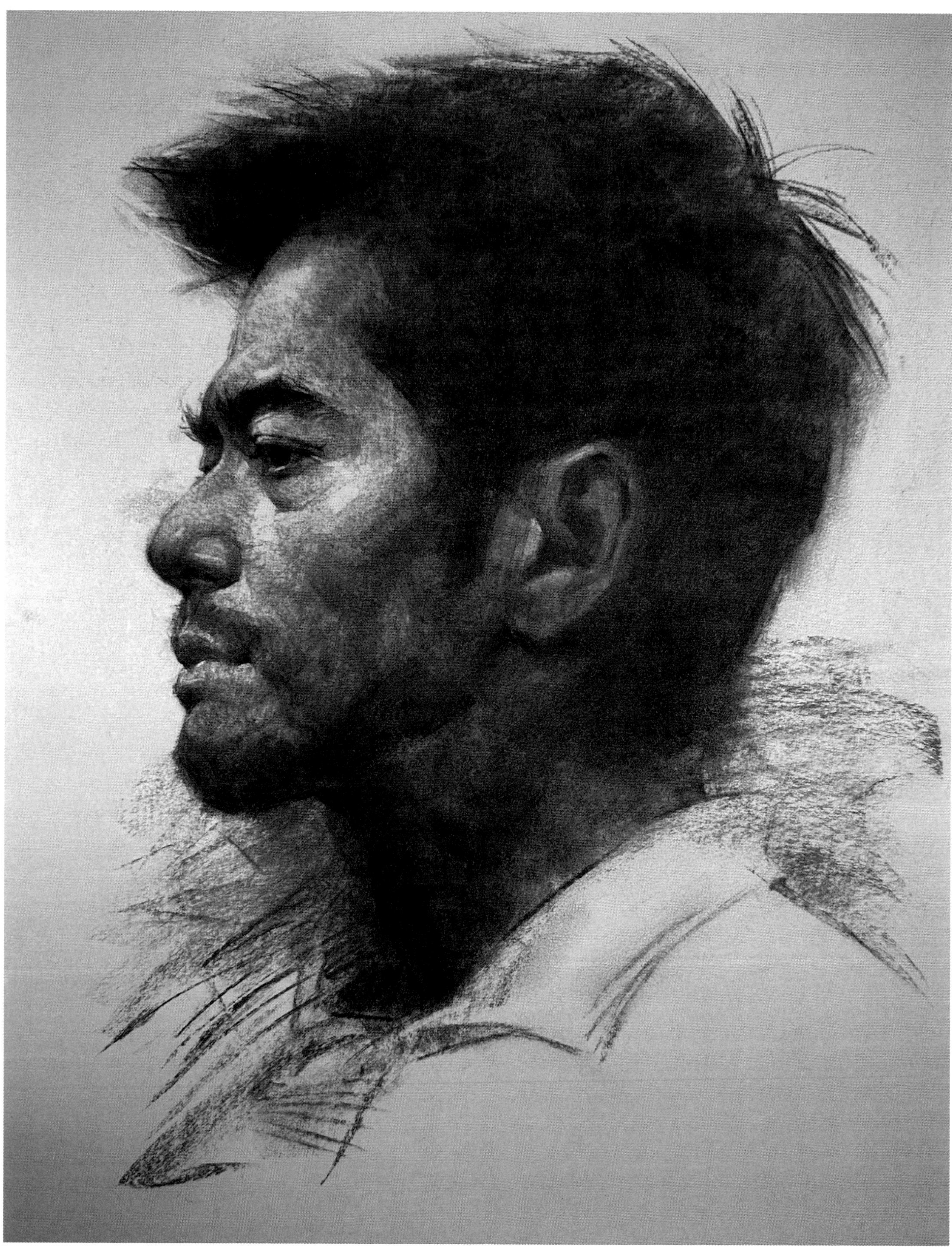

5

CAPTURING EXPRESSIONS

EMOTIONS AND THE FACE

While drawing faces requires consistent effort and improvement over time, it doesn't feel like a tedious task or chore. Instead, the process is enjoyable and engaging. For someone passionate about art, the pleasure and fascination of capturing the unique characteristics and expressions of human faces makes the practice of drawing faces a rewarding and fulfilling activity rather than a laborious job.

People are the most fascinating subjects to study and draw. Every head is a unique assemblage of shapes, lines, and spaces. Each person has a distinctive face. Even the same person, with different expressions, lighting, and clothing, offers an endless array of portraits to capture. There are no boring faces, but you need to acquire the skills to appreciate the enjoyment and challenges of portrait drawing.

The facial muscles can create a vast array of expressions through their movements. Some expressions are pronounced and clear, while others are more subtle and nuanced. Genuine expressions are automatic and reveal the true emotions a person is experiencing. By understanding the underlying muscles and engaging in thoughtful observation and a regular drawing practice, you can draw faces with confidence, broaden your artistic horizons, and express the full range of human emotions.

Let's look at how the face transforms when expressing six of the most universally recognized emotions: happiness, sadness, fear, surprise, anger, and disgust.

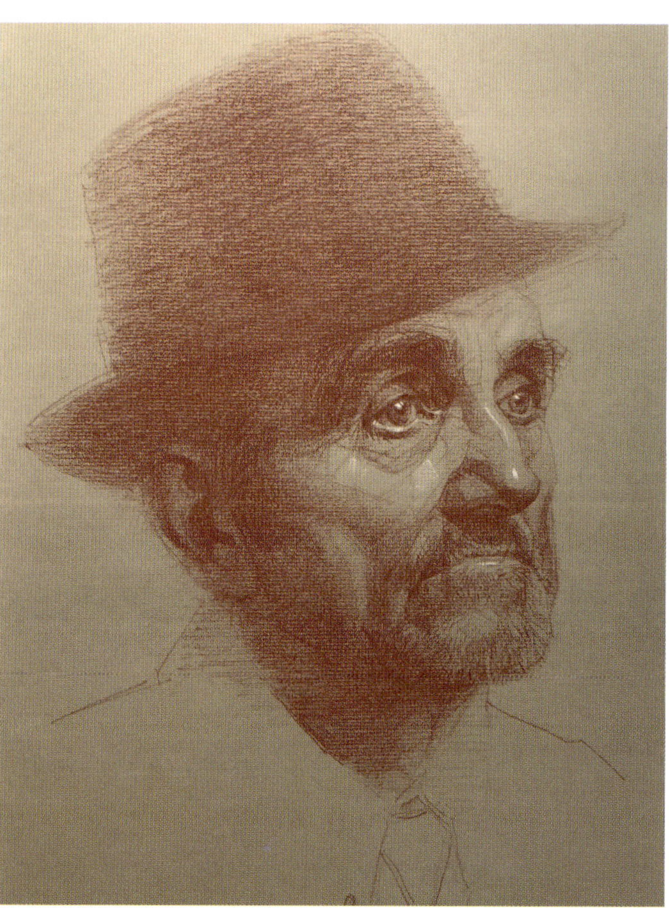

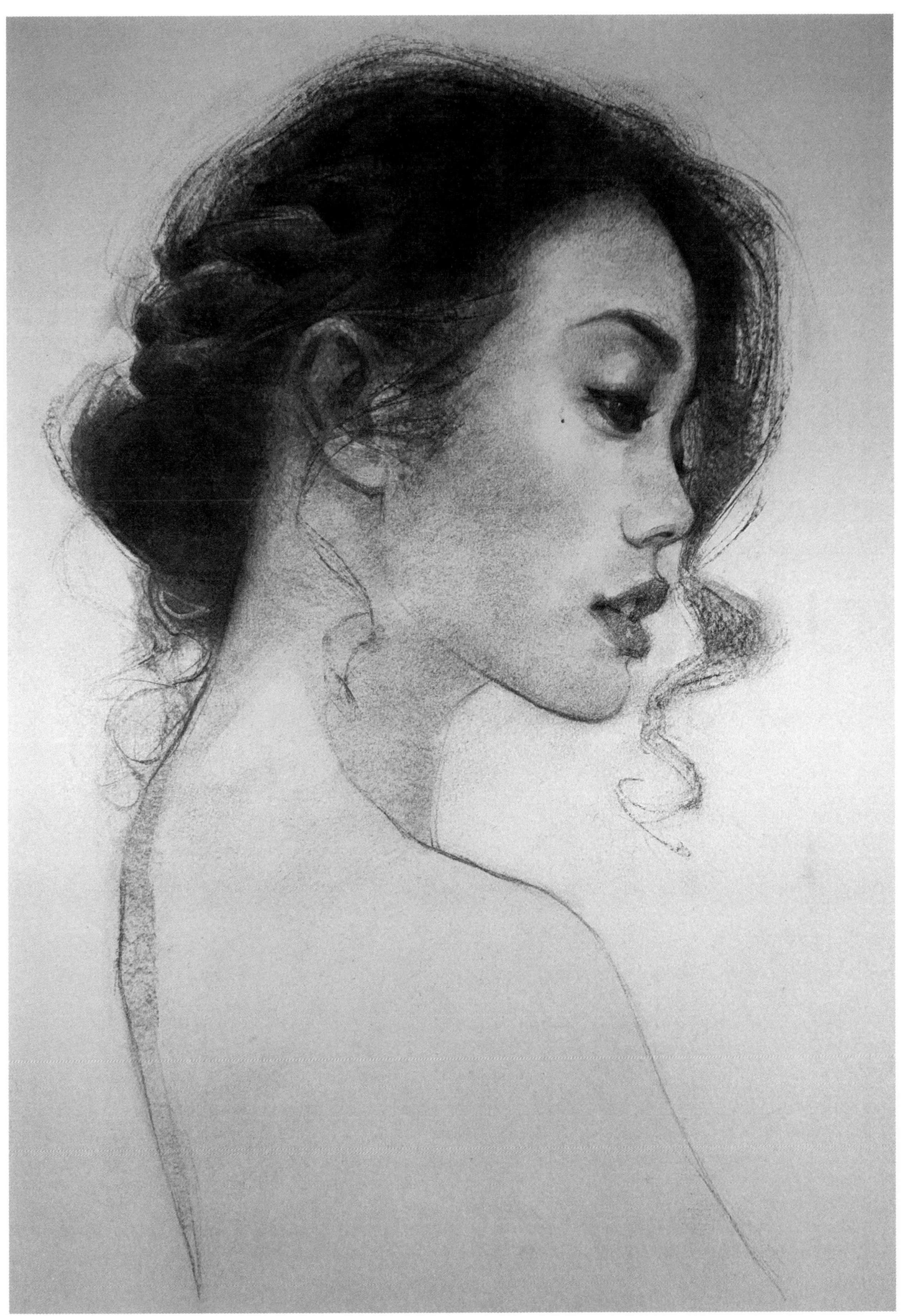

SIX ESSENTIAL EMOTIONS FOR EXPRESSIVE DRAWINGS

HAPPINESS

The expression of happiness is not only pleasant to look at, but it's also efficient, involving just two muscles: the zygomaticus major, which pulls the mouth, and the orbicularis oculi, which narrows the eyes. When we express happiness, the corners of the mouth lift, move outward, and pull back. The nasolabial fold, running from the top of the wing of the nose to the corner of the mouth, deepens. The cheeks lift and puff up, creating wrinkles under the lower eyelid. The eyes narrow, and the lower face broadens and elevates.

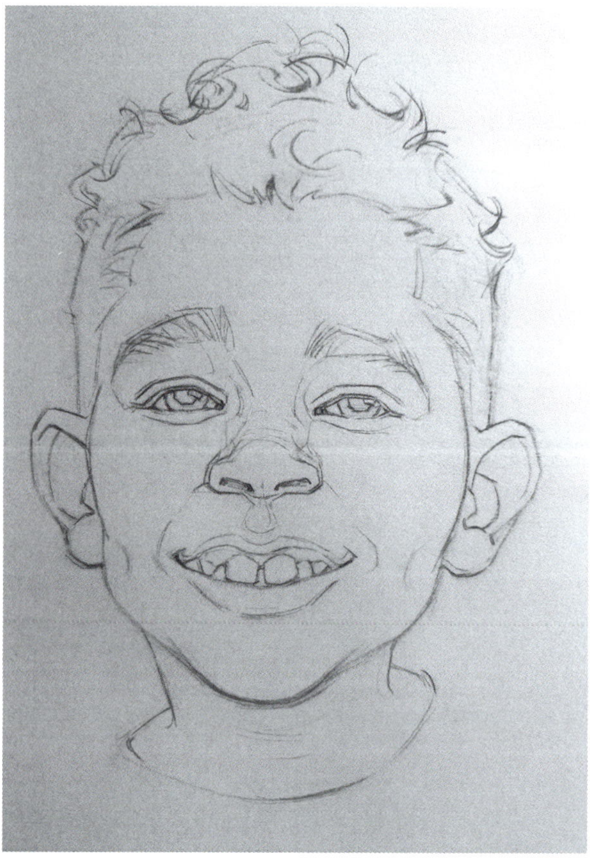

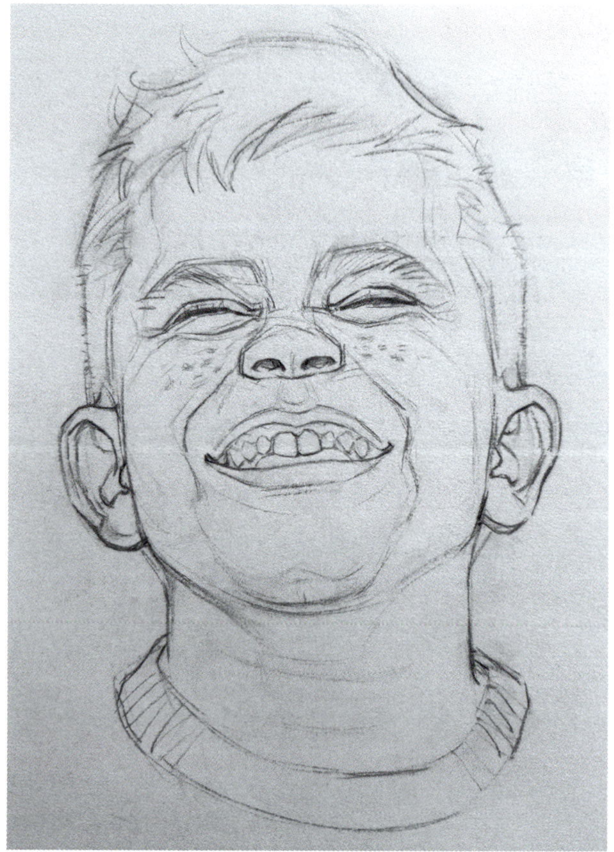

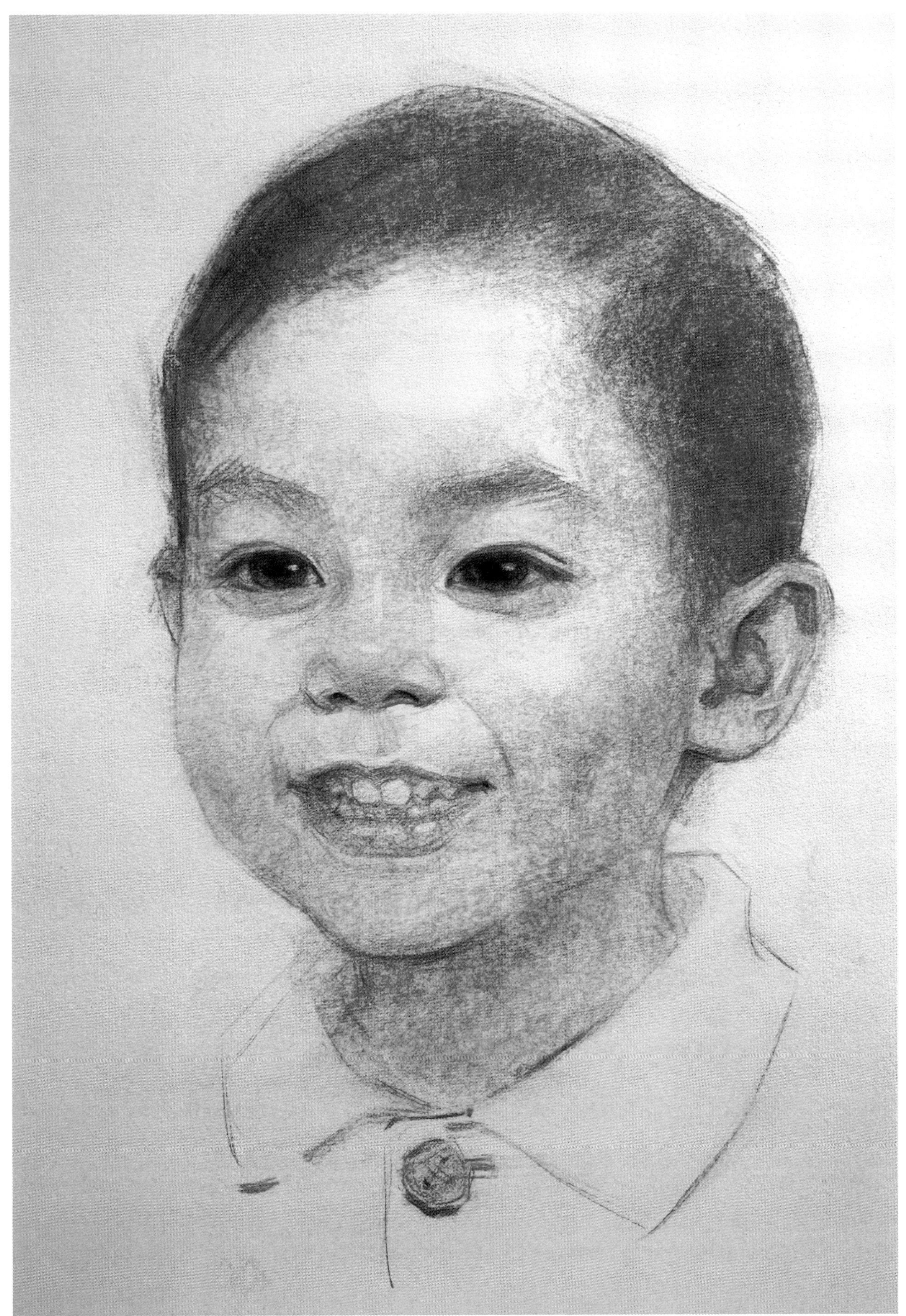

HAPPY EYES

Laughter produces the most pronounced squint, while a slight smile results in a less noticeable squint. When you simply smile, a weak contraction of orbicularis oculi is triggered. The lower eyelid bulges, shortens, and rises up on the eye, covering part of the iris. Crow's-feet wrinkles appear at the outer eye corner, and the cheek bunches up below eye, creating a smile-shaped wrinkle between the cheek and lid.

In laughter, the happy eye is more closed from below. The upper eyelid moves downward only slightly, while the lower eyelid tightens and slides farther up the eye, sometimes reversing direction and arcing upward slightly. Crow's-feet deepen, the nasolabial fold swings farther out than in the basic smile, and the cheek tightens more, creating a sharp highlight on the cheeks.

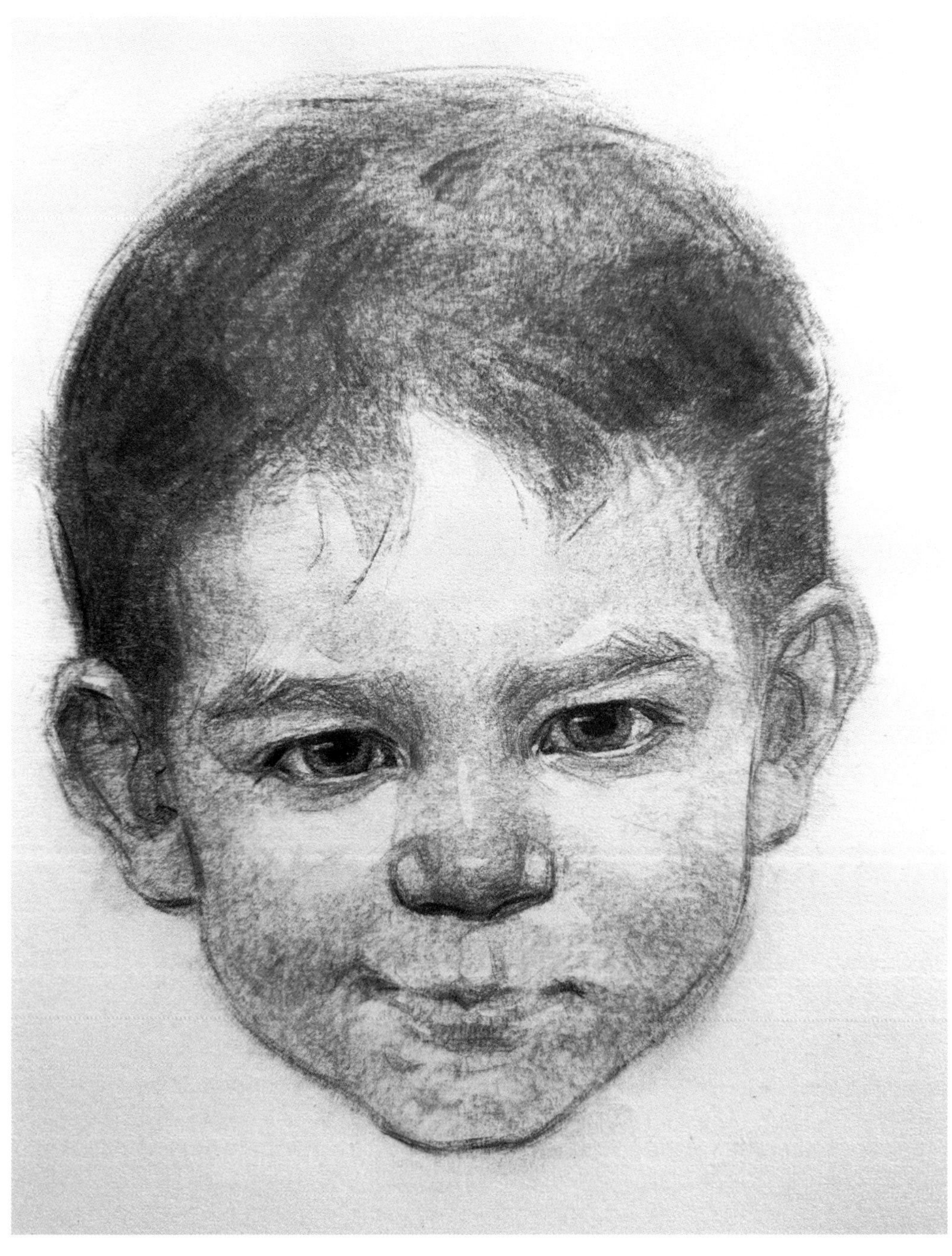

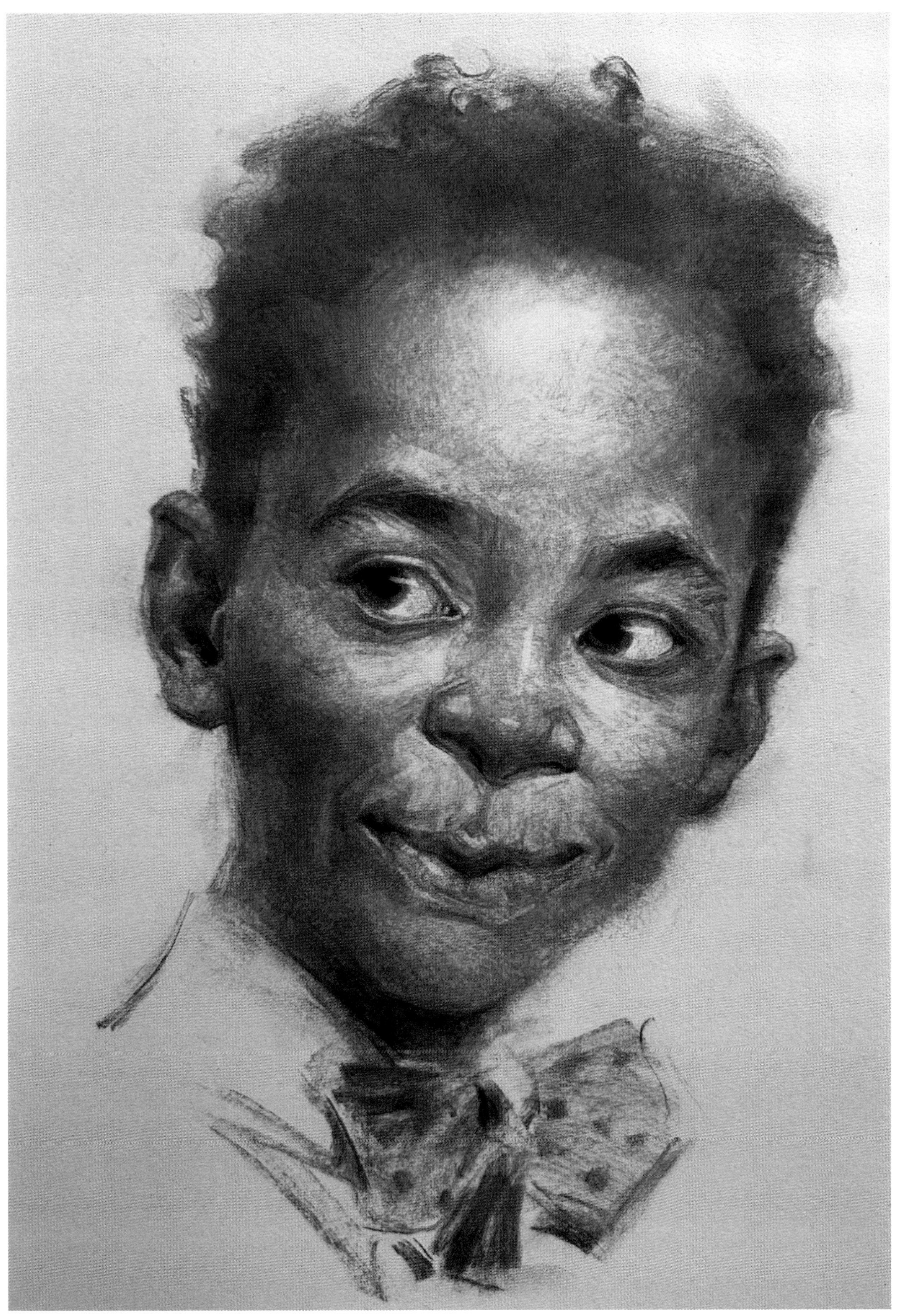

SADNESS

The first expression of sadness begins with a baby's cry. Crying is the baby's way to call for help. The sound of a crying baby is impossible to ignore; the cry protects it. The square-shaped mouth produces a shrill sound that's more penetrating than that of a relaxed, open mouth. As the lower half of the face opens up, the top half closes down. The tightened eyes close. You can't cry with your eyes wide open, nor can you sneeze. The reflexive squinting of the eyes in crying is also instinctive in other expressions where quantities of air are expelled: laughing and coughing.

The contraction of orbicularis oculi muscle tightens up the skin around the eyes, which seems to relieve some of the pressure. The more energetic the cry, the more tightly the muscle compresses, affecting the rest of the face as well. In loud crying, the full contraction of the orbicularis oculi pulls down the brows, raises the cheeks, and may even contribute to squaring the mouth.

The mouth of a crying person is square-shaped due to the upward pull of the sneering muscle, which squares off the upper lip and etches nasolabial folds in the cheeks, and the outward pull of the risorius and platysma muscles, which widen the mouth and stretch the lower lip. The square mouth is often framed by a long crease from nose to chin, resembling a tear's path.

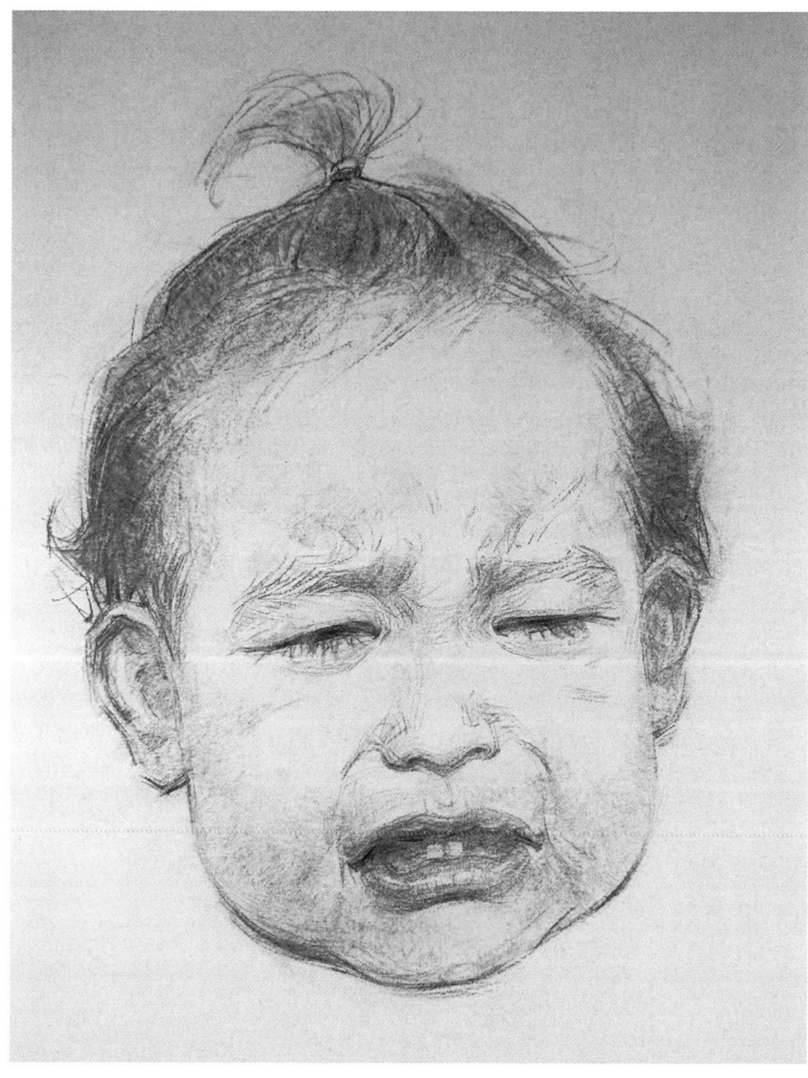

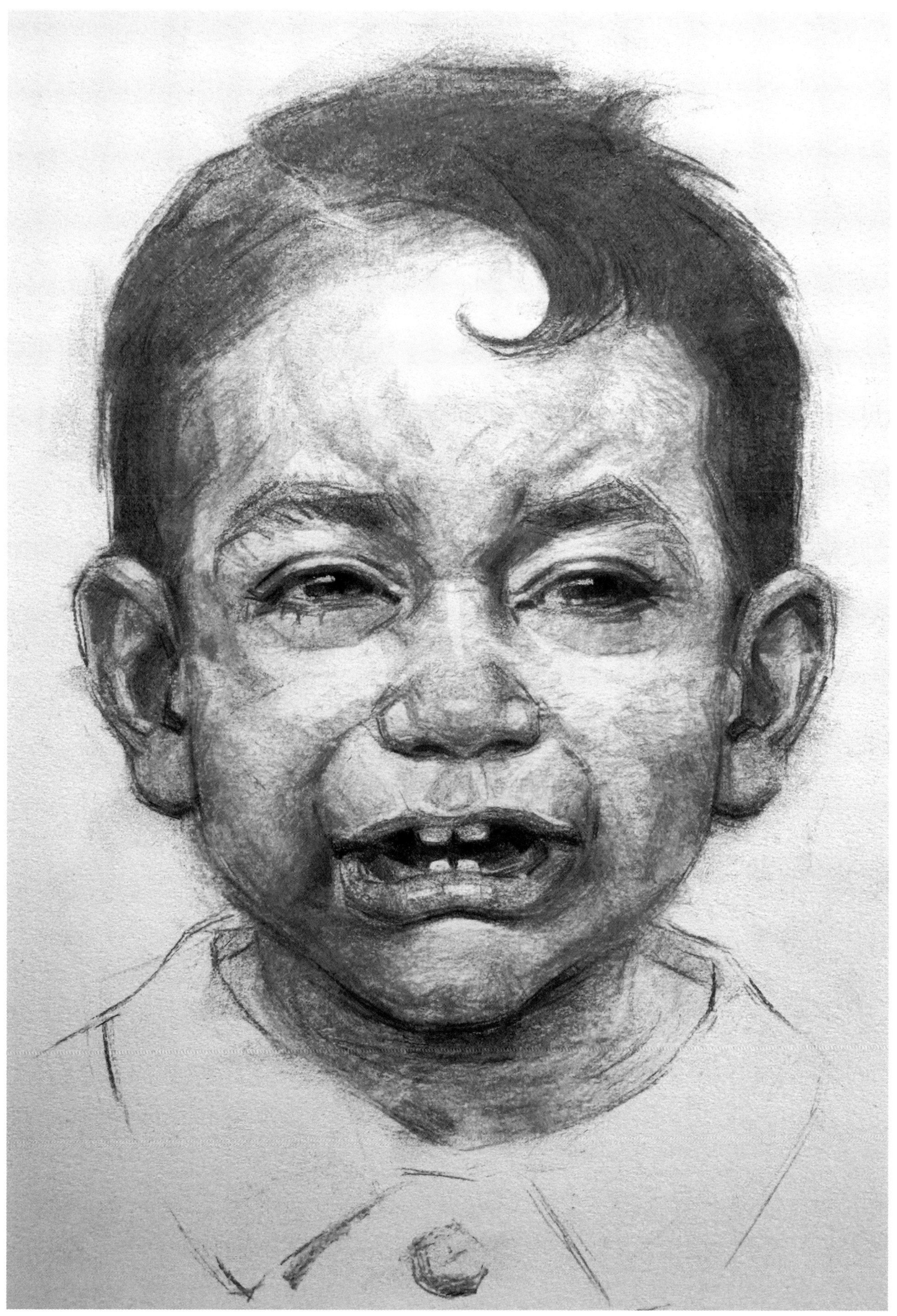

SAD EYES

The expression of the eyes is an essential component of a sad face, changing in shape both above and below. Above the eye, a new skin fold is created by the movement of the eyebrows and partly covers the upper lid. The eyebrows arch upward and gather toward the middle, with the outside corners curving downward. This angularity gives the eyes a less alert, more withdrawn appearance, as the fold slightly pushes down on the eye.

The lower eyelid is also more evident, covering a large portion of the eye. The orbicularis oculi muscle partially contracts, creating a bag under the eye and giving the lid a raised, flattened look.

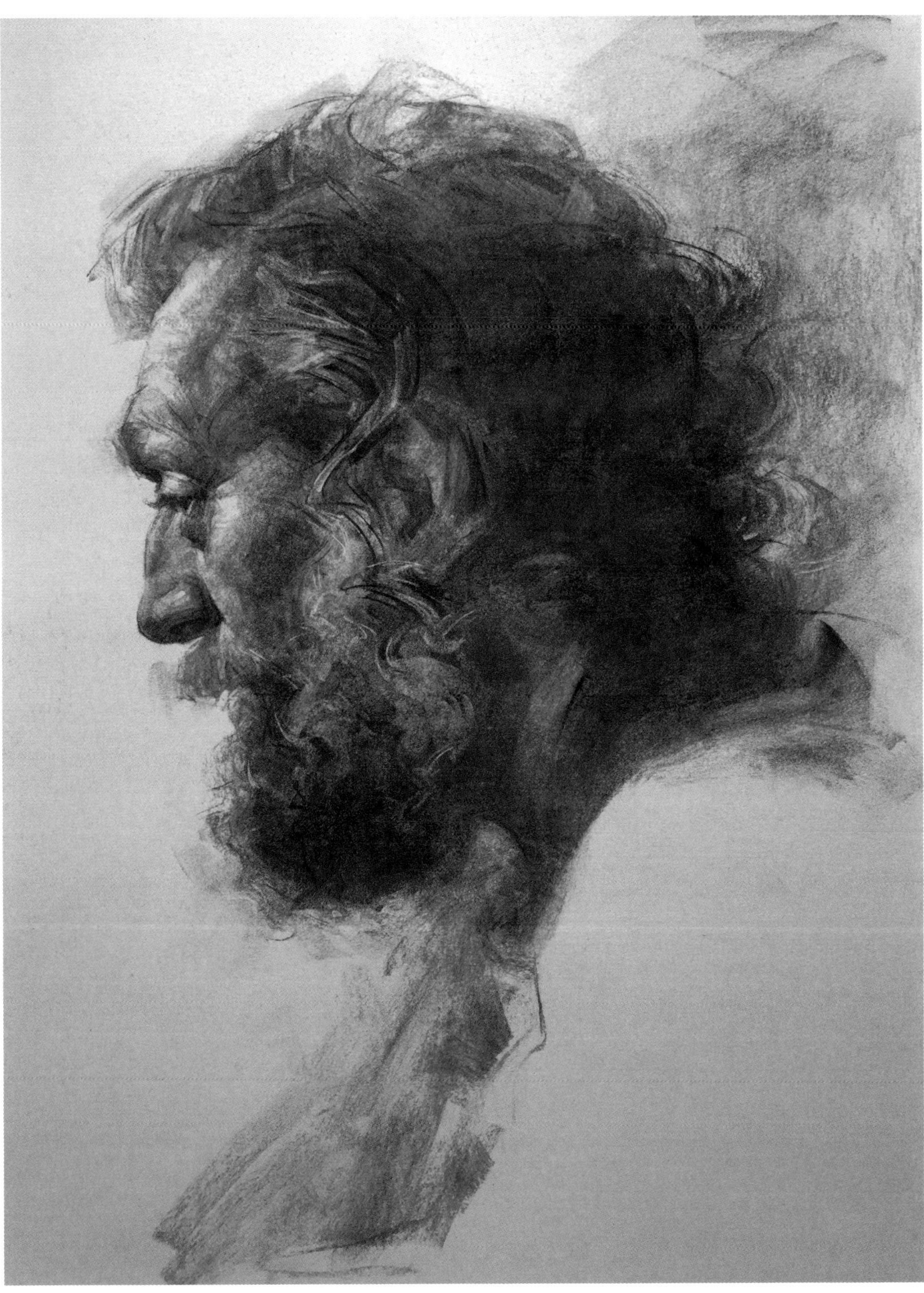

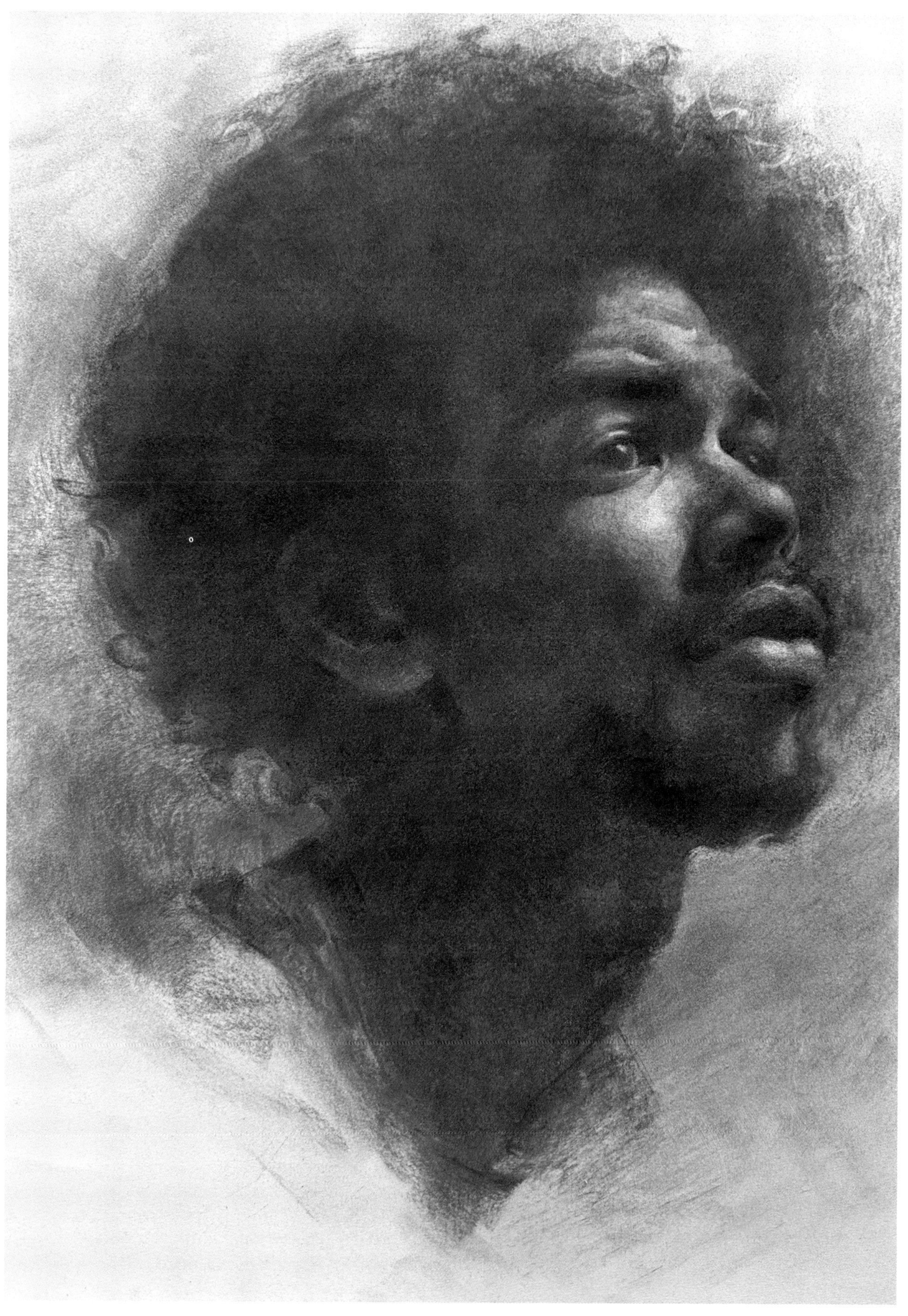

SAD BROWS

The eyebrows are critical when depicting sadness. They are involved in every level of this emotion. The oblique direction of the brows unmistakably indicates grief.

SAD MOUTHS

Facial expressions of sadness are often characterized by the intricate interplay of various facial muscles, particularly the orbicularis oris, risorius, platysma, and mentalis. In such expressions, the mouth tends to undergo specific changes. It may stretch sideways, with the orbicularis oris contracting intensely, resulting in straightened and thinned lips.

Additionally, a characteristic pout may accentuate the expression of sadness, with the center section of upper lip appearing unnaturally long and dropping off quickly at the corners, while the lower lip is slightly thinned.

Moreover, the mentalis muscle, located in the chin region, often accompanies expressions of grief. This muscle acts in tandem with the risorius and platysma muscles, contributing to the stretching of the mouth. When someone is experiencing sadness, whether or not they are crying, the mentalis muscle frequently contracts and relaxes. This action can cause the center of the lower lip to bow and wrinkle the chin when contracting, while the stretched lower lip returns to a straight position on either side of the raised part. These subtle muscular movements contribute to the complex language of human emotions conveyed through facial expressions.

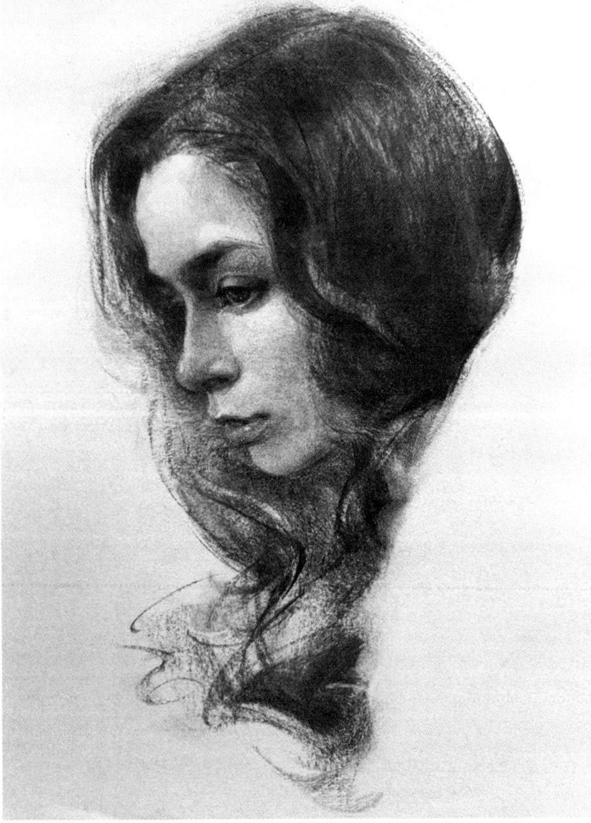

MUSCULAR ACTION: SADNESS

When we express sadness, the inner corners of the eyebrows are raised and drawn together, usually inclining the eyebrows. Horizontal wrinkles form on the center of the forehead. The medial ends of the folds covering the eye, those nearer to the middle of the face, are pulled up, while the lateral parts of those folds, closer to the edges of the face, are pulled down. The corners of the mouth are pulled down at the corners, lengthening the "long face" typical of sadness.

The essence of the crying expression is a stretched mouth and compressed eyes, while the sadness expression is characterized by the pout and upturned eyebrows.

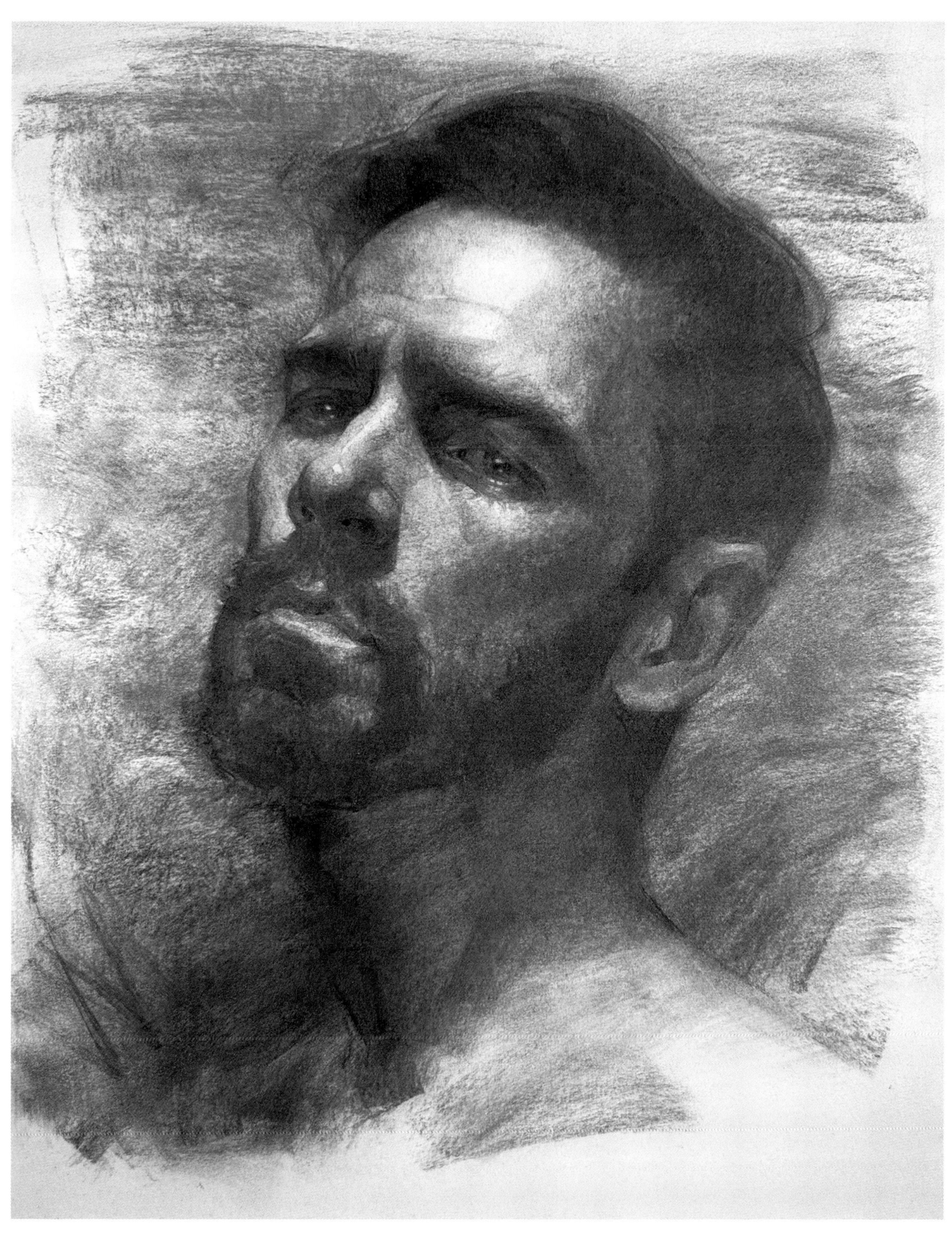

SURPRISE

When we express surprise, our eyebrows lift straight up and arch. In more extreme cases, the upper eyelids rise, exposing the whites above the iris. The lower jaw drops, the mouth opens, the lips become relaxed, and the face elongates.

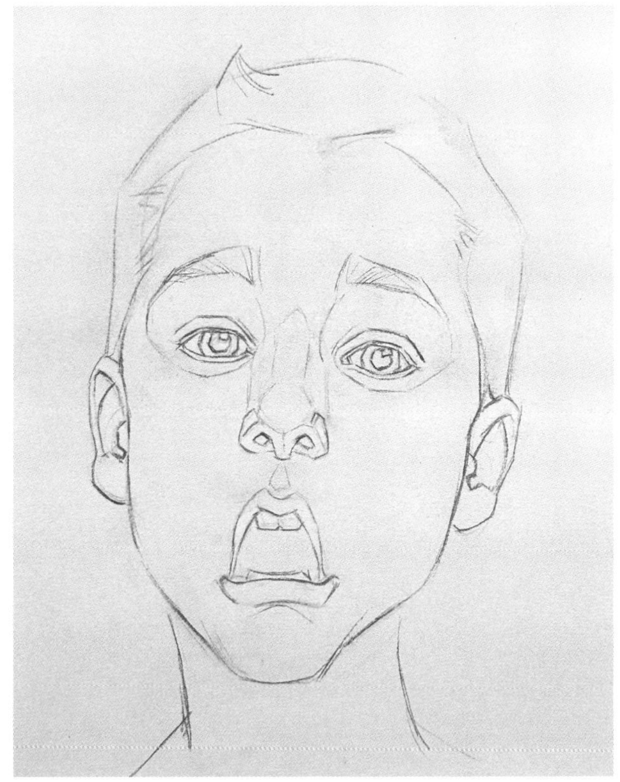

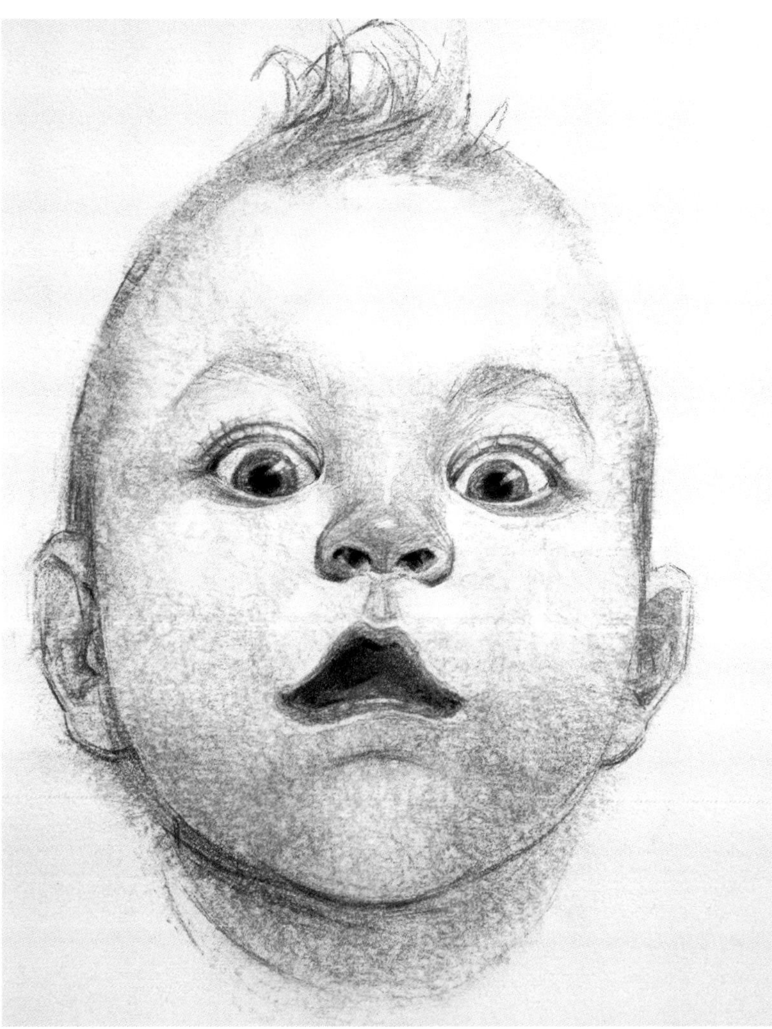

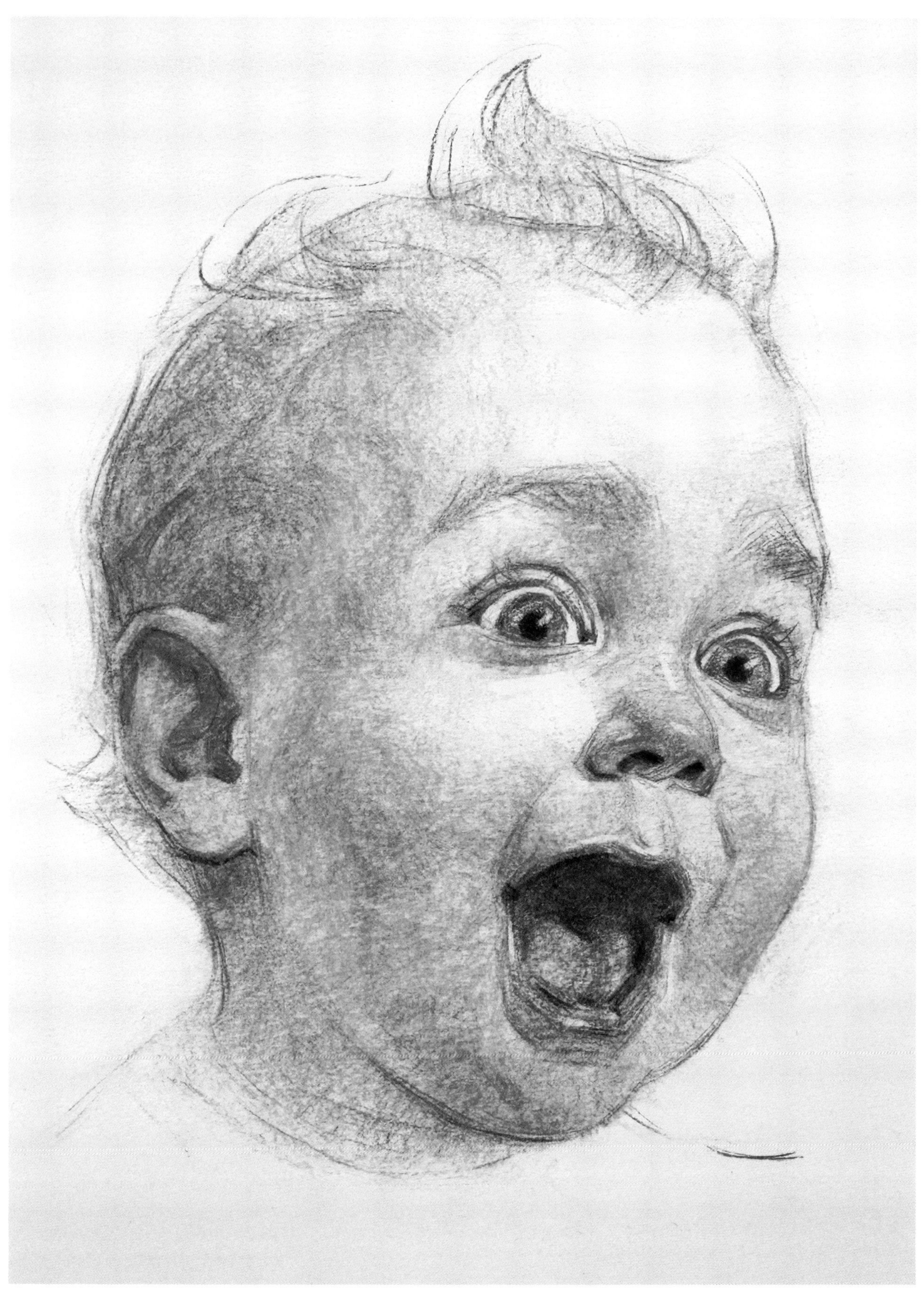

FEAR

In expressions of fear, the eyebrows are raised and drawn together, becoming straight and horizontal with a kink at the medial ends near the center of the face.

Wrinkles form across the entire forehead. The mouth usually opens, and the lower face broadens and flattens, resulting in prominent, rigid folds on the front and sides of the neck.

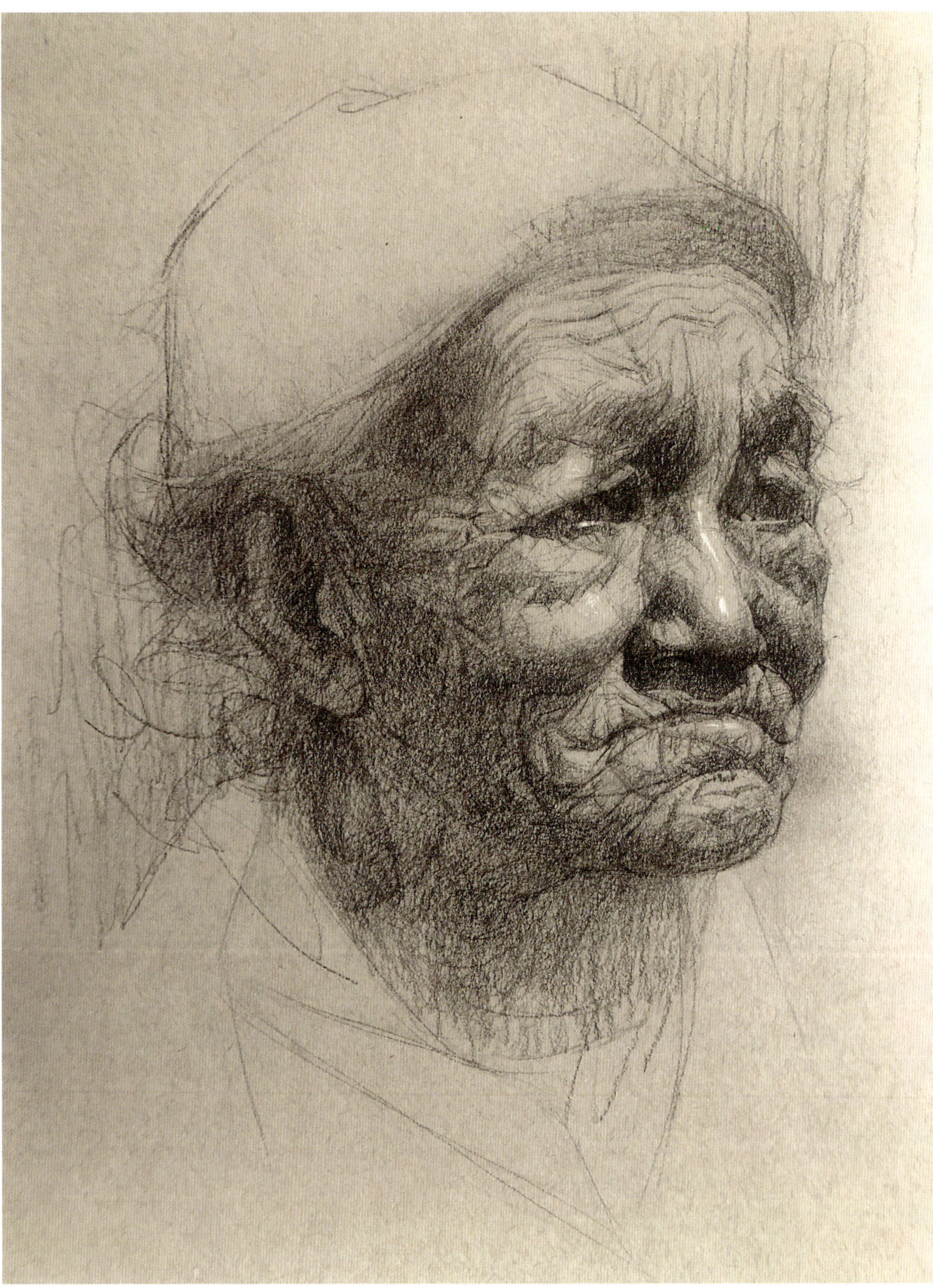

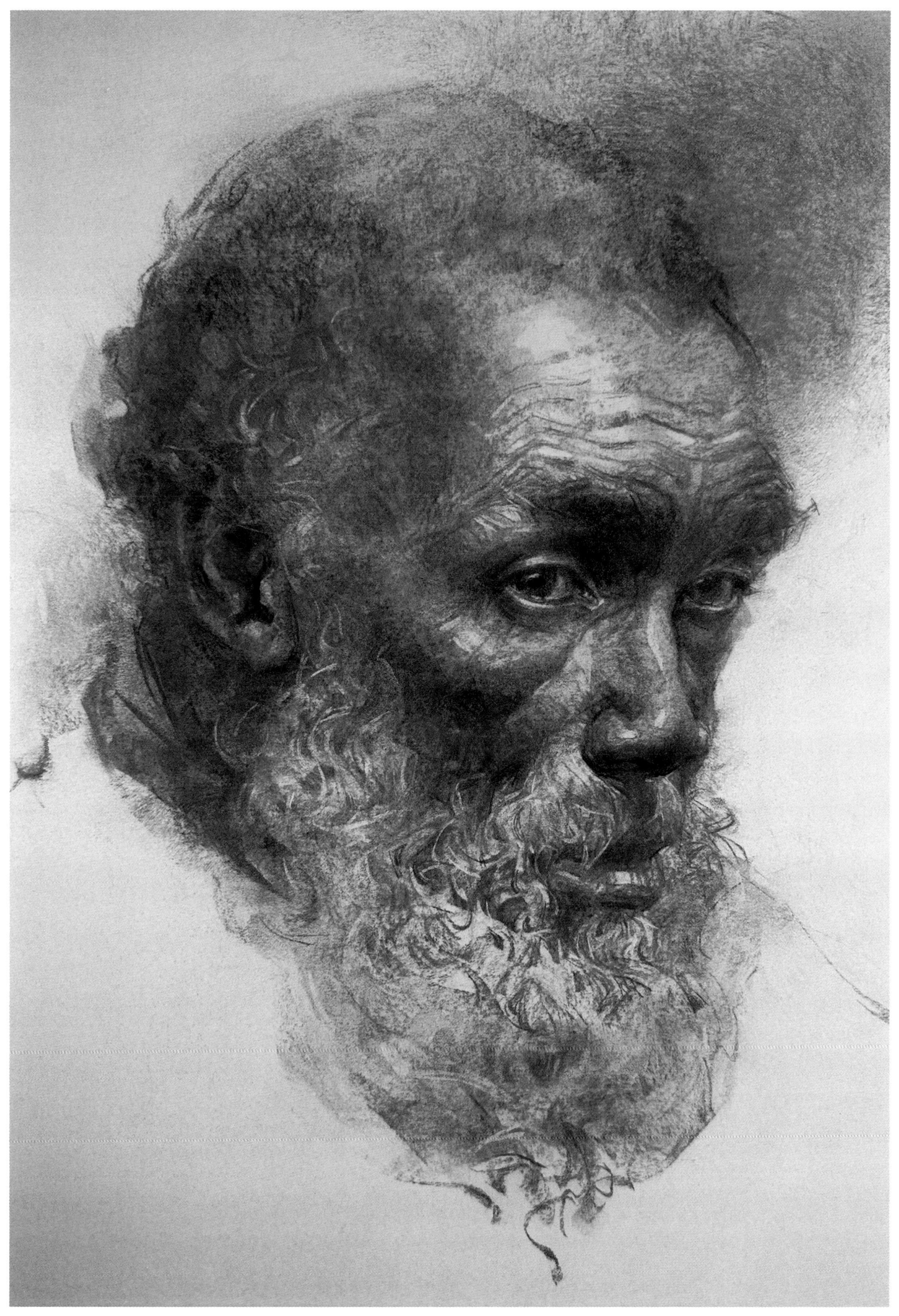

ANGER

Anger is a quick, intense emotion, primarily expressed through the eyes. The intensity of anger in the face hinges on a small detail: the wideness of the eye. There's a direct correlation between the lifting of the upper lid and the perception of anger: the higher the lid is raised, the angrier the expression appears. This effect is heightened when combined with a lowered brow, a well-known indicator of anger.

In facial drawings, a lowered brow paired with a raised eyelid typically signifies subtle anger. This combination gives the eye a penetrating, intense look, often referred to as a glare. However, for the expression of anger to be fully recognized, the glaring eye must be accompanied by an angry mouth. An occasional feature of the angry eye is a taut, straightened lower eyelid, which further intensifies and hardens the gaze.

When all three elements are present—widened eye, lowered brow, and tightened lower eyelid—the resulting expression is one of maximum malevolence.

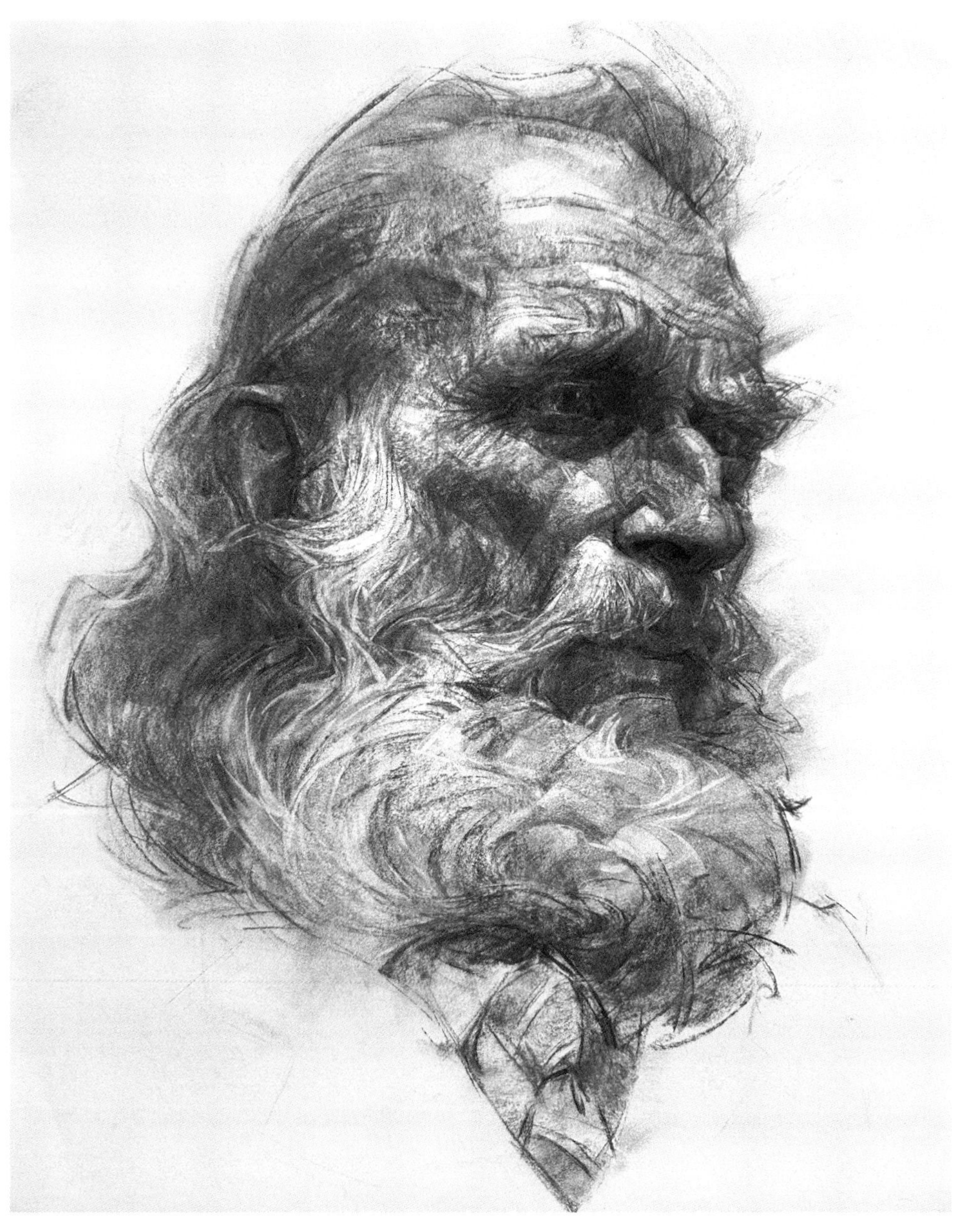

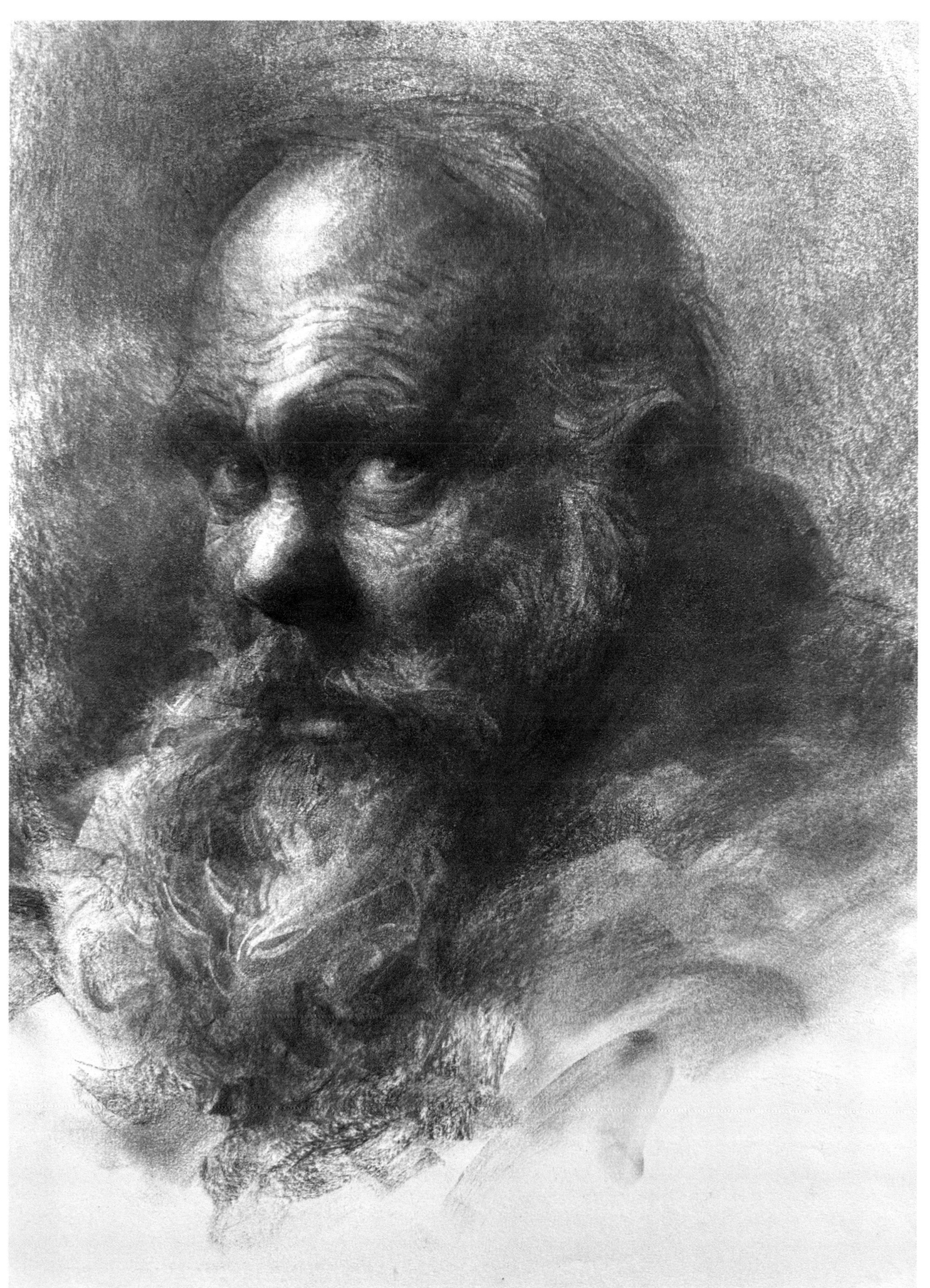

ANGER: COMPRESSED LIPS

When tight lips combine with glaring
eyes and eyebrows pulled down by the
contraction of the corrugator muscle, the
resulting expression can be described as
furious, irate, or simply angry. Closing
your mouth with extra force involves
the orbicularis oris (the lip presser), the
mentalis (the chin muscle), and the often the
triangularis, which is the muscle most often
associated with frowning. The combination
of muscle actions is known as the *three-
muscle press.*

In this expression, the lips narrow down
to a single, straight line, with the lower lip
pushed forward. Bulges appear both above
and below the lips, and the triangularis
creates a hooklike mound. The mentalis
muscle causes the chin to appear roughened.

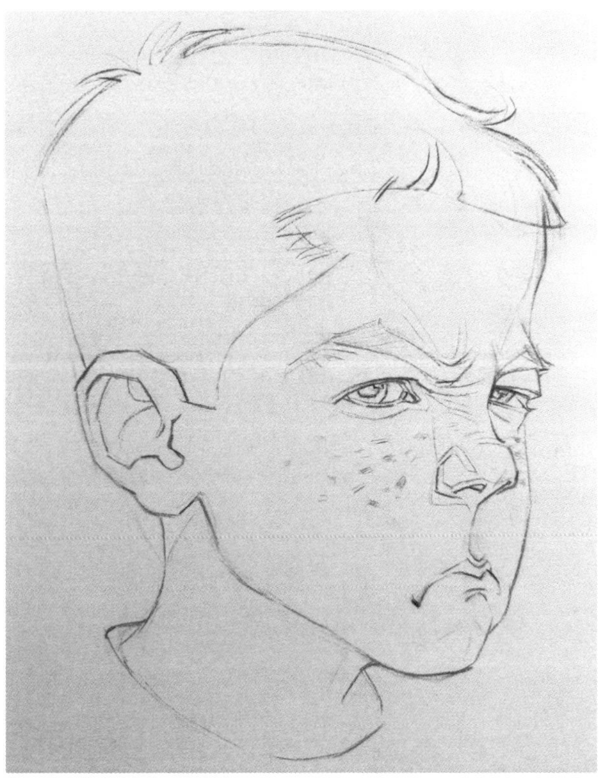

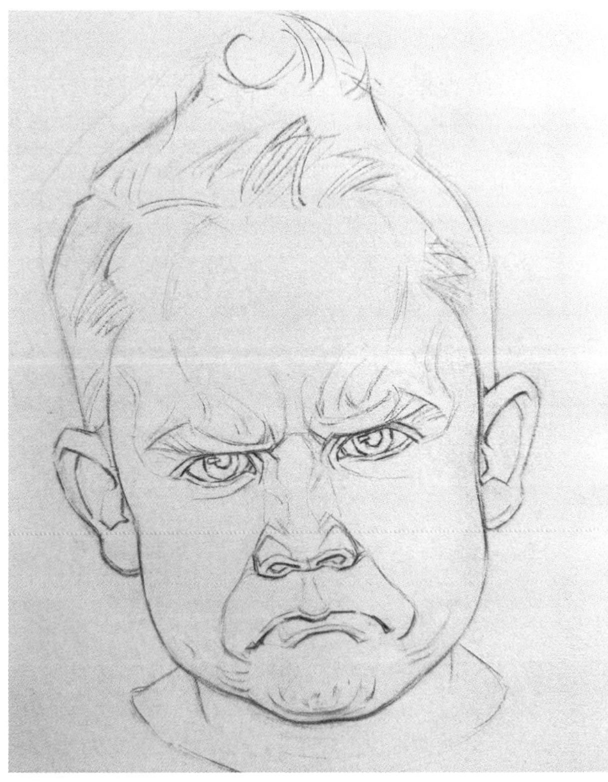

FACIAL EXPRESSIONS FOR ARTISTS

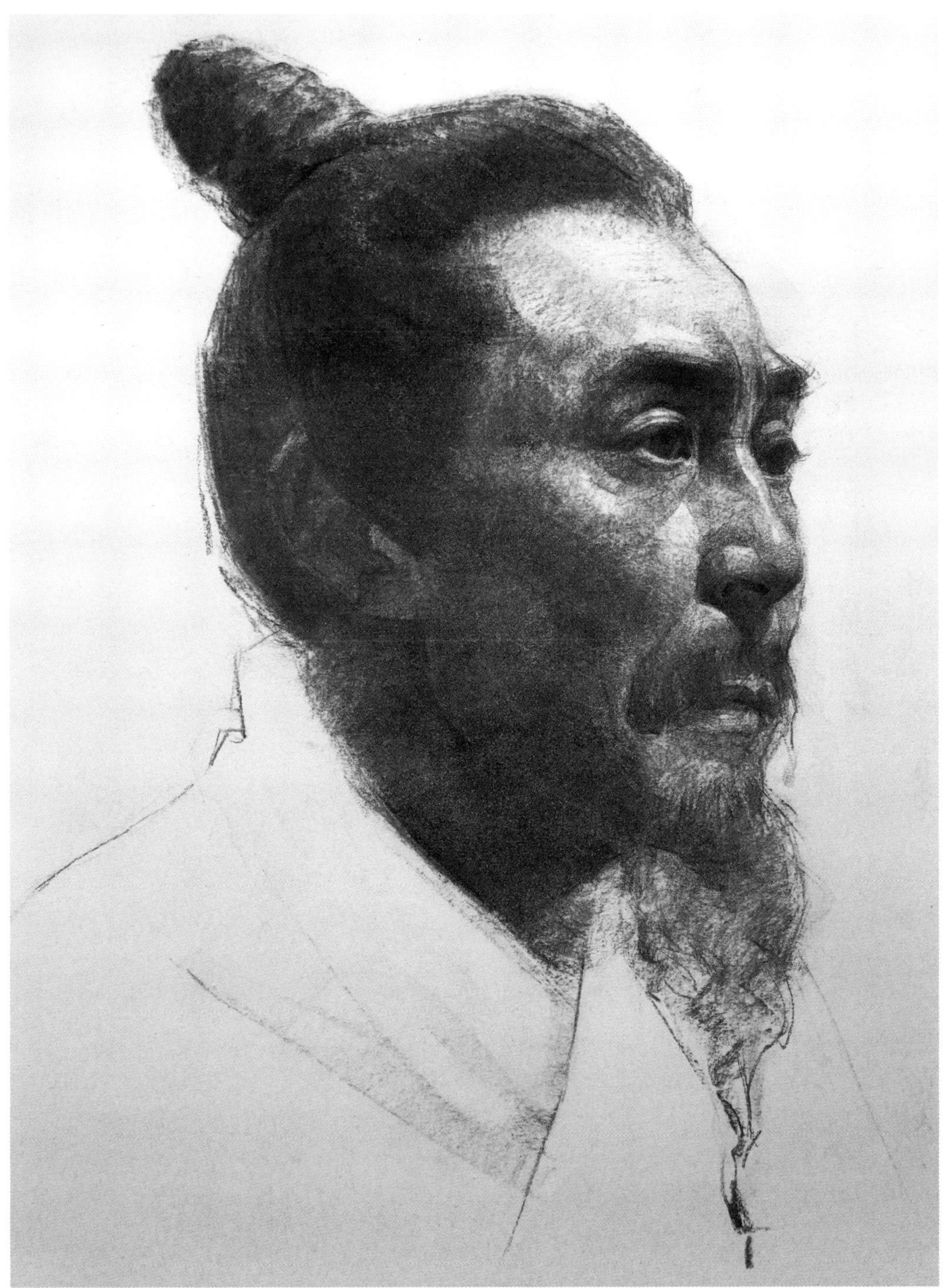

MUSCULAR ACTION: ANGER

When we express anger, the inner ends of the eyebrows are pulled down and drawn together. The nostrils flare, the mouth forms a square shape, exposing the teeth, the lips become tense, and the neck veins bulge. In expressions of rage, fierce, glaring eyes are almost always accompanied by a mouth shaped for shouting: lips tensed, teeth bared, and jaw dropped. The nose also contributes to the angry look, distorted into a sneer by the sneering muscle, with flared nostrils.

DISGUST

In expressions of disgust, the middle portion of each side of the upper lip is pulled up, causing the skin on the bridge of the nose to wrinkle. The front of the cheeks rise and bulge, forming wrinkles below the lower eyelids. As the cheeks push upward, the eye openings become narrower. When these muscles contract intensely, they can part the lips, revealing the upper teeth.

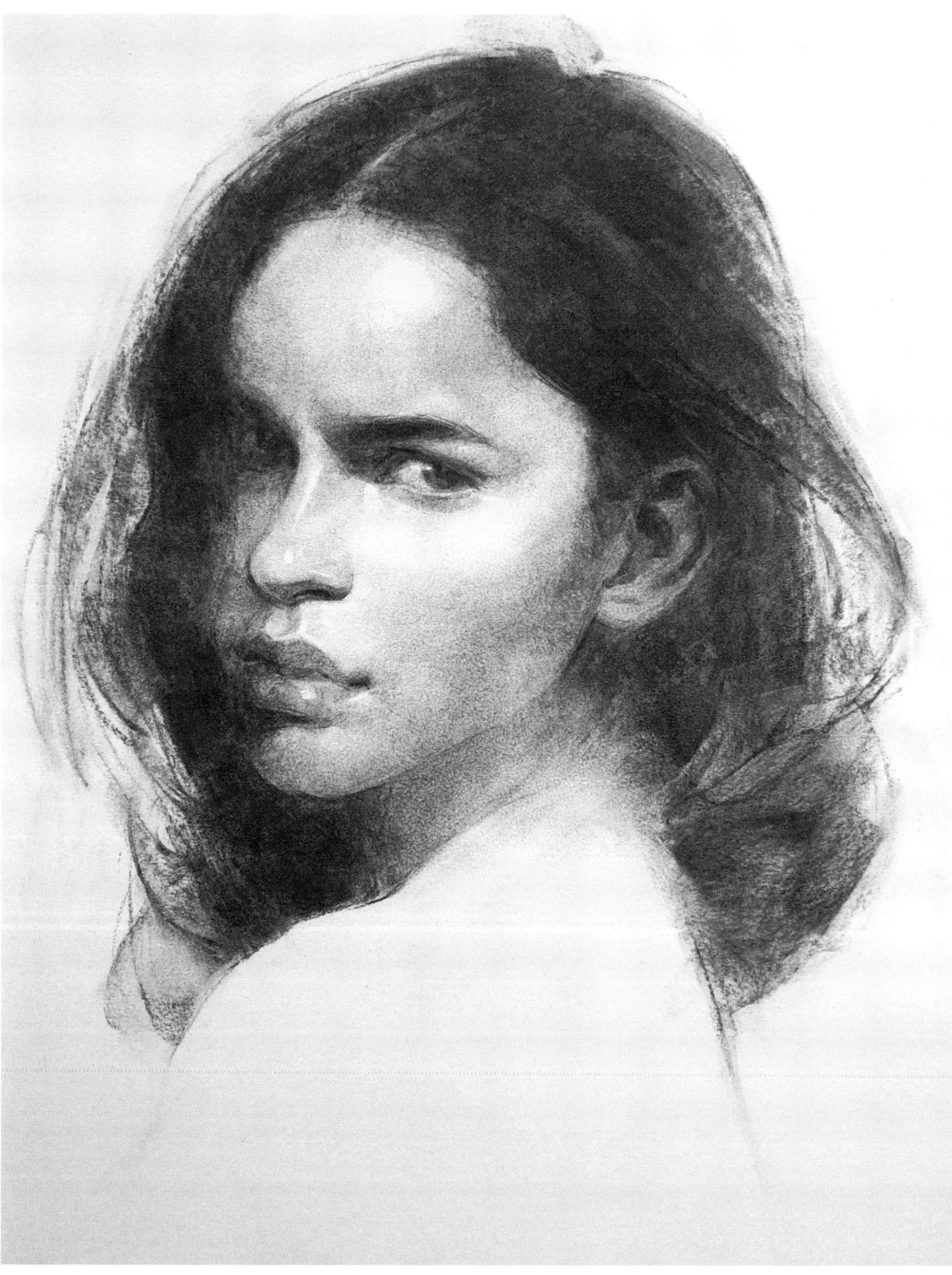

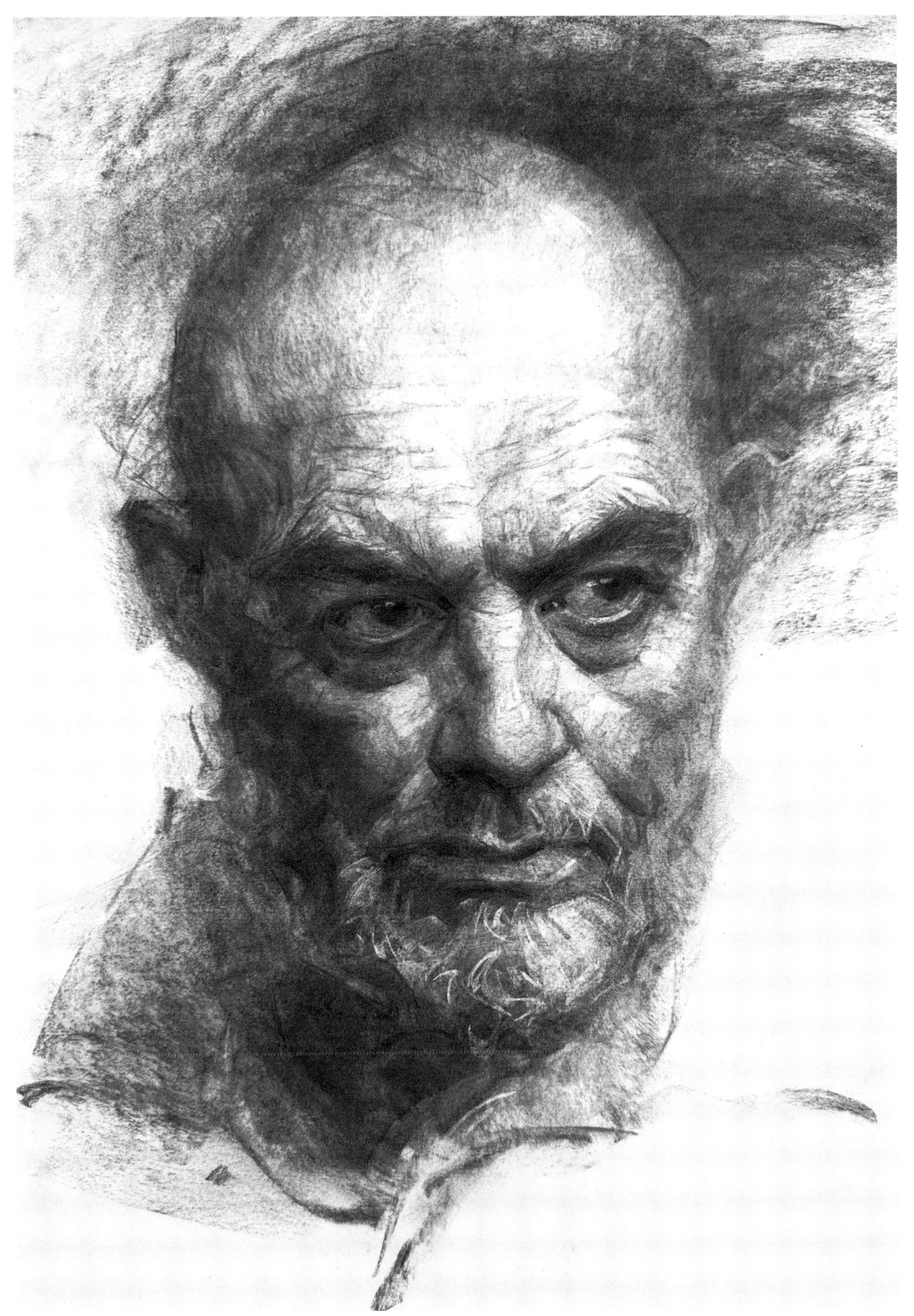

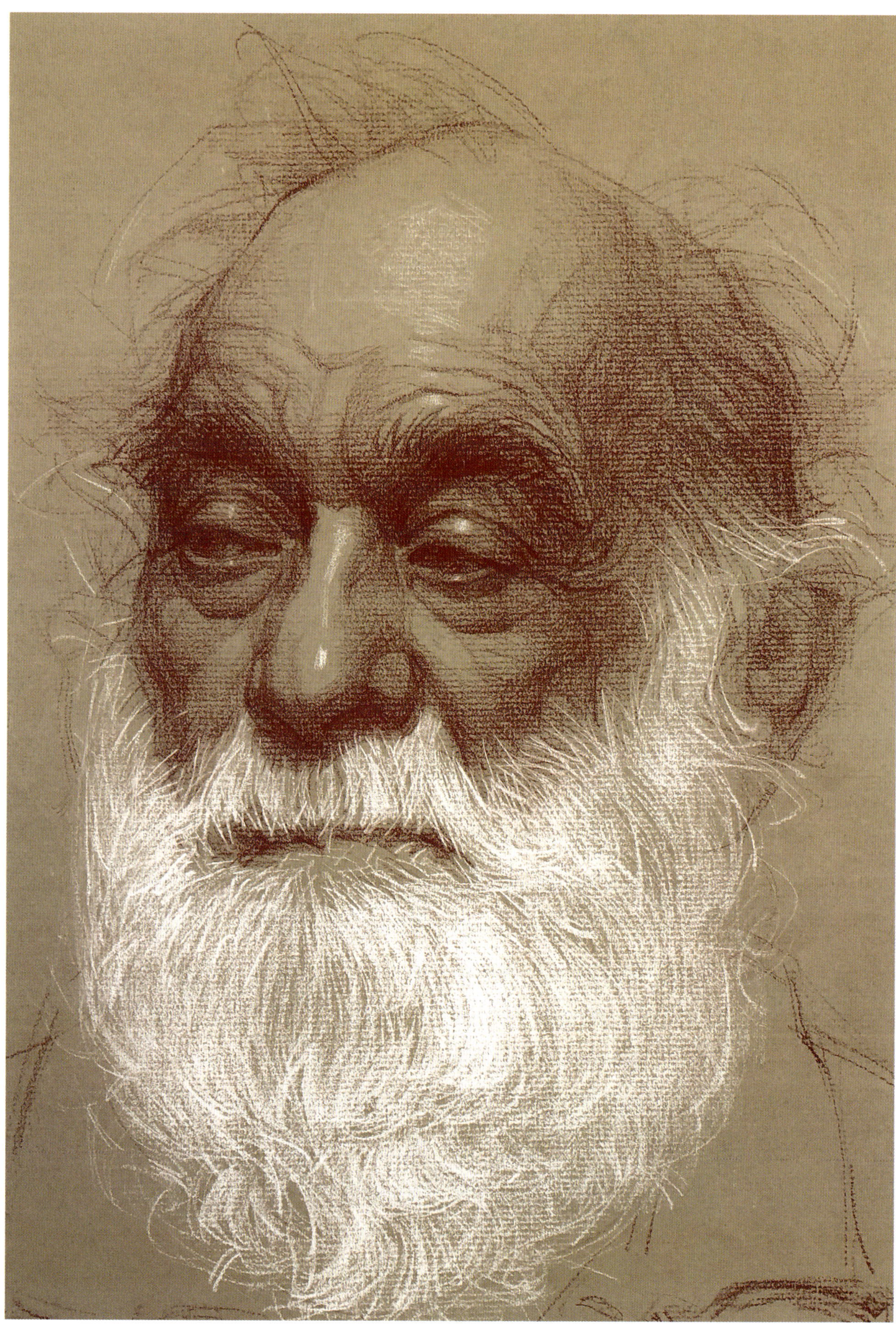

MUSCULAR ACTION: DISGUST

Here are the names of the muscles involved and their basic functions:

1. **Corrugator supercilii:** This muscle lowers the brow.
2. **Orbicularis oculi:** This muscle squints the eye.
3. **Levator labii superioris alaeque nasi:** This muscle raises the cheeks, nose wings, and upper lip, deepens the nasolabial fold, and triggers 1 and 2.
4. **Mentalis:** This muscle pushes up the lower lip and wrinkles the chin.

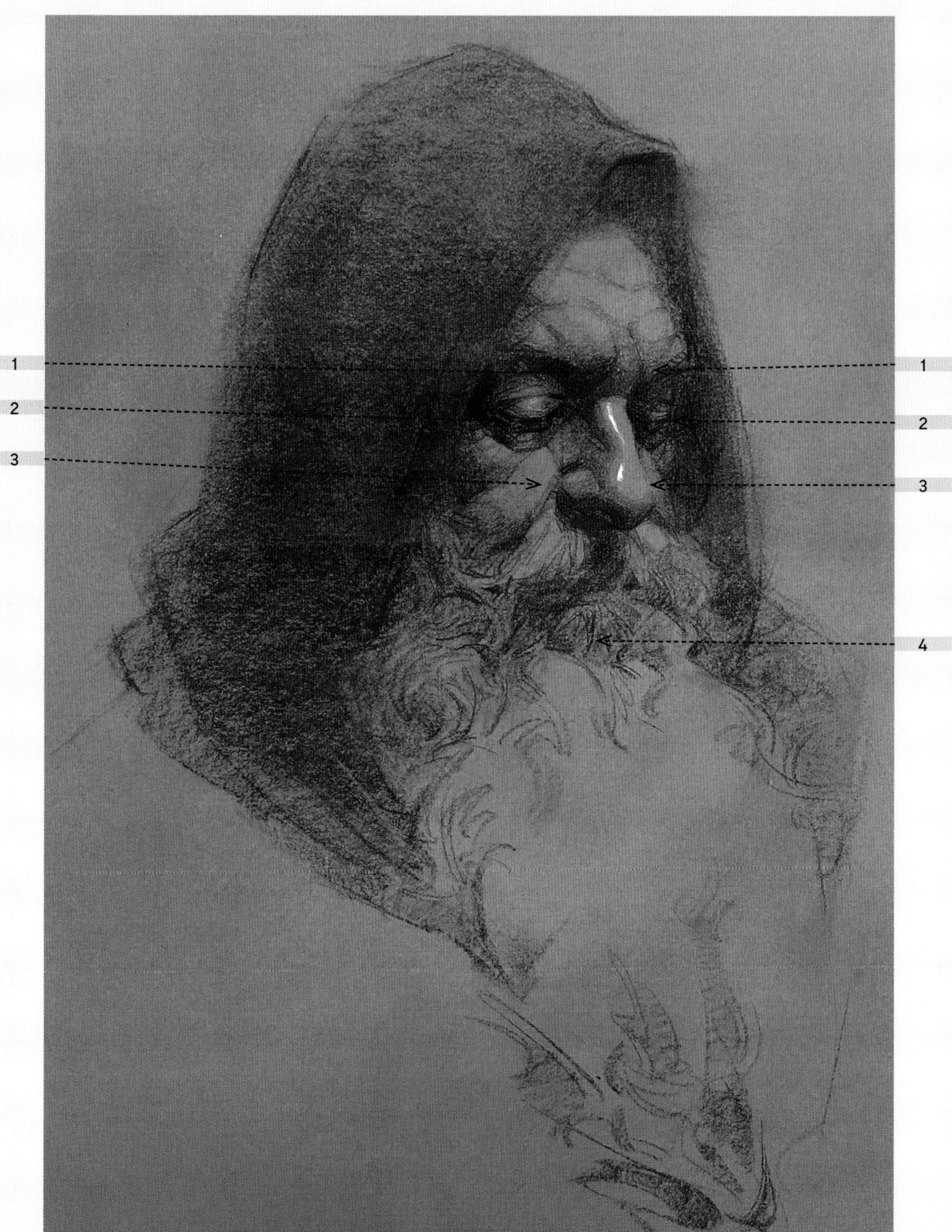

DRAWING EXPRESSIONS AT EVERY STAGE OF LIFE

As a person progresses from newborn to old age, their appearance changes significantly, making it challenging to accurately determine their age. To capture these distinctions correctly, artists must study how time affects our faces. The aging process varies among individuals and is influenced by numerous factors, including genetics, ethnicity, health, and living conditions. For example, a person who has been overexposed in the sun may appear to age more quickly that the person who faithfully uses sunscreen and spends limited time in the sun.

For simplicity, we will summarize the long process of incremental changes into a few key stages. However, nothing can replace the careful observation of real individuals. Study the people around you. Note that children can develop at varying rates, though most tend to converge by adulthood. Try estimating their age and pay attention to the cues that guide your estimation.

BABIES AND CHILDREN

Drawing babies is almost a unique branch of art due to the distinct features and proportions that set them apart from older children and adults. Their round faces, large eyes, small noses, and chubby cheeks require a specific approach and keen observation to accurately capture their innocence and delicate characteristics. This specialized focus on depicting infancy involves understanding the subtle nuances and differences in their anatomy and expressions, making it a specific and challenging area within the broader field of art.

In my experience, I discovered that many of the facial landmarks I rely on when drawing older people simply are much less visible when drawing children. When I was a student, I thought, "A face is a face; who cares how old it is?" But it turned out that age *does* indeed matter and in fact makes a huge difference. Children have a significant amount of baby fat, which obscures their mandible, maxilla, zygomatic bones, and the facial muscles like the masseter and the modioli at the corners of the mouth. Instead of these defined structures, children's faces feature a soft, doughy expanse across their cheeks, with surface forms blending together to the point of near invisibility.

Failing to account for these subtleties will result in an overly simplified, plastic, mannequin-like appearance that never looks quite right. It's essential to describe the structure that is present, but overdeveloping these facial subforms, even slightly, can make children appear aged and haggard. Additionally, the neck plays an important role in indicating age. Children's necks are slender and shorter, whereas longer necks suggest an older age.

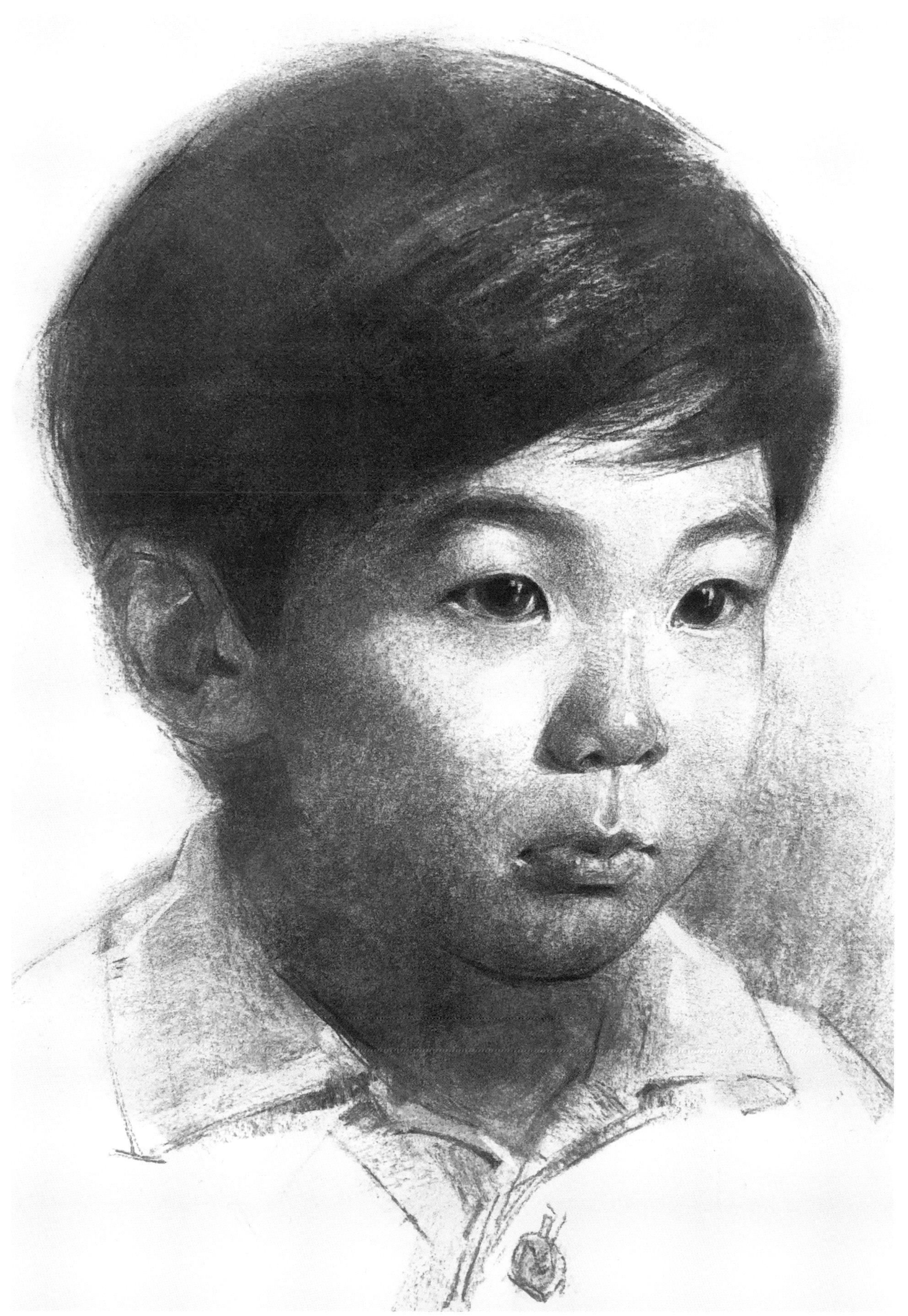

I enjoy drawing open smiles on children. Capturing children's first ventures in the world is truly endearing. I suggest focusing on the same details as when drawing adult smiles: the shapes of the teeth and gums and the dark triangles at the corners of the mouth. Observe the differences in size and shape between the baby teeth of the five-year-old and the adult teeth of the eight-year-old. A missing front tooth is a common characteristic of a seven-year-old that can be used to indicate their age.

This is the subtle balancing act that's required when drawing children: providing enough description of the forms hidden beneath the baby fat without overdoing it and inadvertently adding years of wear and tear to a child's face. After all my experience drawing children, I feel I've adjusted to the unexpected challenges that come with it. These challenges are part of why, after all this time, I'm still motivated to draw children, even though it was tricky at first. I enjoy drawing children and capturing their innocent gazes on paper, emphasizing their cheerfulness and unique energy. Children inspire me. They've opened my eyes to new perspectives, and I've learned so much from them. Being able to capture a moment of pure happiness and youthfulness in the life of a baby or child is truly spectacular.

Portraits of children also make wonderful pictures for framing. When drawings of children are skillfully done, most families are delighted with them, so it can be a great marketing tool. My clients have shared the sentiment that when their children look back at the beautifully drawn portraits of themselves, they'll be reminded of their loving and happy upbringing. Children's portraits capture, celebrate, and record precious moments, creating timeless keepsakes that the clients will cherish forever. I believe a child or baby portrait makes an ideal gift for occasions such as birthdays, Christmas, or Valentine's Day. Moreover, the classic appeal of a handsomely drawn portrait ensures that it will always be popular, making it a lasting and memorable gift.

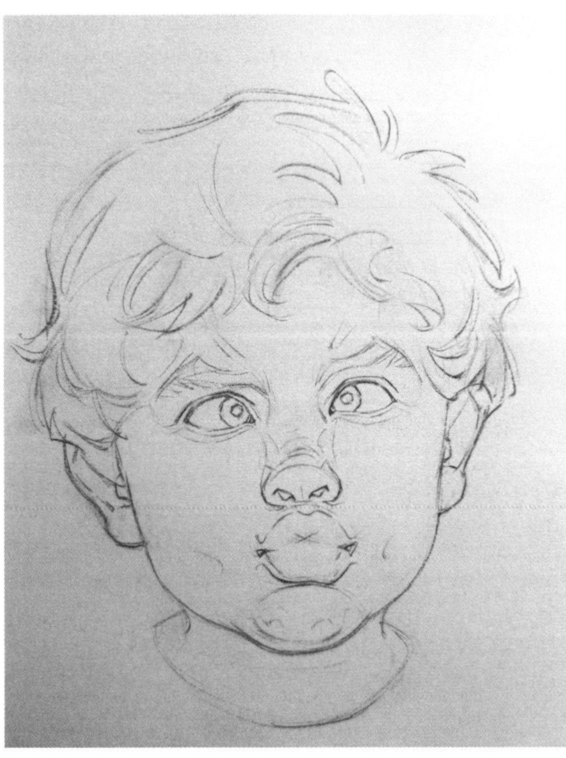

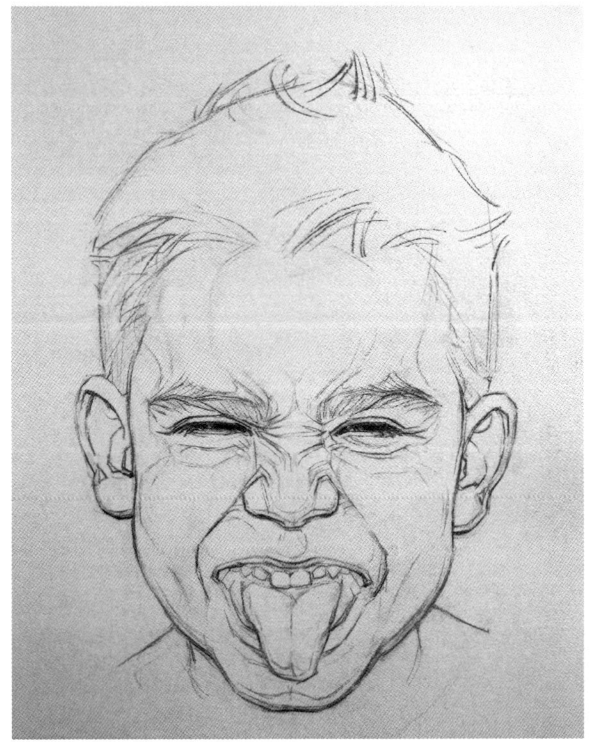

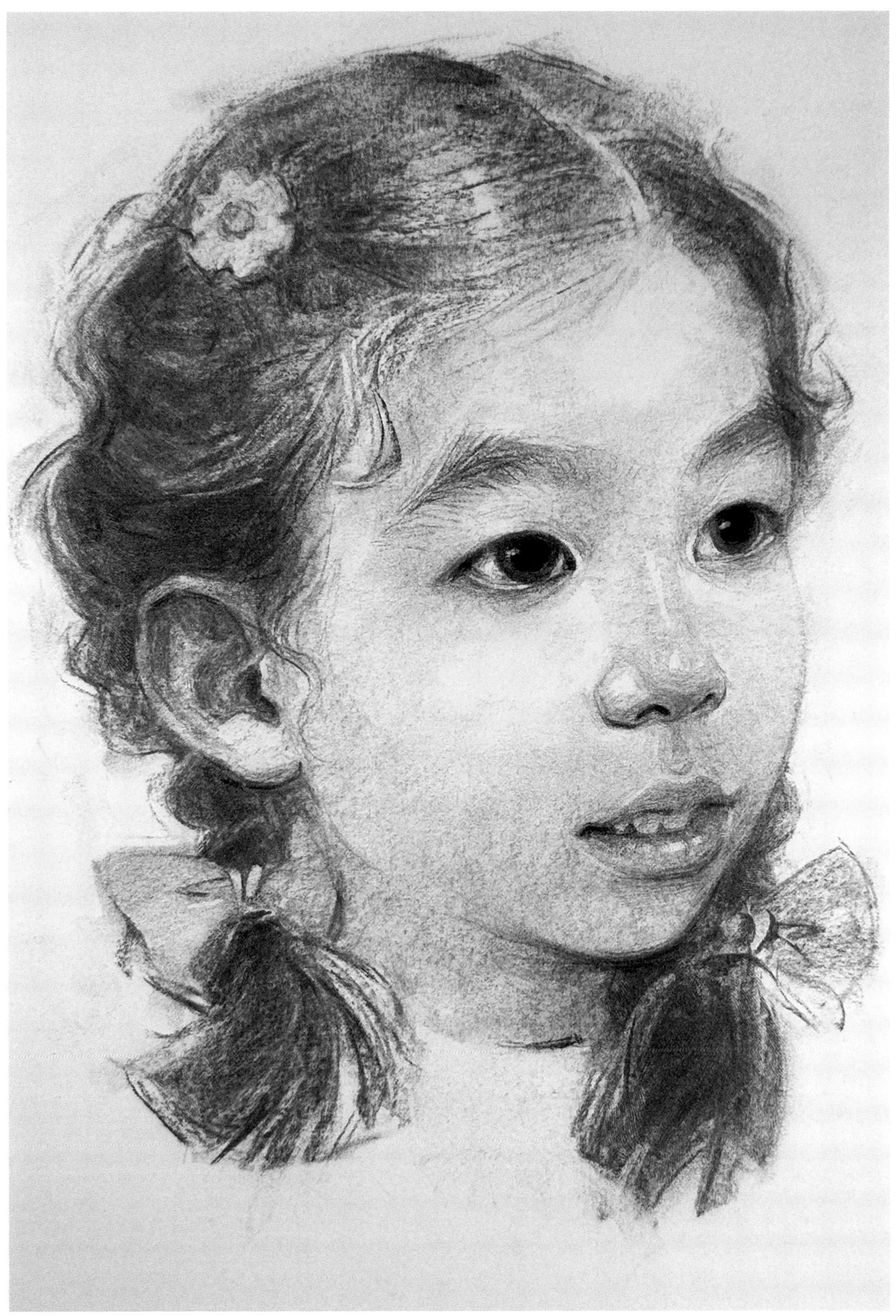

BABIES
(AGES ONE MONTH TO ONE YEAR)

A baby's skull needs to be flexible to navigate the birth canal and accommodate the rapidly growing brain. As a result, it consists of several parts that take a few years to fuse into a single structure. In newborns, the skull may look slightly misshapen. At this stage, there's essentially no difference in the skull between boys and girls.

Drawing a baby may seem challenging, but it primarily involves dealing with different proportions. This applies to all children. They aren't simply smaller adults. Their physique is distinct, and capturing these accurately is essential for drawing younger age groups correctly. The diagram below outlines the facial structure for children up to one year old.

For nearly the first twelve months of their lives, healthy babies accumulate fat all over their bodies—faces, legs, arms, hands, feet, and everywhere in between. Most babies' cheeks are so plump that a big smile merely creates little folds near their mouth, which is characteristic of the smiles of young children.

As children grow taller and their muscles and physical skills develop, they gradually lose their baby fat. Babies typically have skin folds on their wrists, ankles and the bent parts of their arms and legs, with dimples appearing at the elbows instead of visible bones. In a baby, you'll mostly see curves. Pay particular attention to the spot where the contour of the cheek ends and the curve of the chin begins. The farther below the mouth this spot is, the younger the child appears. Always draw the curve under a child's chin convex, never concave. Babies and small children often have overlapping creases between the chin and neck.

A baby's cranium is larger in proportion to the face, giving them a big, full forehead. Unlike adults, a baby's eye level is below the halfway mark of their head. Their eyes are about 75 percent of their full size, but with smaller openings and a smaller head, giving them a big and widely spaced appearance. Babies have larger pupils, more pronounced eyelashes, and fully developed irises, which makes the eyes appear large and button-like. Their face takes up only about a quarter of the head, with the nose, mouth, and chin closer together. The nose is more upturned, and the brow ridge and cheekbones are barely visible. The eyebrows are usually light and delicate. As babies grow more hair, they appear older, despite their proportions changing only slightly.

In general, babies' faces are smooth and round, with small facial bones. Remember to keep the bridge of the nose low and concave, with the two small round nostrils spaced widely apart. Let the upper lip protrude, place the ears fairly low, and draw the chin round and tucked under. Keep the cheeks high and full. Epicanthic folds may be more visible in the development stages during the childhood

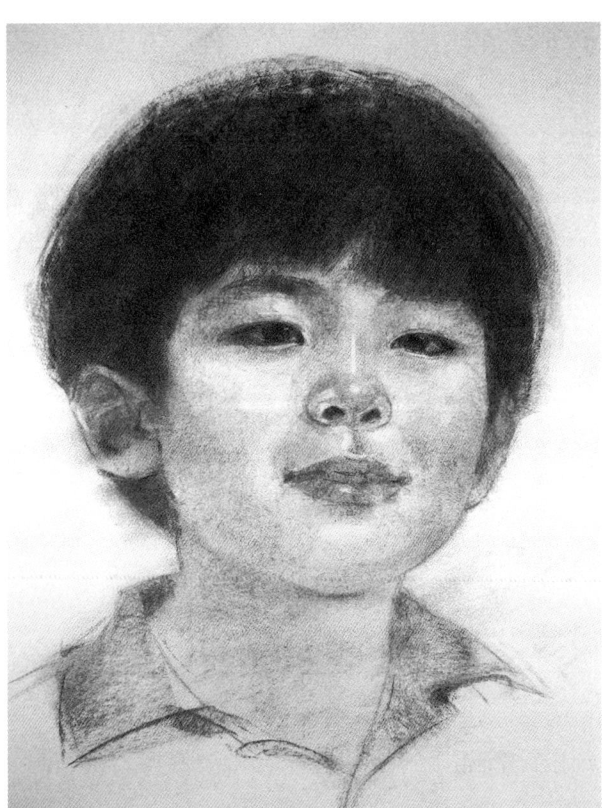

of any race, especially before the nose bridge fully develops. Note the length of the eyelashes and keep the eyebrows subtle.

As the child grows, the lower part of the face, from the eyes down, expands downward and outward in proportion to the cranium. The eyes appear higher on the face as the nose and jaw lengthen. The jawline and chin are initially receding and underdeveloped, while the jawbone, cheekbones, and bridge of the nose are comparatively smaller. The cartilages of the nose grow faster than the bone structure, often causing the nose to turn up as the bridge remains rounded.

By the time we reach our teens, our eyes are at the halfway level like an adult's. It's as if the lower features, and the rest of the body, catch up with the cranium. This is why understanding facial proportions is important for capturing a child's age accurately.

As the child grows past their first year, their facial features gradually shift upward, although the eyes still don't reach the midline. The baby develops a neck, which is small, thin, and short as compared to the head. A child's shoulders are narrow, and their hair grows in thick enough to cover the head. The mouth looks pouty, with the top lip tending to protrude. The upper lip is longer, and the still receding chin sits well under the lips. Baby fat often results in a small double chin. By the age of two or three years, the child typically has a complete set of baby teeth.

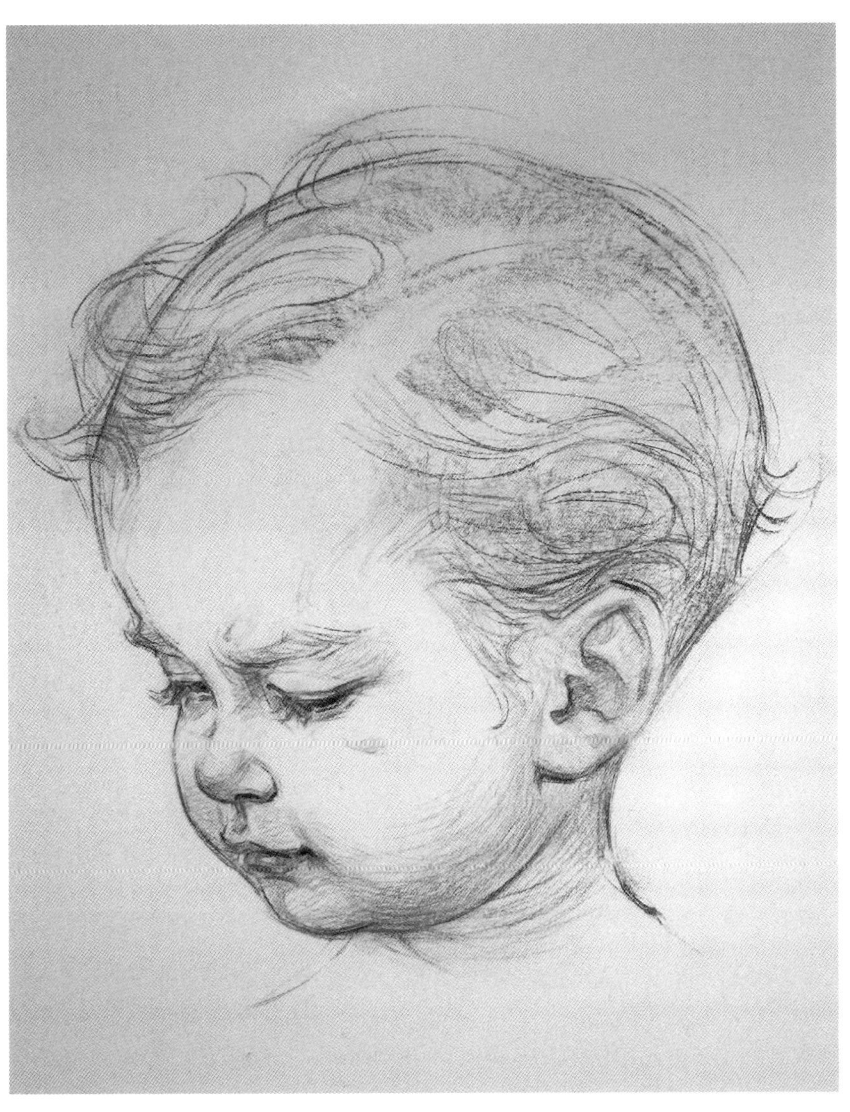

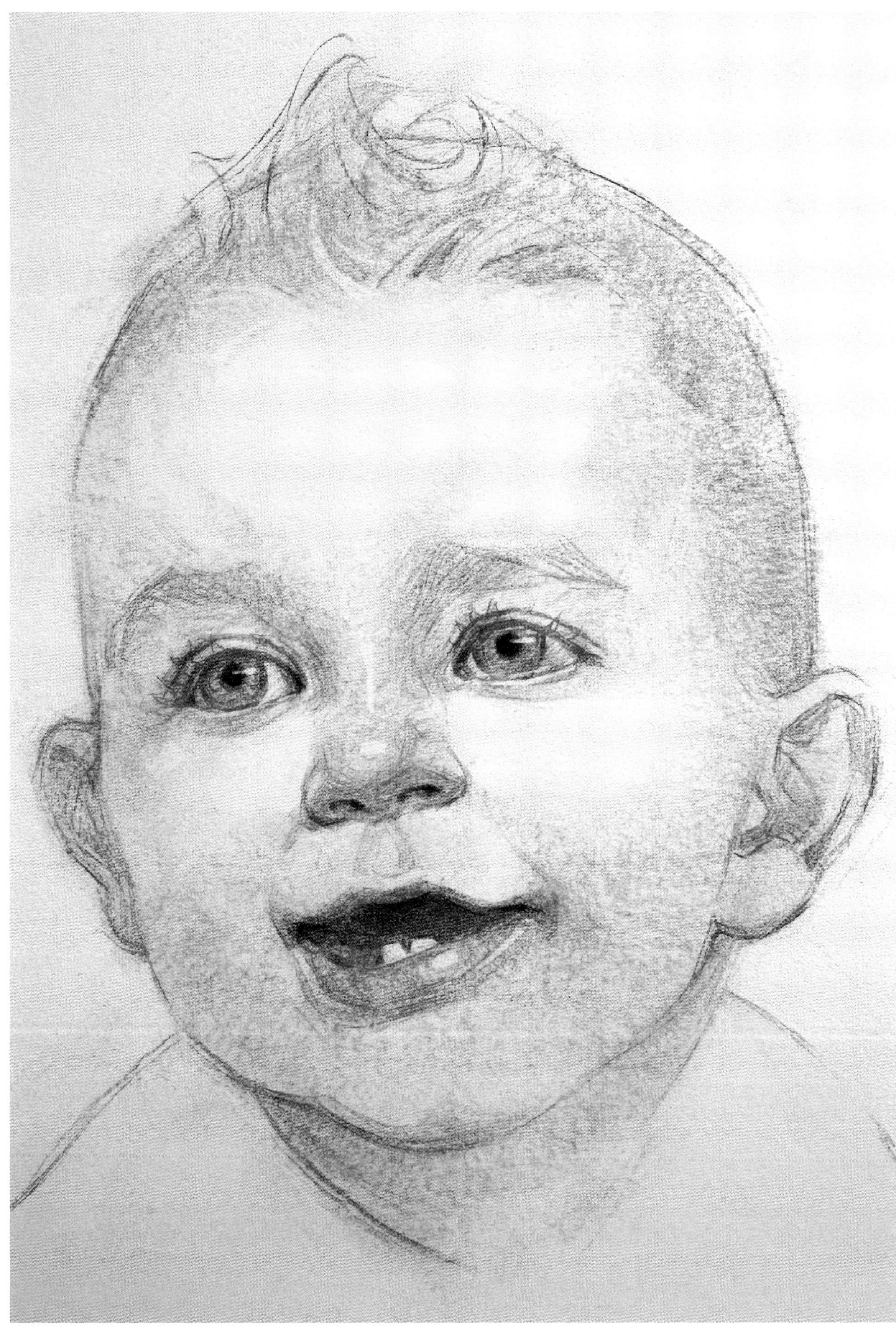

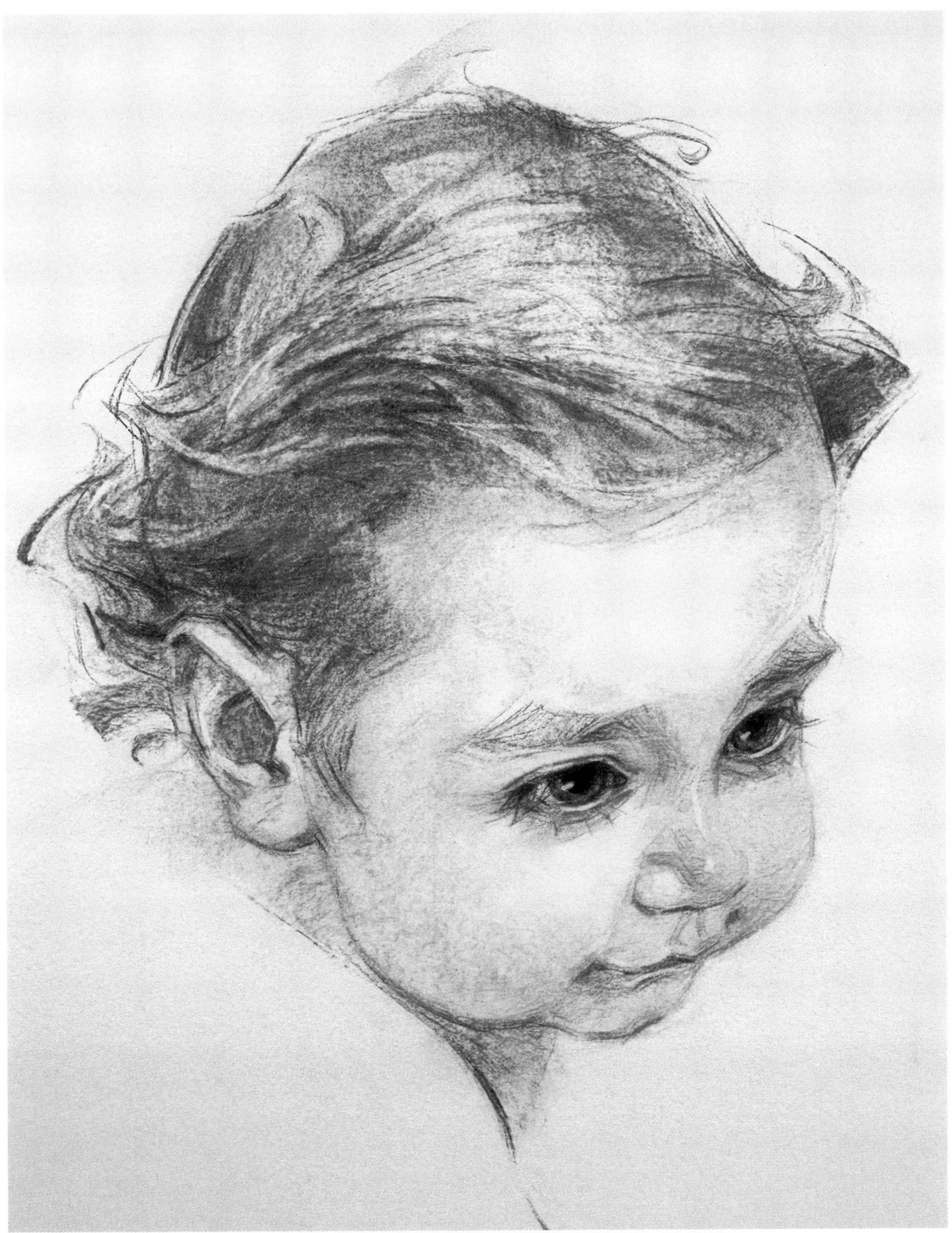

TIPS ON DRAWING BABIES

The key is to keep it simplified and smooth. Most often, babies have round faces, big sparkling eyes, no wrinkles, and cute dimples. They also have fuller hair, small noses, and their facial expressions and posture reflect their youthful charm. Artists can easily become sentimental when drawing babies, and it's important to be cautious of being overly emotional, which can lead to distortions or inaccuracy. This sentimentality can apply to any endearing, large-eyed creature. Stay vigilant to keep it realistic!

SMALL CHILDREN
(AGES ONE TO SEVEN)

Before puberty, boys and girls often appear quite similar and are mainly distinguished by cultural cues like hairstyles and clothing. Generally, the faces of young children are smooth and round, but girls tend to have slightly rounder contours, such as a higher forehead and a softer jawline. However, the proportions remain similar for both sexes.

The term toddler typically refers to a child approximately one to three years old, whereas a child three to five years old is called a preschooler. The word *toddler* is derived from "to toddle," meaning to walk unsteadily, like a child of this age. In the toddler stage, children tend to grow thicker hair and eyebrows, while still maintaining their chubby cheeks and puckered lips. As they move past this phase, they often appear slimmer because they shed their baby fat before their muscles start developing. This slender look persists into preadolescence.

At this stage, the child typically boasts a full head of hair, which grows particularly well over the temples. This emphasizes their large cranium but maintains a small-looking face . The face tends to become relatively narrower, although it remains petite,

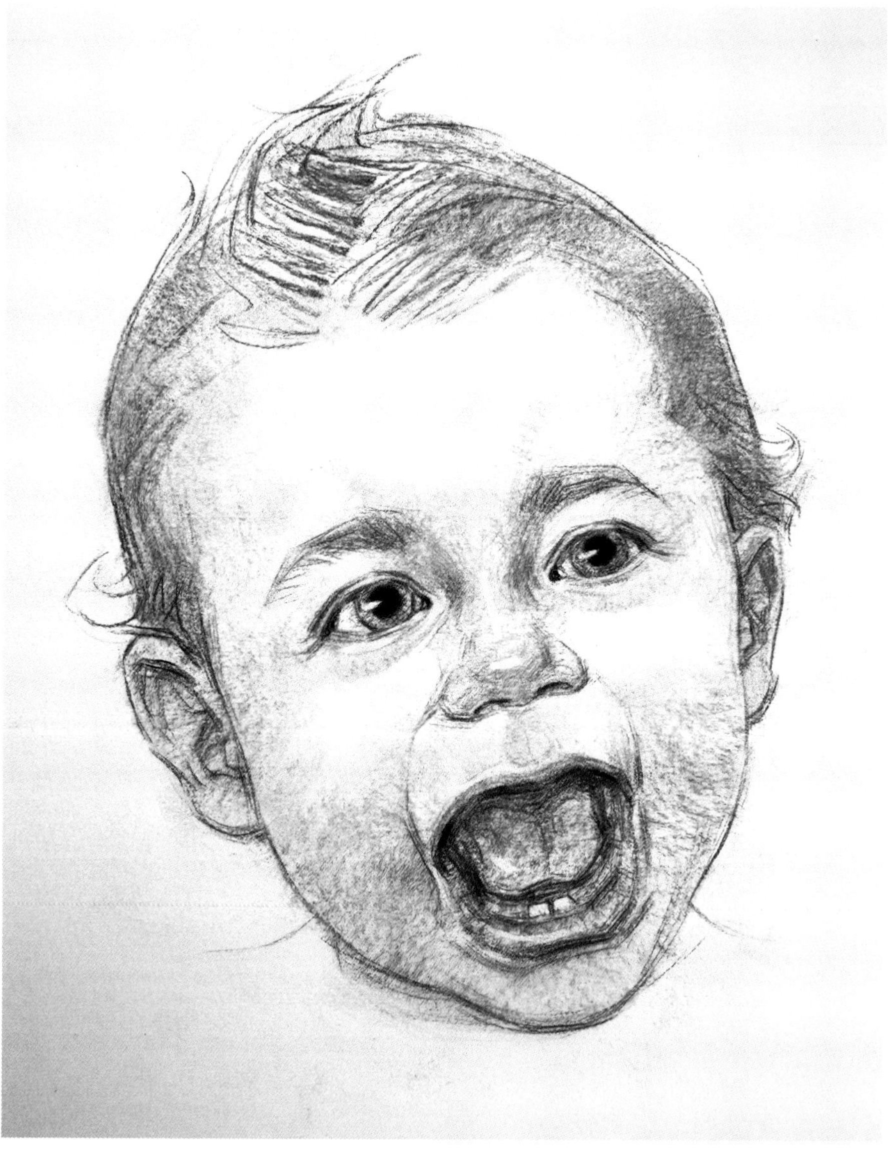

occupying less space compared to an adult's face. The nose undergoes lengthening, and the bridge begins to take shape. Ears, in particular, start growing ahead of other features and may appear prominent, especially in boys, giving them that awkward "jug-eared" look. *Jug-eared* refers to having ears that protrude prominently from the head, resembling the handle of a jug.

As the head grows, the eyes may appear smaller than before, with the irises also seeming proportionally smaller, but they still remain notably large and are often adorned with long eyelashes. Due to the underdeveloped trapezius muscle, the neck may appear thin, making the head seem relatively big. At around four years of age, the chin and jawline begin to develop in preparation for the eruption of permanent teeth, which can result in gaps between the existing baby teeth. Notably, the nostrils and the upper lip tend to grow, with the upper lip appearing somewhat shorter.

While the ears continue to grow, they are typically fully developed by the age of ten or twelve. Despite this, the distance between the nose and ears may still appear wide.

Children's heads often seem to project backward due to their small necks and the underdeveloped muscles attaching to the base of the skull. Typically, contour lines are softer and rounder in girls, accentuating their facial femininity, while boys often have more angular features, contributing to a rugged appearance. A closer hairline tends to enhance a boy's boyishness, whereas a larger forehead can emphasize a girl's girlish charm. Traditional hairstyles like little pigtails with ribbons and bangs remain timeless, while loose or curly hair is also popular. The delicate structure of children's ears and brows should be reflected in drawings, keeping them light and transparent. Dimples are often a prominent characteristic in children's illustrations, as is a missing front tooth.

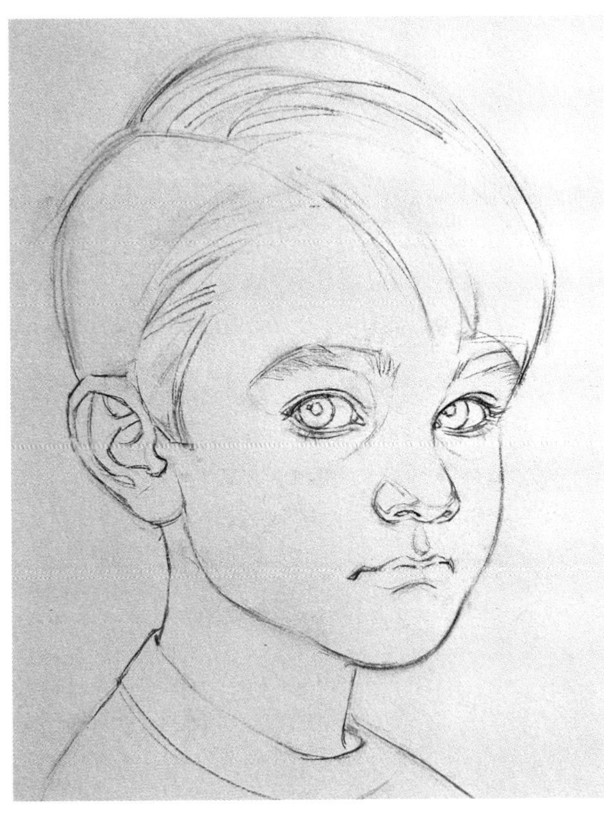

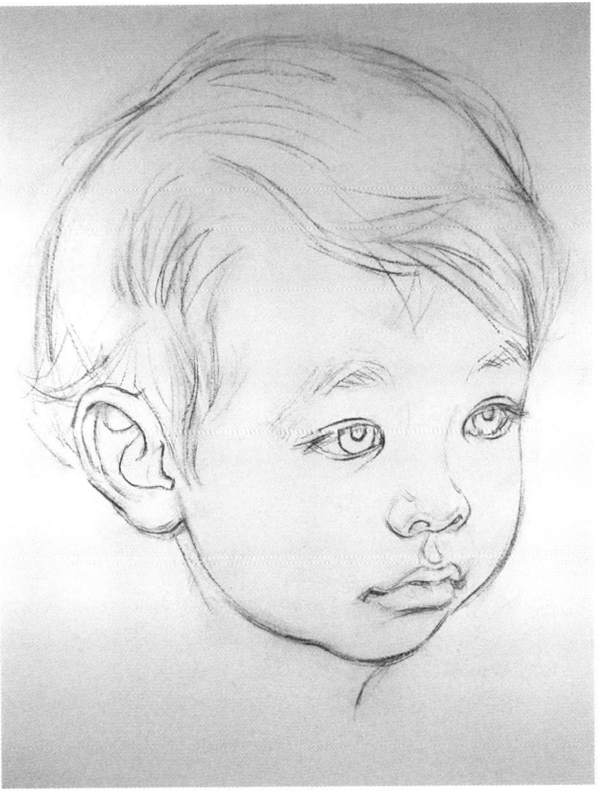

TIPS ON DRAWING SMALL CHILDREN

Remember to avoid drawing any sharp and prominent jawline or chin. Try to keep it softer and rounder at the edges. Children's heads are still small, adding to the cuteness and youthfulness of the subject.

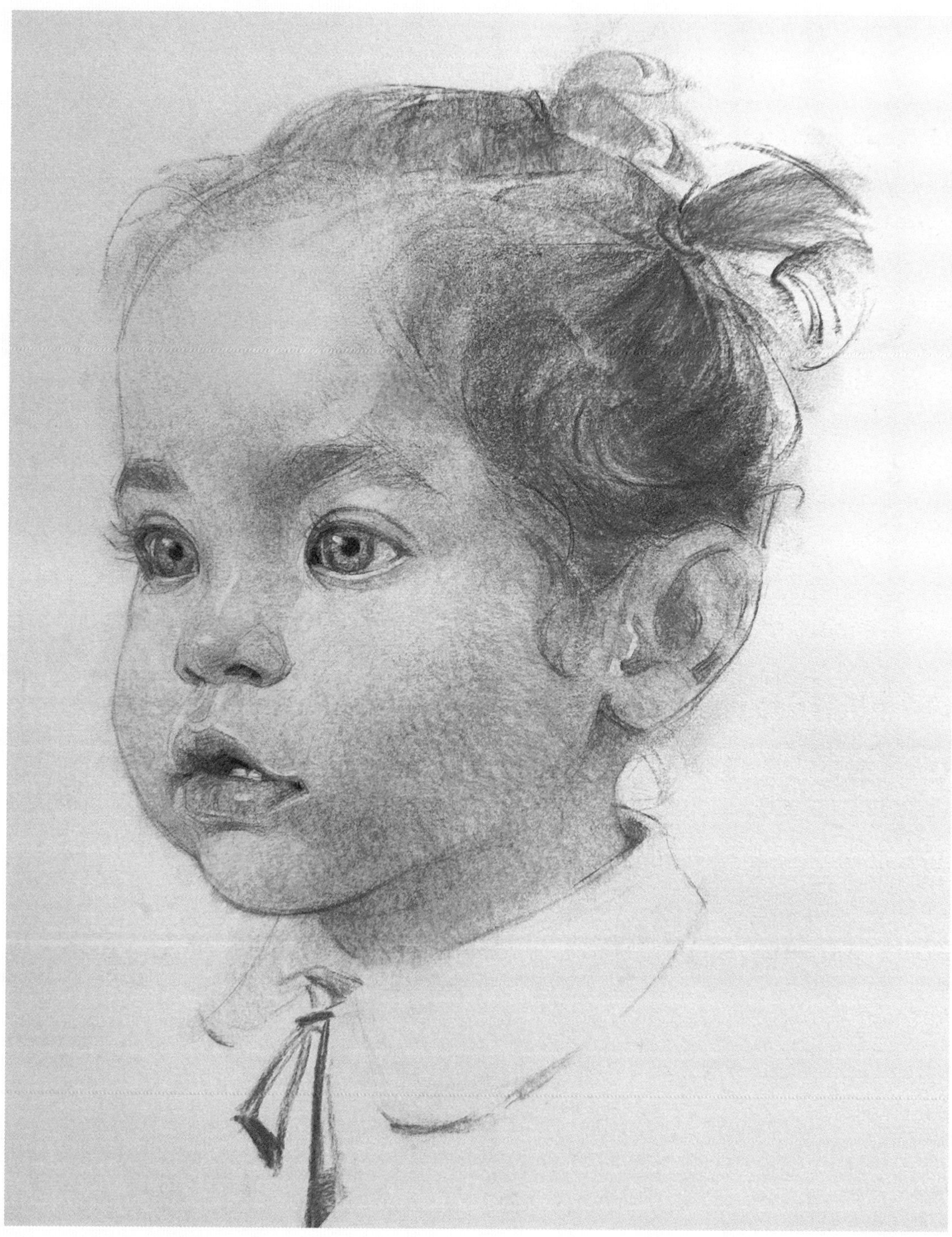

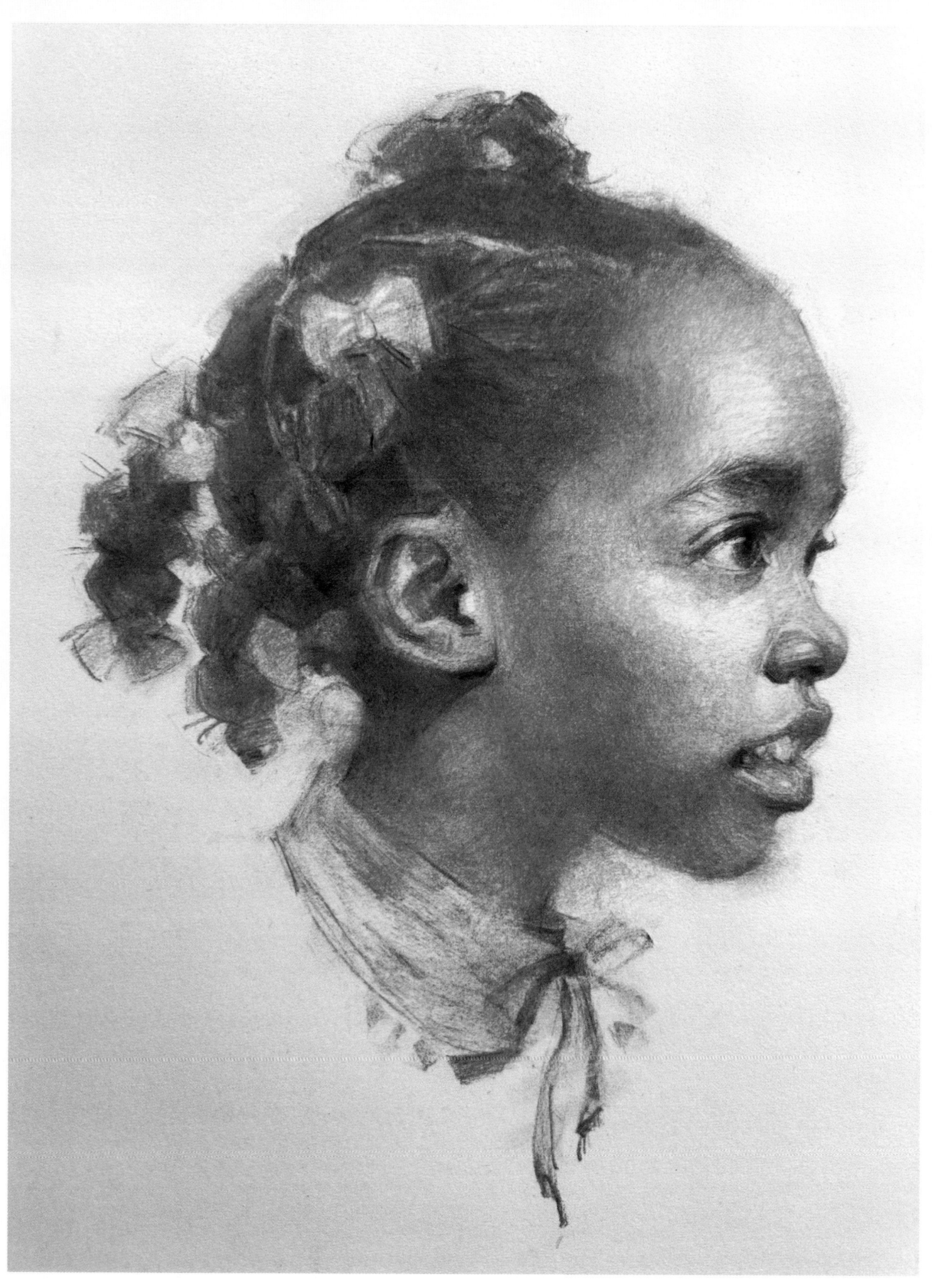

TWEENS
(AGES EIGHT TO TWELVE)

Children between the ages of eight and twelve are often referred to as *tweens* or *preteens*. This term reflects the interval where they are considered too old to be young children yet too young to be teenagers. This stage marks the transition from childhood to adolescence, characterized by a sense of mischief and carefree happiness. Their boundless energy often manifests in physical activity and lively expressions, reflecting the exuberance of this in-between phase.

Children transition into tweenhood due to both physical and behavioral changes. At this age, it's helpful to depict the neck and shoulders, as the "large head, skinny body" appearance is still prominent, distinguishing tweens from teenagers. The top of the eyes now reaches the halfway line of the face, though they are not yet perfectly centered, and the hairline remains slightly elevated, and the hair tends to be unruly. The mouth loses its puckered appearance and many of its baby-like features, marking further progression toward maturity. By this stage, the second set of teeth begins replacing the baby teeth. The baby teeth gradually make way for permanent adult teeth between the ages of six to twelve, often resulting in the front teeth appearing larger.

Boy's undergo significant development in their ears, and the characteristic jug-eared appearance typically fades out at puberty as their bodies mature. While the jawline develops during this time, it's important

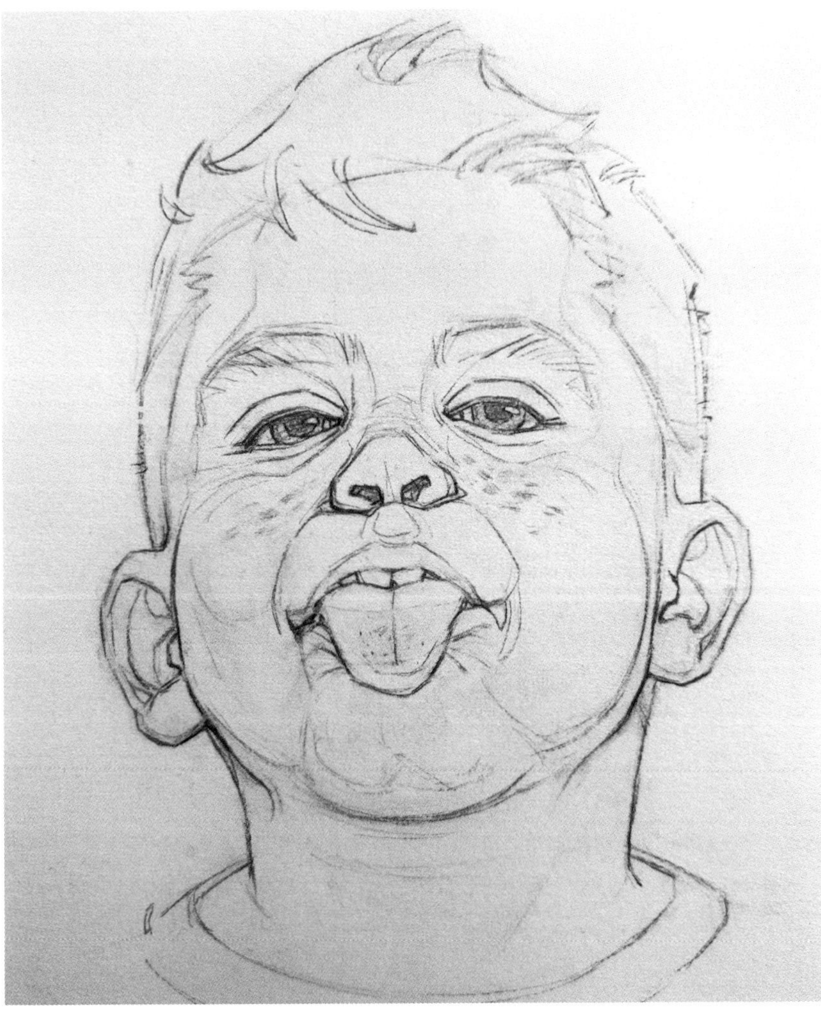

not to make the corners below the ear too square, as this can prematurely age them, making them look more like teenagers. To maintain a youthful appearance, it's advisable to keep the corners of the jaw rounded. The bone at the bridge of the nose tends to develop more slowly, so many boys retain a sightly upturned nose until well into their teens. Additionally, the nostrils develop, and the cartilages of the nose spread during this period.

Girls typically begin puberty about one year earlier than boys, and as a result, their faces tend to mature slightly sooner. Girls often have higher foreheads and hairlines than boys, along with rounder cheeks. The lips are fuller and should be drawn curved rather than thin or angular. When drawing a young girl's face, it's important not to make the mouth too large or too dark to maintain proportion and delicacy. This is the age of freckles, but don't overdo it.

Children at this age are full of curiosity. With the onset of puberty during this stage, they experience significant changes during this transition, not only physically, but also mentally and emotionally. Children are exploring new interests and striving to establish their identities as individuals during the tween years. This period is marked by increased independence, often characterized by a willingness to test boundaries and engage in more risk-taking behaviors.

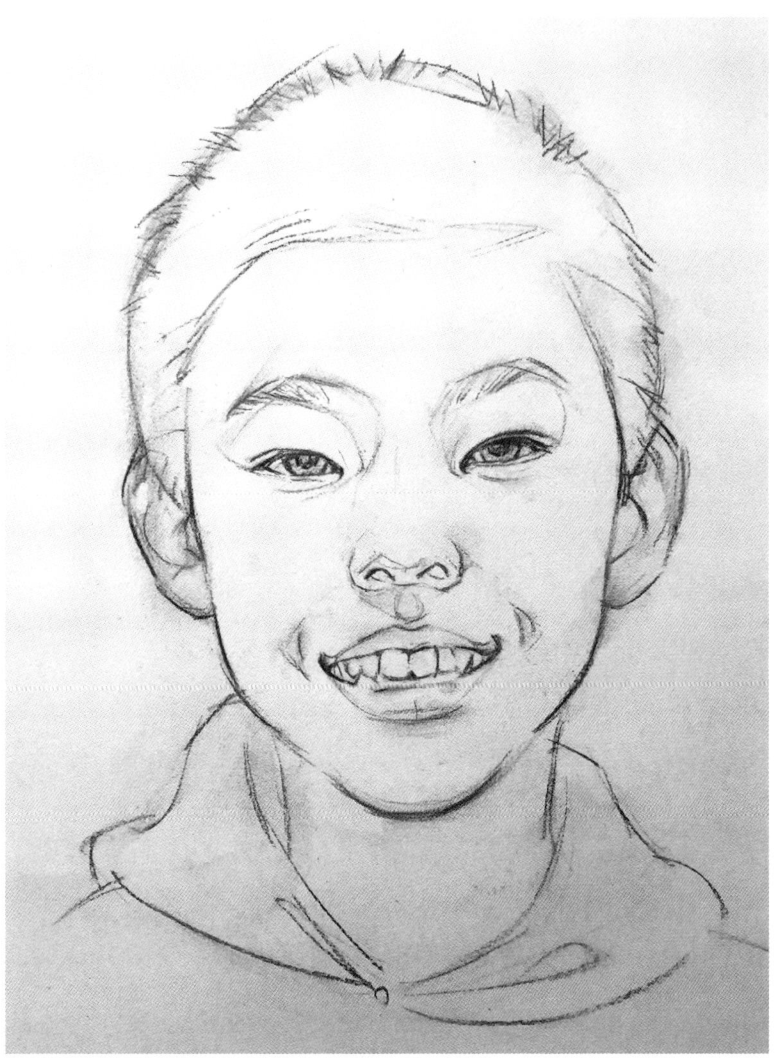

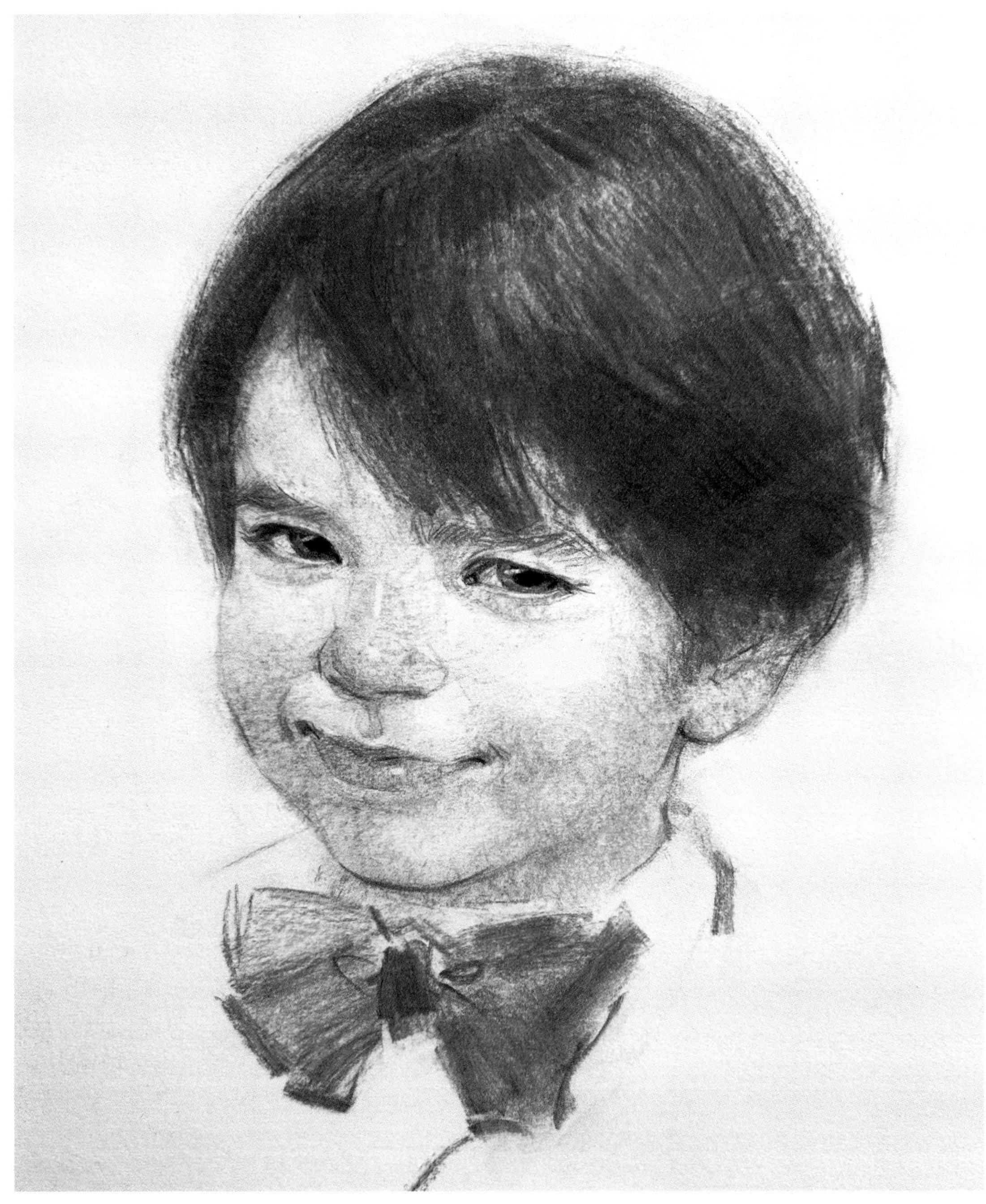

TIPS ON DRAWING TWEENS

Drawing the subject's head in outline form first allows you to focus on the age and expression accurately before adding details like tone and shading. If the outline doesn't appeal to you or doesn't feel right, there's no need to proceed with adding tone, as it won't effectively enhance a flawed foundation. In fact, sometimes leaving a head in outline form can convey a certain charm or character that may be lost in a fully finished drawing. Trust your instincts and prioritize getting the outline just right before moving on to more detailed work.

When adding tone, make sure to keep it to a minimum so as not to obscure the radiance of youth.

TEENAGERS
(AGES THIRTEEN TO NINETEEN)

Adolescence, often referred to as the teenage years or simply *teens*, is a period marked by significant social, emotional, and relationship changes. These transformations occur primarily due to puberty, which typically spans from thirteen to nineteen years old. While it's convenient to categorize these changes under a single heading, it's important to recognize the complexity and variability within this age group. During the teenage years, the high cranium characteristic of childhood gradually disappears as the skull continues to grow.

By this stage, teenagers generally have proportions similar to adults, but their youthful freshness and energy set them apart. Despite reaching adultlike physical proportions, teenagers retain a distinct vibrancy and vitality that distinguishes them from older adults. During the teenage years, the eyes may still seem slightly larger in proportion to the rest of the face. While the structure of the nose and jawline is nearing maturity, it's not as pronounced or as heavy as in fully developed adults. Although the ears no longer appear large, they seem smaller in relation to the entire head compared to childhood. The cartilage of the ear becomes more defined, and the ears lose some of their roundness, adopting more angular lines. The soft features of childhood give way to greater angularity and slightly stronger contours. Brows tend to thicken, and the lips reach their full size and shape. Additionally, the chin becomes more prominent and takes on a more permanent form but continues to develop until the age of twenty or more. The cranium doesn't reach its maximum growth until full maturity.

In boys, the bone structure becomes more pronounced during adolescence, though it shouldn't be emphasized as much as in an adult man's head. The cheeks typically remain smooth without significant definition of the

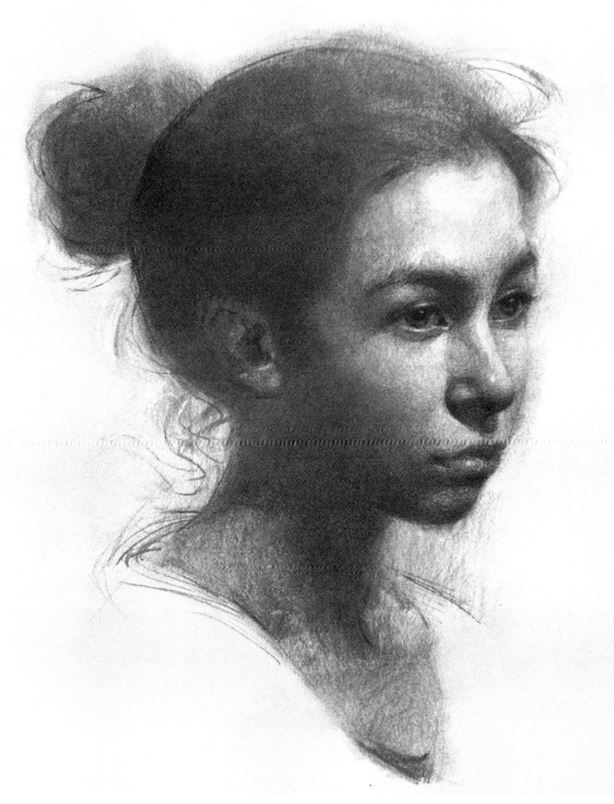

muscles. However, the jawline undergoes considerable development in a relatively short period. As boys mature, the neck thickens, and the Adam's apple becomes prominent. Around age fifteen or sixteen, boys may start to notice the onset of soft facial hair, particularly on the lip and chin, which is a common change associated with puberty.

On the other hand, girls tend to be more rounded, sleek, and fair in appearance. The prevailing quality in their faces is youthfulness, characterized by smoothness, freshness, and vigor. Girls' faces typically exhibit few lines and wrinkles, reflecting their exuberance and vitality.

Both genders can experience acne, a condition associated with fluctuating hormone levels during puberty. As their bodies undergo growth spurts at varying rates and they grapple with self-identity uncertainties, teenagers may appear awkward and gangly. Human diversity, including differences in height, strength, and other physical attributes, becomes increasingly evident as individuals progress toward their fully developed adult state. Typically, the body reaches physical maturity around the ages of eighteen to twenty-one.

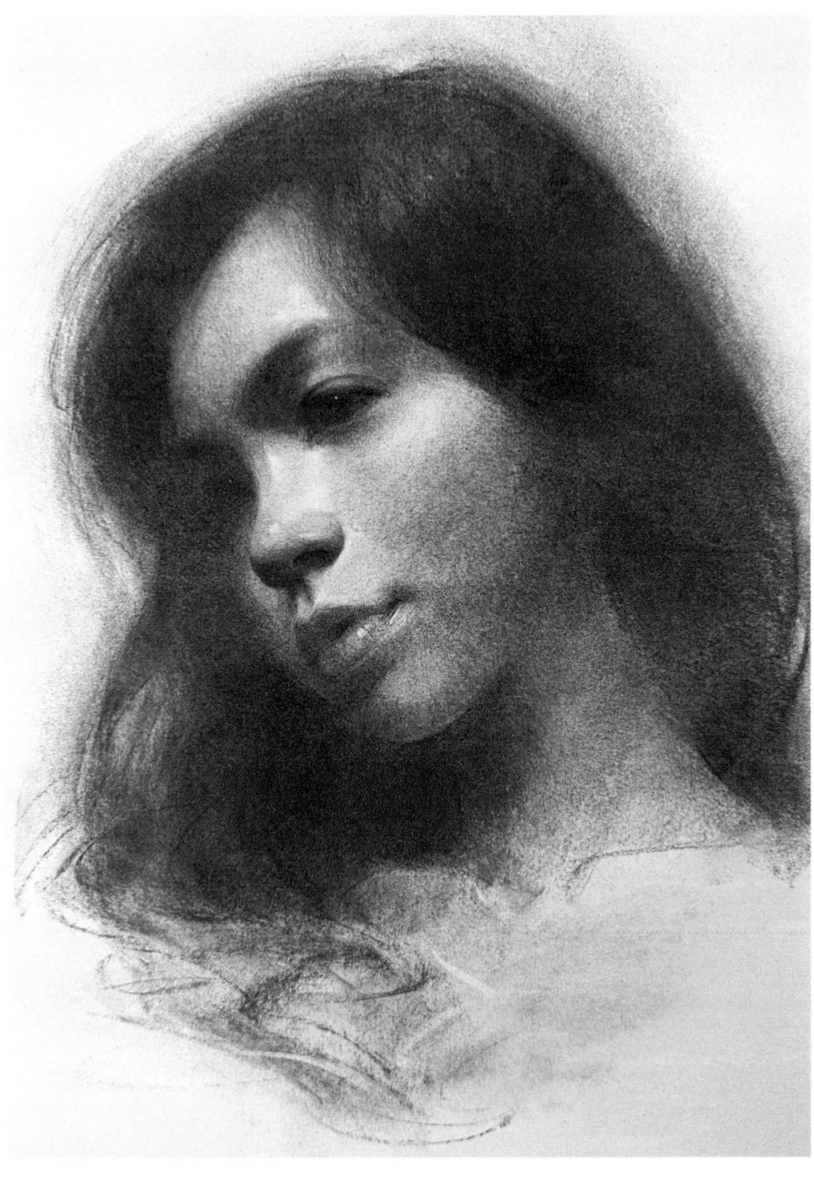

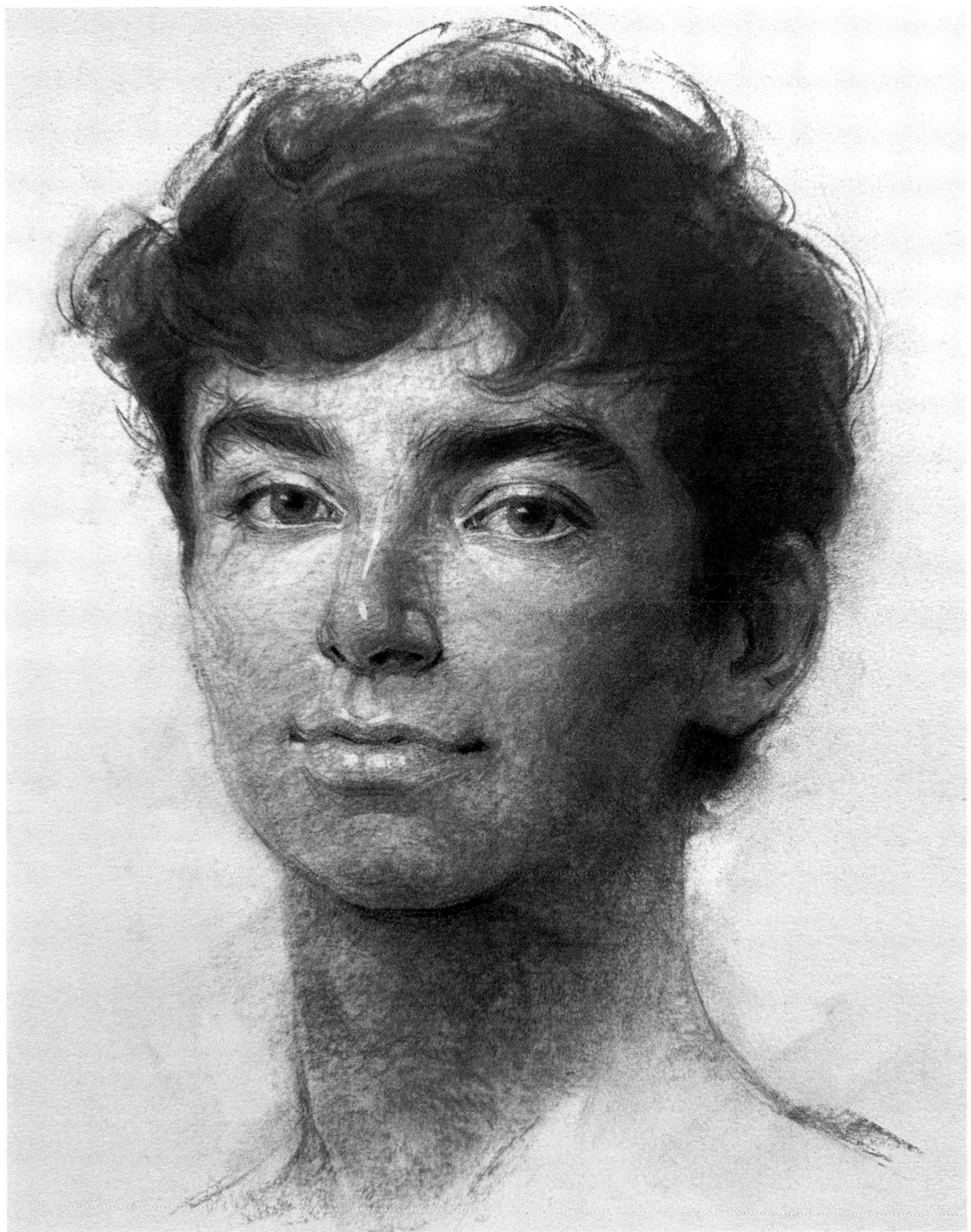

TIPS ON DRAWING TEENAGERS

When drawing teenagers, several key elements come into play, including line, form, value, perspective, and composition. In vine charcoal, lines can be manipulated to expressively vary in thickness, adding depth and character to the drawing.

Focus on using meaningful contour lines and minimal tone. Remember to keep the lines soft and don't add too much definition to the jawline or cheekbones—it will make your subject look much older. You want to capture the subject at this precise stage of life.

OLDER PEOPLE

Exploring the intricacies of older faces can be truly captivating. Unlike younger faces that often appear smooth, the lines and marks on an older face tell stories of a lifetime's worth of emotions and experiences. These facial details are shaped by years of expressions and movements, with factors like repeated muscle contractions leading to forehead lines and external influences like sun exposure contributing to further aging.

As we age, significant changes take place in the structure and appearance of our faces. The skull may lose volume, resulting in larger eye sockets and a more define jawline. Skin loses its elasticity and firmness, causing it to sag and develop wrinkles. This process can alter the overall shape of the head, with fine wrinkles appearing across the face. Additionally, features like cheekbones and jawlines may become more pronounced, while the nose may appear larger over time. Ears continue to grow, leading to longer earlobes and increased hair growth inside the ears. Sagging flesh around the chin and jawline can create jowls, and loose skin on the neck is often referred to as a *turkey neck*.

Capturing these intricate details in art requires an understanding of facial forms and how they change over time. By observing and depicting these features accurately, artists can create lifelike portraits of elderly individuals that convey the unique character of aging.

Furthermore, as we age, several changes occur in specific facial features. Lips tend to become thinner, and wrinkles develop above and below them. The philtrum, the indentation between the nose and upper lip, may flatten out over time. Hair often turns grey or white, eyebrows may lose color and definition, and the skin texture may become rougher. Age spots can also appear on the face and other areas of the body.

These natural changes are part of the aging process and contribute to the distinct appearance of older individuals. When portraying older faces in art, it's crucial to accurately capture this transformation to create authentic and realistic representations.

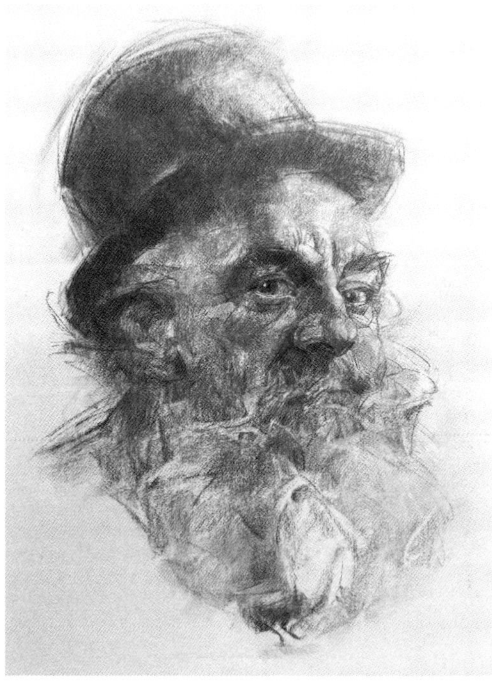

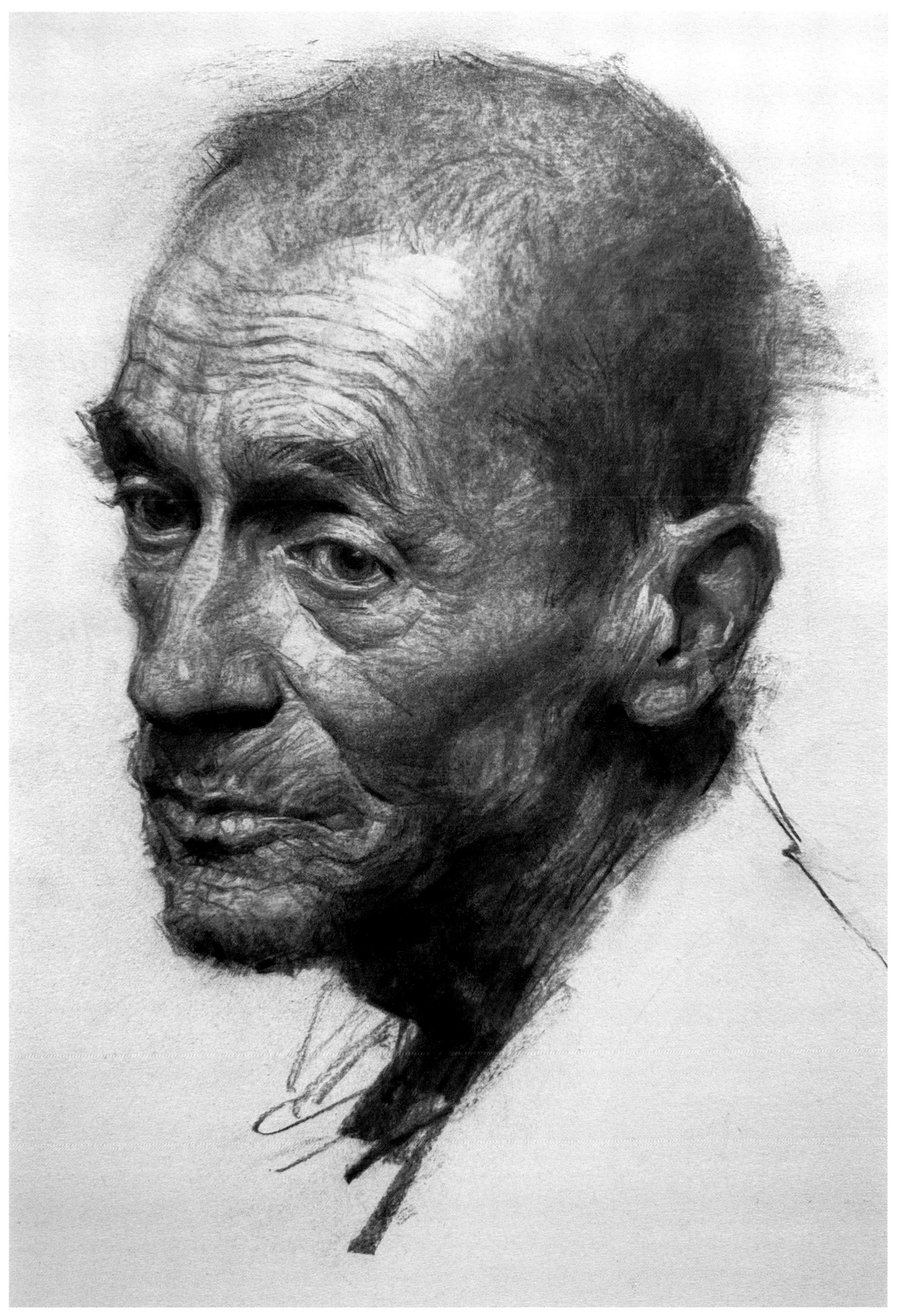

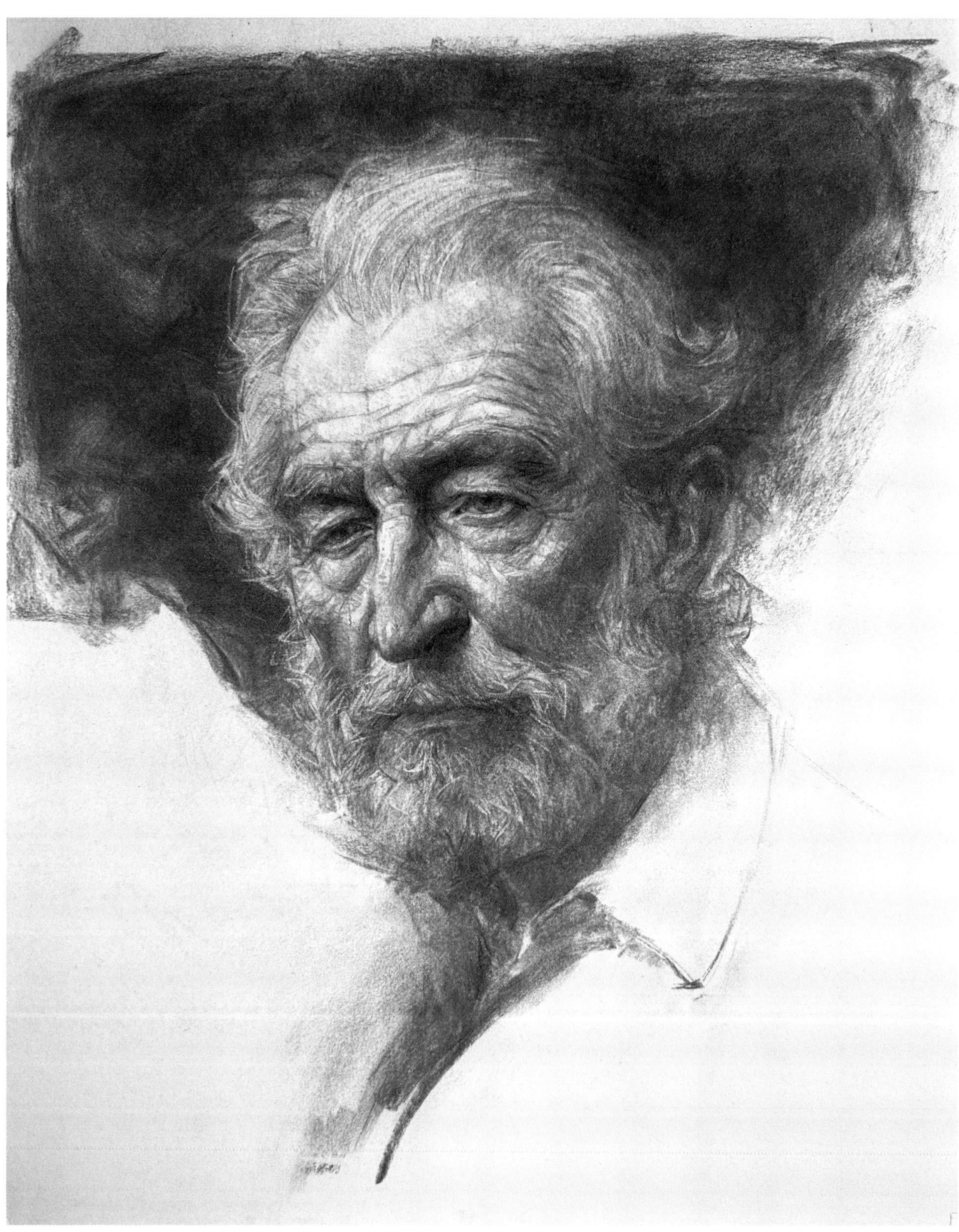

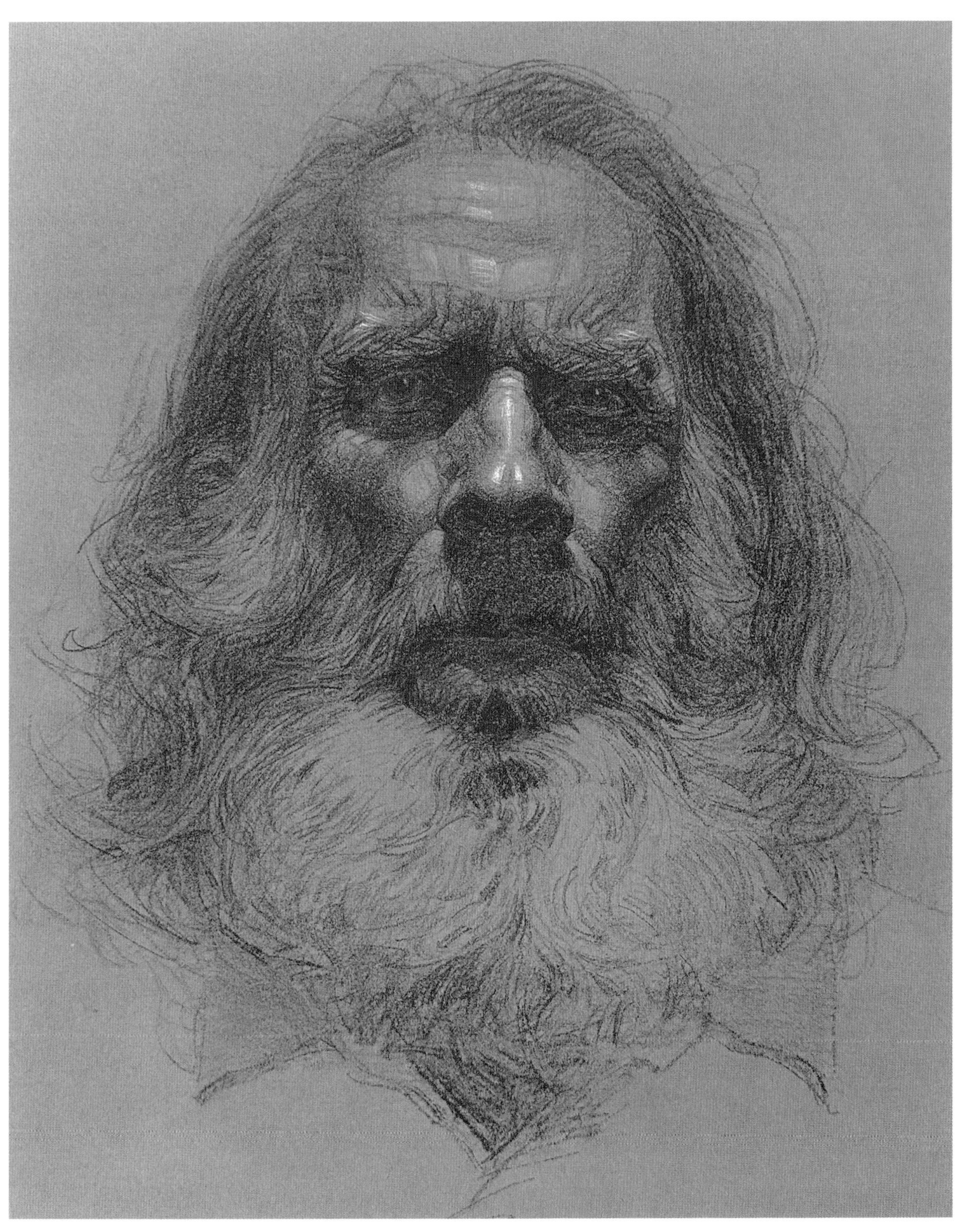

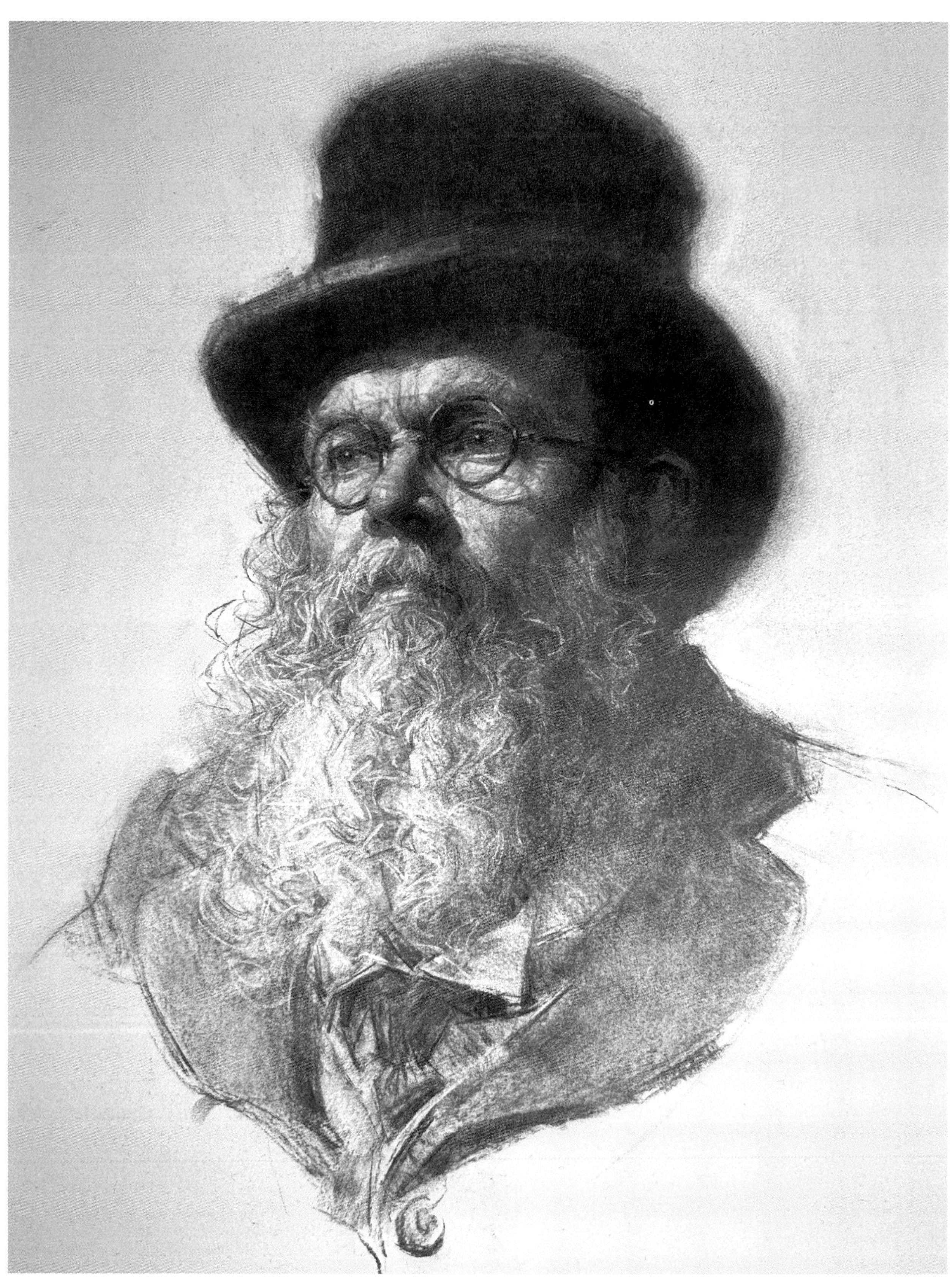

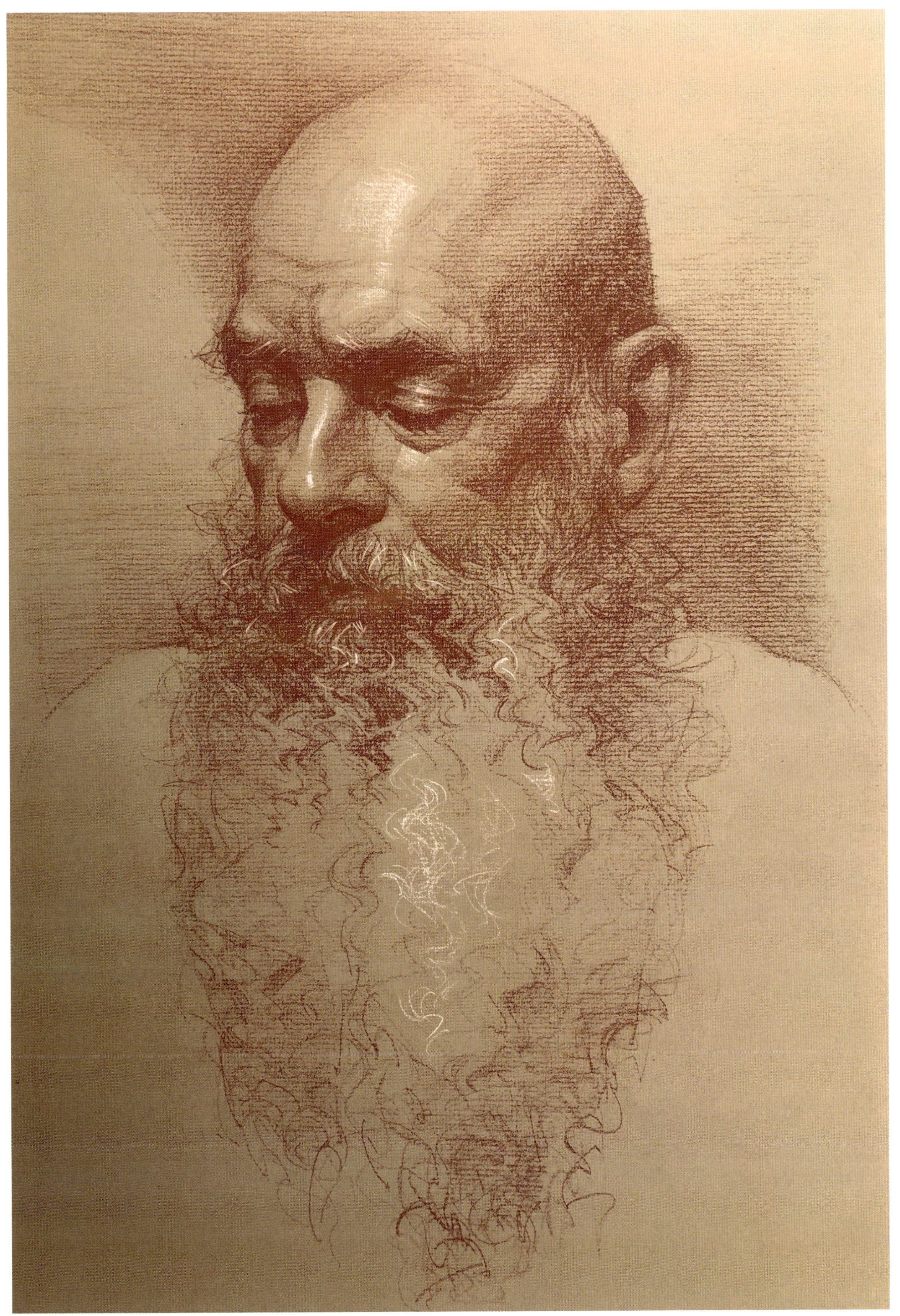

SELF-PORTRAIT CHALLENGE

During the challenging times of the pandemic, like so many other people, I found myself grappling with a range of difficult emotions. Stress, anxiety, and depression became constant companions, casting a shadow over daily life. Yet, amidst this turmoil, I discovered a beacon of solace and expression in art. Turning to self-portraiture, I embarked on a journey of introspection and self-discovery, using my own image as both subject and canvas.

Self-portraiture, I quickly learned, is far more than just a technical exercise. It's a deeply personal and introspective process—one that transcends mere representation to delve into the depths of the human psyche. At its core, a self-portrait is a reflection of the artist's innermost self, a raw and unfiltered expression of thoughts, feelings, and experiences.

For me, creating self-portraits during the pandemic was a form of catharsis—an opportunity to confront and process the myriad emotions swirling within. Each stroke of the pencil or brush became a meditation, a means of channeling my inner turmoil into tangible form. Through the act of drawing or painting myself, I found a sense of agency and control in a world that often felt chaotic and uncertain.

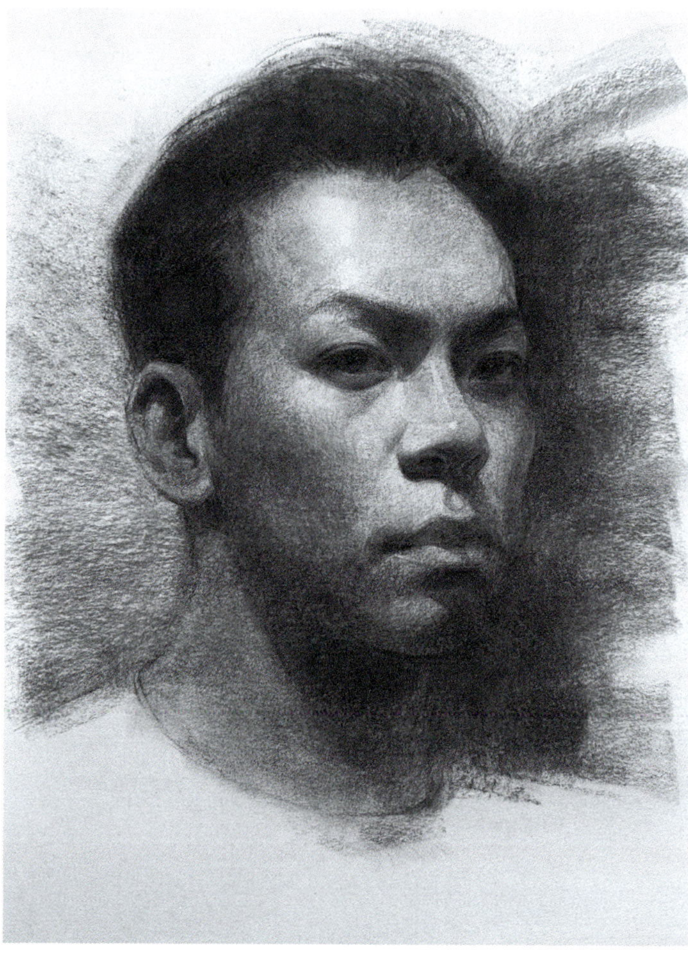

But self-portraiture is not merely a therapeutic exercise. It's also a profound act of self-exploration and self-acceptance. As I scrutinized my own image in the mirror, I was forced to confront my insecurities, vulnerabilities, and imperfections. Yet, in doing so, I also discovered a newfound appreciation for my own unique beauty and humanity.

In the process of creating self-portraits, I came to understand that authenticity is far more valuable than perfection. Each line, each wrinkle, and each flaw told a story—a testament to a life lived and experiences endured. Through my self-portraits, I sought not to hide or disguise these imperfections, but to embrace them as integral parts of my identity.

Moreover, self-portraiture allowed me to explore and express a range of emotions that words alone could not capture. In the depths of my darkest moments, my self-portraits became a mirror of my innermost thoughts and feelings—a silent witness to my struggles and triumphs.

Ultimately, creating self-portraits during the pandemic became an act of self-love and self-compassion—a testament to my resilience and strength in the face of adversity. Through my art, I learned to embrace my own humanity, with all its complexities and contradictions, and to find beauty in the midst of chaos.

So, as we navigate the uncertainties of life, I encourage you to embrace the transformative power of self-portraiture. Look beyond the surface and dare to explore the depths of your own soul. For in the act of creating art, we discover not only ourselves but also the boundless potential of the human spirit.

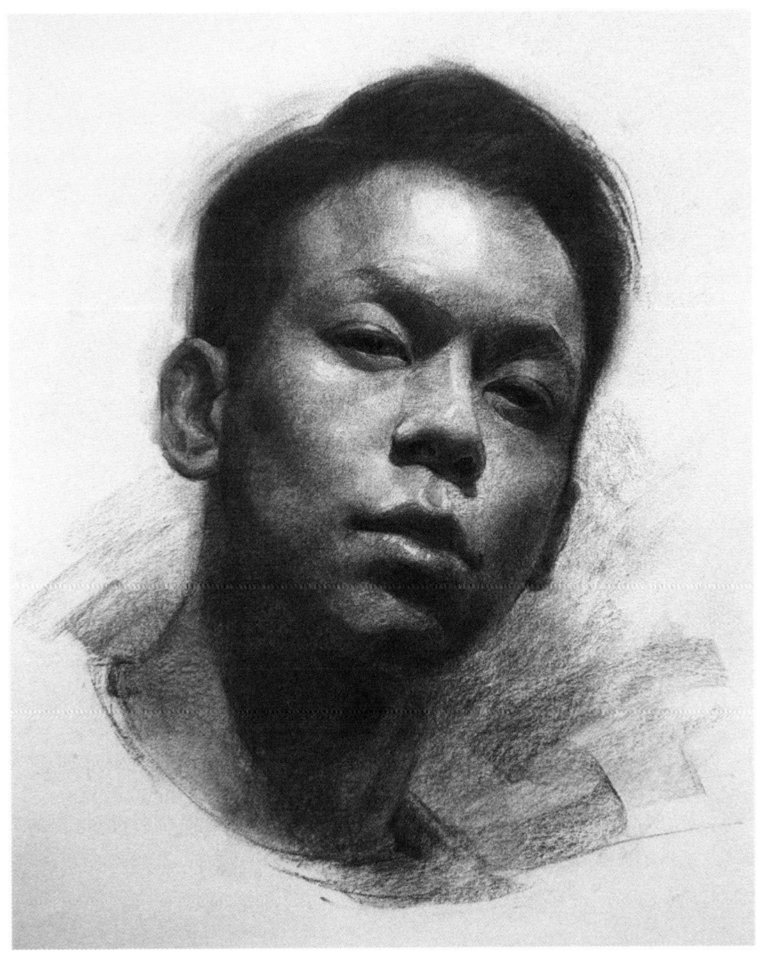

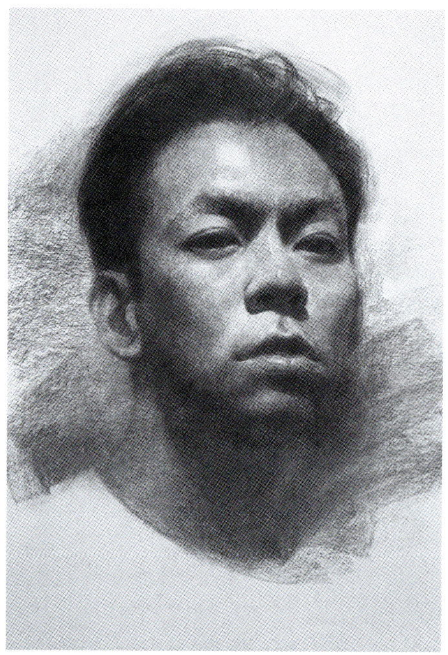

ABOUT THE AUTHOR

Oliver Sin is a distinguished alumnus of the Academy of Art University in San Francisco, California, where he earned a bachelor of fine arts in illustration. Upon graduating in 1996, he embarked on his professional journey as a computer-game concept artist with LucasArts. From 2001 to 2022, Oliver made a significant impact as an art professor at his alma mater, contributing to the university's School of Fine Arts and 2D Animation programs.

Oliver's passion for art was evident from an early age. He began drawing at just three years old and has always been particularly captivated by portraiture, a form of expression he has continuously honed, both as an educator and as a personal pursuit.

Oliver's first art book, *Drawing the Head for Artists*, was published in 2019 and then translated into Spanish, Dutch, and German in 2020. Furthering his educational endeavors, his instructional DVD titled *Portrait Drawing Simplified* through Streamline Publishing was released in April 2022.

Oliver's exceptional talent has been recognized on prominent platforms. Notably, two of his portraits were commissioned for the cover of *Time* magazine's "100 Women of the Year" project, featured in the March 2020 issue. His skill in portraiture was also honored with the First Place in Drawing award at the Portrait Society of America's International Art Competition in 2021 for his vine charcoal portrait of his father. In recognition of his sustained excellence and contributions to fine art portraiture, Oliver was awarded Signature Status by the Portrait Society of America in 2022.

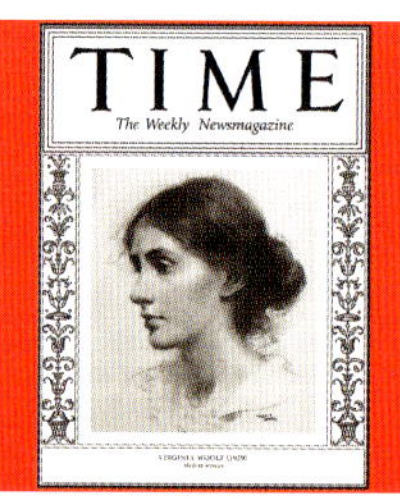

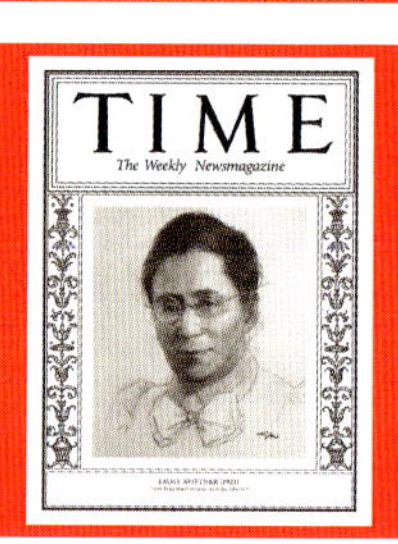

Oliver offers workshops and classes around the country and overseas.. For further information, please visit www.oliversinart.com.

ACKNOWLEDGMENTS

From the depths of my heart, I extend my sincerest gratitude to Zhaoming Wu, Henry Yan, and Huihan Liu. These extraordinary mentors have been my guiding art heroes since 2011. Their boundless wisdom, patience, and kindness have not only honed my skills but also deeply enriched my perspectives on art and life. Their mentorship has illuminated paths I never knew existed and has continually inspired me to push the boundaries of my creativity, striving for portrait drawings that genuinely touch the human spirit.

I am eternally grateful to my long-time friend Ivan Chan. Her constant belief in me as an artist, ever since our college days, always offers me hope and encouragement. Ivan's keen insights and steadfast support have accompanied me throughout my artistic journey, pushing me to pursue my dreams relentlessly against all odds.

My profound appreciation extends to Joy Aquilino, Quarry Books' editorial director, and the entire staff, who have been instrumental in bringing this book to fruition. This book might have remained nothing more than a passing idea had it not been for Joy's initial encouragement. Your dedication, patience, and unwavering support throughout this long and intricate process have been vital. I am deeply grateful for your belief in my work and for making this dream a reality.

To my family, friends, students, and fans from social media, your encouragement and support has been the wind beneath my wings. A special thanks goes to the many professional models who have graciously posed for me in various guises. Their artistic creativity and remarkable presence breathed life and soul into the images in this book. Their contributions have been invaluable in transforming my vision into reality.

Lastly, I offer my heartfelt gratitude to my parents and dear family, especially my brother, Kelvin, whose absolute faith in my talents has been a source of immense strength. Kelvin, your constant presence and belief in me have fueled my passion and perseverance. You have been my steadfast companion whose bond will always be the dearest and closest to me.

This journey has been one of profound learning and discovery. Each step has revealed new insights, challenged my understanding, and fostered growth beyond my expectations. Your belief in me has driven me to relentlessly pursue excellence. I promise to continue walking this path tirelessly, with a heart full of gratitude, determination, and humility. Our walk together compels me to strive for greater heights and to create art that resonates deeply with the human experience.

Thank you all, from the bottom of my heart.

Sincerely,
Oliver Sin

INDEX

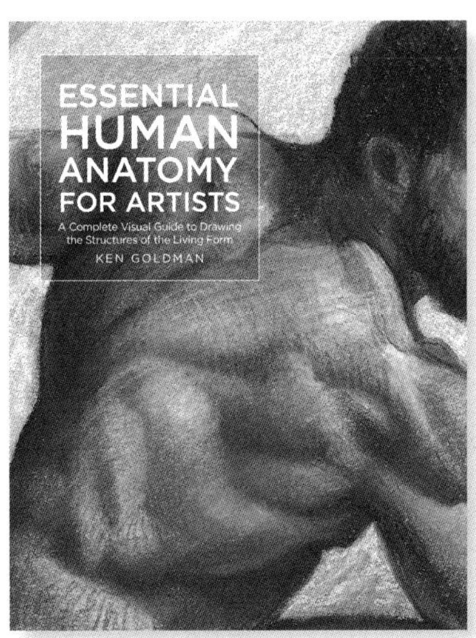

Essential Human Anatomy for Artists
978-1-6315-9959-0

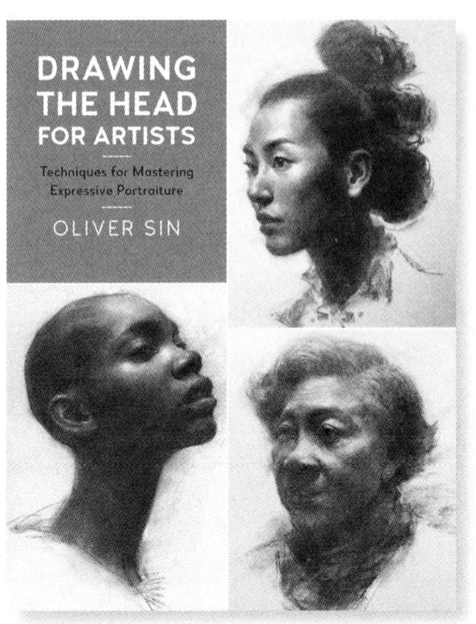

Drawing the Head for Artists
978-1-63159-692-6

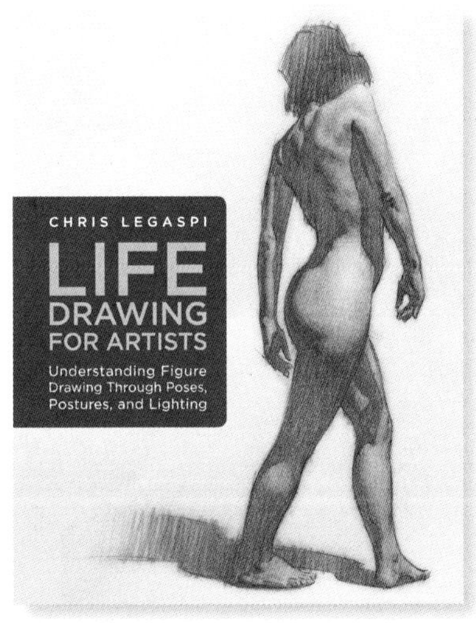

Life Drawing for Artists
978-1-63159-801-2

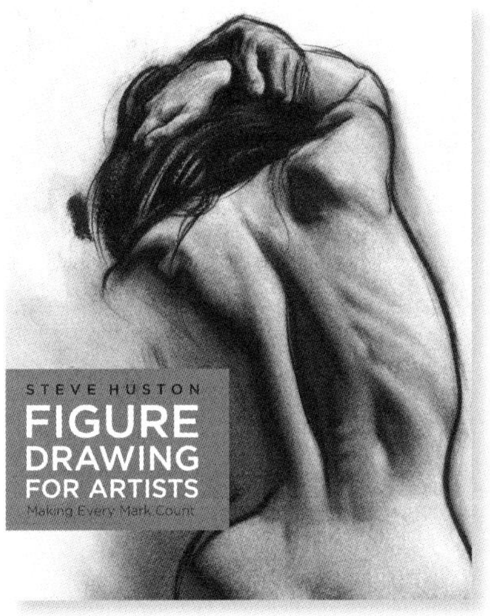

Figure Drawing for Artists
978-1-63159-065-8

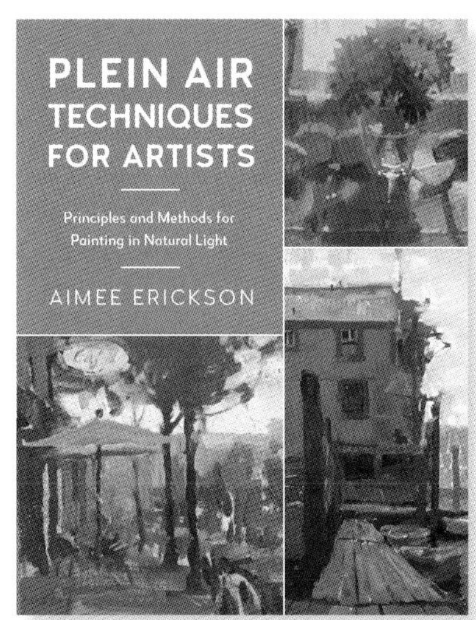

Plein Air Techniques for Artists
978-0-7603-7935-6

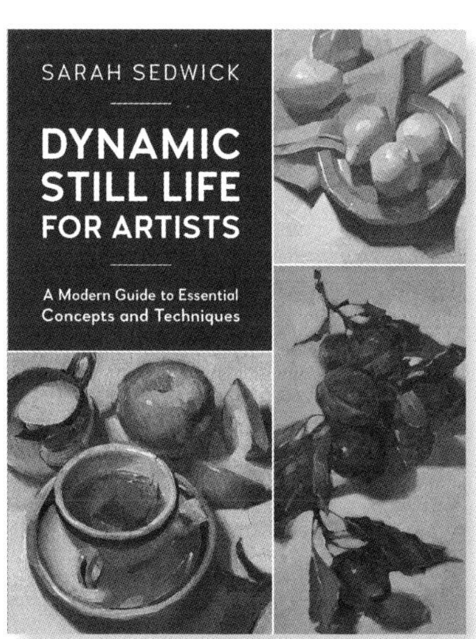

Dynamic Still Life for Artists
978-0-7603-7700-0

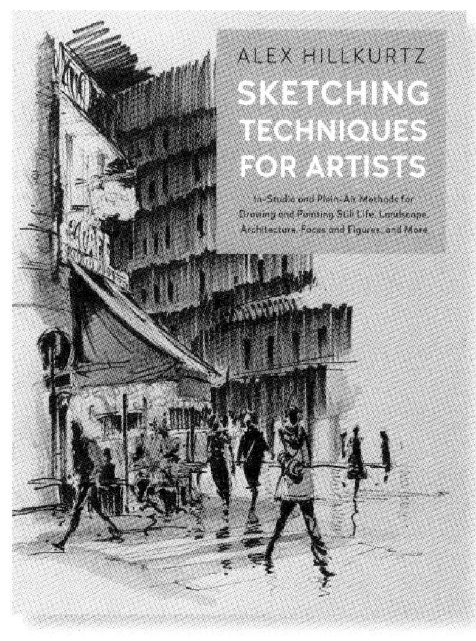

Sketching Techniques for Artists
978-1-63159-924-8

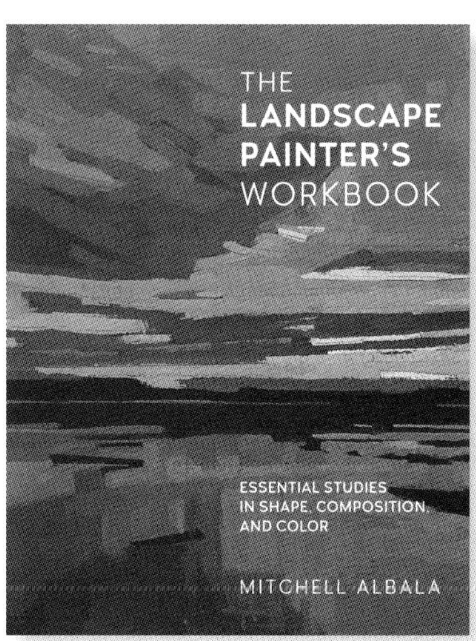

The Landscape Painter's Workbook
978-0-7603-7135-0

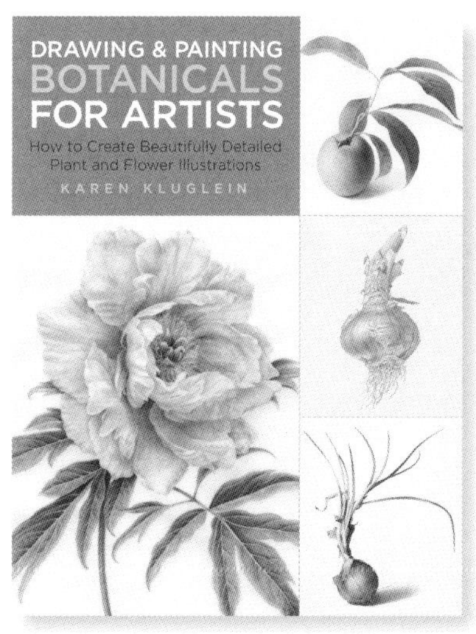

Drawing and Painting Botanicals for Artists
978-1-63159-857-9

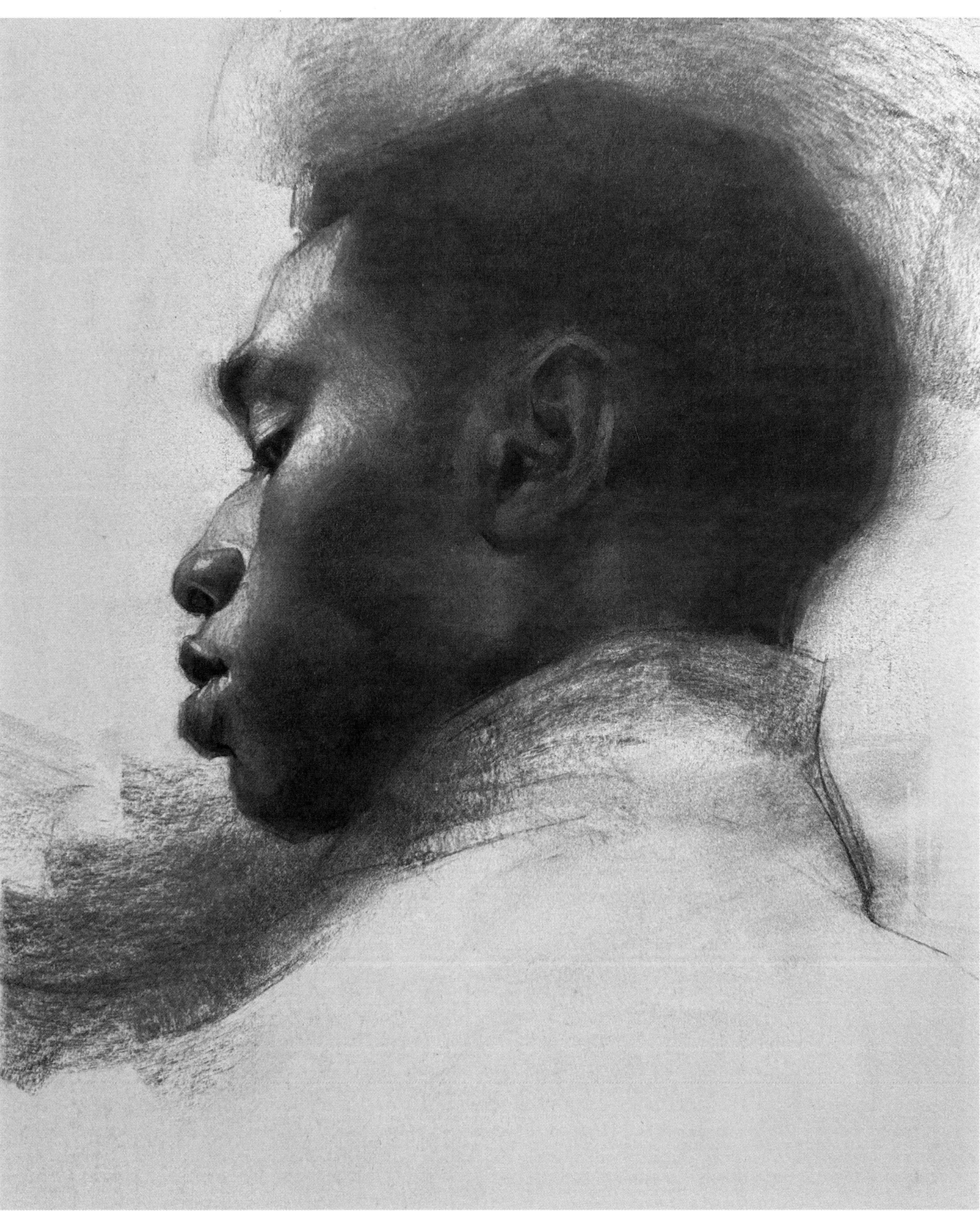